Cisco LAN Sw Configuration Handbook

Steve McQuerry, CCIE No. 6108
David Jansen, CCIE No. 5952
Dave Hucaby, CCIE No. 4594

Cisco Press

800 East 96th Street

Indianapolis, IN 46240

Cisco LAN Switching Configuration Handbook

Steve McQuerry, David Jansen, David Hucaby

Copyright © 2009 Cisco Systems, Inc.

Published by:
Cisco Press
800 East 96th Street
Indianapolis, IN 46240 USA

Printed in the United States of America

First Printing June 2009

Library of Congress Cataloging-in-Publication data is on file.

ISBN-13: 978-1-58705-610-9

ISBN-10: 1-58705-610-0

Warning and Disclaimer

This book is designed to provide information about the configuration of Cisco Catalyst switches. Every effort has been made to make this book as complete and as accurate as possible, but no warranty or fitness is implied.

The information is provided on an "as is" basis. The authors, Cisco Press, and Cisco Systems, Inc. shall have neither liability nor responsibility to any person or entity with respect to any loss or damages arising from the information contained in this book or from the use of the discs or programs that may accompany it.

The opinions expressed in this book belong to the author and are not necessarily those of Cisco Systems, Inc.

Trademark Acknowledgments

All terms mentioned in this book that are known to be trademarks or service marks have been appropriately capitalized. Cisco Press or Cisco Systems, Inc., cannot attest to the accuracy of this information. Use of a term in this book should not be regarded as affecting the validity of any trademark or service mark.

Corporate and Government Sales

The publisher offers excellent discounts on this book when ordered in quantity for bulk purchases or special sales, which may include electronic versions and/or custom covers and content particular to your business, training goals, marketing focus, and branding interests. For more information, please contact: **U.S. Corporate and Government Sales**   1-800-382-3419   corpsales@pearsontechgroup.com

For sales outside the United States please contact: **International Sales**   international@pearsoned.com

Feedback Information

At Cisco Press, our goal is to create in-depth technical books of the highest quality and value. Each book is crafted with care and precision, undergoing rigorous development that involves the unique expertise of members from the professional technical community.

Readers' feedback is a natural continuation of this process. If you have any comments regarding how we could improve the quality of this book, or otherwise alter it to better suit your needs, you can contact us through email at feedback@ciscopress.com. Please make sure to include the book title and ISBN in your message.

We greatly appreciate your assistance.

Publisher: Paul Boger

Associate Publisher: Dave Dusthimer

Executive Editor: Brett Bartow

Managing Editor: Patrick Kanouse

Senior Development Editor: Christopher Cleveland

Project Editor: Seth Kerney

Editorial Assistant: Vanessa Evans

Book and Cover Designer: Louisa Adair

Composition: Mark Shirar

Indexer: Tim Wright

Cisco Representative: Eric Ullanderson

Cisco Press Program Manager: Anand Sundaram

Technical Editors: Ron Fuller, Don Johnston

Copy Editor: Apostrophe Editing Services

Proofreader: Language Logistics, LLC

CISCO

Americas Headquarters
Cisco Systems, Inc.
San Jose, CA

Asia Pacific Headquarters
Cisco Systems (USA) Pte. Ltd.
Singapore

Europe Headquarters
Cisco Systems International BV
Amsterdam, The Netherlands

Cisco has more than 200 offices worldwide. Addresses, phone numbers, and fax numbers are listed on the Cisco Website at **www.cisco.com/go/offices.**

CCDE, CCENT, Cisco Eos, Cisco HealthPresence, the Cisco logo, Cisco Lumin, Cisco Nexus, Cisco StadiumVision, Cisco TelePresence, Cisco WebEx, DCE, and Welcome to the Human Network are trademarks; Changing the Way We Work, Live, Play, and Learn and Cisco Store are service marks; and Access Registrar, Aironet, AsyncOS, Bringing the Meeting To You, Catalyst, CCDA, CCDP, CCIE, CCIP, CCNA, CCNP, CCSP, CCVP, Cisco, the Cisco Certified Internetwork Expert logo, Cisco IOS, Cisco Press, Cisco Systems, Cisco Systems Capital, the Cisco Systems logo, Cisco Unity, Collaboration Without Limitation, EtherFast, EtherSwitch, Event Center, Fast Step, Follow Me Browsing, FormShare, GigaDrive, HomeLink, Internet Quotient, IOS, iPhone, iQuick Study, IronPort, the IronPort logo, LightStream, Linksys, MediaTone, MeetingPlace, MeetingPlace Chime Sound, MGX, Networkers, Networking Academy, Network Registrar, PCNow, PIX, PowerPanels, ProConnect, ScriptShare, SenderBase, SMARTnet, Spectrum Expert, StackWise, The Fastest Way to Increase Your Internet Quotient, TransPath, WebEx, and the WebEx logo are registered trademarks of Cisco Systems, Inc. and/or its affiliates in the United States and certain other countries.

All other trademarks mentioned in this document or website are the property of their respective owners. The use of the word partner does not imply a partnership relationship between Cisco and any other company. (0812R)

About the Authors

Steve McQuerry, CCIE No. 6108, is a technical solutions architect with Cisco Systems focused on data center solutions. Steve works with enterprise customers in the Midwestern United States to help them plan their data center architectures. Steve has been an active member of the internetworking community since 1991 and has held multiple certifications from Novell, Microsoft, and Cisco. Steve holds a BS degree in physics from Eastern Kentucky University. Prior to joining Cisco, Steve worked as a consultant for various companies and as an independent contractor with Global Knowledge, where he taught and developed coursework around Cisco technologies and certifications.

David Jansen, CCIE No. 5952, is a vertical solutions architect for manufacturing for U.S Enterprise Segment. David has more than 20 years experience in the information technology industry. He has held multiple certifications from Microsoft, Novell, Checkpoint, and Cisco. His focus is to work with Enterprise customers to address end to end manufacturing architectures. David has been with Cisco for 11 years, and working as a manufacturing architect for the past year has provided unique experiences helping customers build architectural solutions for manufacturing connectivity. David holds a BSE degree in computer science from the University of Michigan (Go Blue!) and an MA degree in adult education from Central Michigan University.

David Hucaby, CCIE No. 4594, is a lead network engineer for the University of Kentucky, where he works with healthcare networks based on the Cisco Catalyst, IP Telephony, PIX, and VPN product lines. Prior to his current position, David was a senior network consultant, where he provided design and implementation consulting, focusing on Cisco-based VPN and IP Telephony solutions. David has BS and MS degrees in electrical engineering from the University of Kentucky.

About the Technical Reviewers

Ron Fuller, CCIE No. 5851 (Routing and Switching/Storage Networking) is a technology solution architect for Cisco specializing in data center architectures. He has 18 years of experience in the industry and has held certifications from Novell, HP, Microsoft, ISC2, SNIA, and Cisco. His focus is working with Enterprise customers to address their challenges with comprehensive end-to-end data center architectures. He lives in Ohio with his wife and three wonderful children and enjoys travel and auto racing.

Don Johnston has more than 20 years of technical, management, consulting, and training experience in networking. He is a CCSI and has developed well-received courses and labs. As a consultant, Don successfully designed LANs and WANs, installed, provided troubleshooting expertise, and managed technical staff for insurance brokerage, reinsurance, and marketing companies. An instrument-rated pilot, Don and his family live in the Chicago area.

Dedications

Steve McQuerry: This work is dedicated to my wife and children. Becky, thank you for your love and support as we continue our life together; I look forward to each new chapter we write together. Katie, you are an amazing young lady. I'm excited for all that life has in store for you; keep your work ethic, and you will be successful. Logan, you have never believed that there was anything you couldn't accomplish. That drive and spirit will allow you opportunities beyond your imagination. Cameron, you have a thirst for learning that will serve you well. Keep finding ways to channel your quest for knowledge, and you will have a challenging and rewarding future.

David Jansen: This book is dedicated to my loving wife Jenise and my three children; Kaitlyn, Joshua, and Jacob. You are the inspiration that gave me the dedication and determination to complete this project. Thank you for all your love and support.

Dave Hucaby: This book is dedicated to my wife Marci and my two little daughters, Lauren and Kara. For girls who have never seen a Catalyst switch, they sure encouraged me to keep at the writing I enjoy. I'm so grateful to God, who gives endurance and encouragement (Romans 15:5) and who has allowed me to work on projects such as this.

Acknowledgments

Steve McQuerry: The publishing industry is filled with a great group of people who are as much responsible for the finished product as those who have their names on the front of the book. I would like to take this time to thank the individuals responsible for helping me with my part of this book.

First, I would like to thank my friend and coauthor Dave Hucaby. I can't think of anyone I've worked with in my entire career as dedicated and focused as you are. More important than your focus and dedication to your work, however, is your focus on the importance of God, family, and friendship. I am blessed by having you for a friend. I hope we can continue to find ways to keep working together in the future.

David Jansen, thank you for jumping into the mix on the revision of this work. You are a great friend and coworker. Cisco is one of the most amazing places I've ever worked, and it's people like you, who are wicked smart and a lot of fun to work with, that make it such a great place. I look forward to working on other projects in the future.

As always, I want to thank Brett Bartow. I don't think we could finish a book without Brett's consistency and his follow-through. Thanks for the opportunity, and thanks for keeping us motivated. It is truly a pleasure to work with you.

Chris Cleveland, it is always a pleasure to work with you. Thanks for putting up with me on yet another project. Your expertise as a development editor is unsurpassed; I appreciate your hard work and professionalism. Thank you for making us look good!

To our technical editors—Don Johnston and Ron Fuller—thanks for the sharp eyes and excellent comments. It was great having you as part of the team.

A special thanks to the fine professionals at Cisco Press. You guys are the best in the industry!

Thanks to my manager at Cisco, Scott Sprinkle. I appreciate your guidance and your trust in my ability to juggle the many work tasks along with extra projects like working on a book.

I want to thank my wife and children for the support they offer for all my projects and for the patience and understanding they have when I work late and act a little grouchy the next day.

Most important, I want to thank God, for giving me the skills, talents, and opportunity to work in such a challenging and exciting profession.

David Jansen: This is my first book, and it has been a tremendous honor to work with the great people at Cisco Press. There are so many people to thank; I'm not sure where to begin. I'll start with Brett Bartow: Thank you for getting me started in the writing industry; this is something I've always wanted to do. I appreciate your patience and tolerance on this project. I really appreciate you keeping me on track to complete the project in a timely manner.

Thanks to Chris Cleveland and Steve McQuerry for helping me learn the formatting and style along with the writing process in general. I never knew how much was involved in writing a book. I'd also like to extend a special thanks to Steve for giving me all the hard chapters. I now know why you asked for me to help on the project.

I would like to extend a special thanks to David Hucaby. Steve tells me that you were the true creator of the Field Manual series of books, and I appreciate the opportunity to continue to work on this project in your absence.

Thanks to our technical reviewers Don Johnston and Ron Fuller. Thank you both for all the great comments and insight. Don, it was a pleasure to work with you, and Ron, even though we have our differences of opinions about college football, thanks for being a great friend and coworker.

To all the people at Cisco Press behind the scenes, thank you for all your help and support on this project.

I want to thank my family for their support and understanding while I was working on this project late at night and being patient with me when my lack of rest may have made me a little less than pleasant to be around.

I would like to thank God for giving me the ability to complete such a task with dedication and determination and for providing me the skills, knowledge, and health needed to be successful in such a demanding profession.

Dave Hucaby: Once again, it is my good pleasure to be involved in writing a Cisco Press book. Technical writing for me is great fun, although it's hard to write a book strictly on lunch hours and after the rest of the family goes to bed. I gratefully acknowledge the good people at Cisco Press for allowing me to work on this project and for their encouragement, patience, and diligence to produce fine work.

In particular, I would like to thank Brett Bartow for making this project a goal we could meet. Writing a book such as this is a long and difficult process. Brett always gives us a feel for the big picture, while keeping us on track with the details. I am also very grateful to work with Chris Cleveland again. Chris is probably the hardest working person I know and is a wonderful editor. Somehow, he can take in rough-hewn chapters and turn out smooth text.

I would like to acknowledge the hard work and good perspective of our technical reviewers: Ron Fuller and Don Johnston. The reviewers have done a superb job of catching us in inaccuracies and helping us to better organize the technical information. I'm glad I was on the writing end and not the reviewing end!

I would like to express my thanks to my coauthors Steve McQuerry and David Jansen. It's been a pleasure sharing the writing load with them.

Contents at a Glance

Contents

Icons Used in This Book

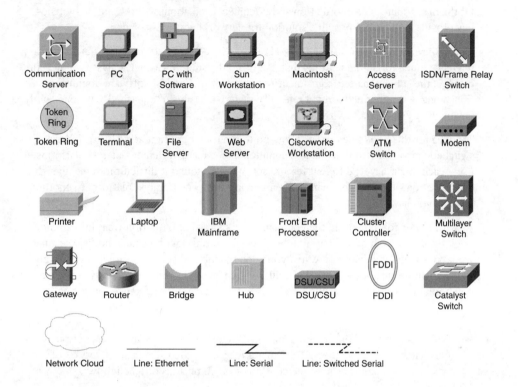

Command Syntax Conventions

The conventions used to present command syntax in this book are the same conventions used in the IOS Command Reference. The Command Reference describes these conventions as follows:

- **Boldface** indicates commands and keywords that are entered literally as shown. In actual configuration examples and output (not general command syntax), boldface indicates commands that are manually input by the user (such as a **show** command).

- *Italic* indicates arguments for which you supply actual values.

- Vertical bars (|) separate alternative, mutually exclusive elements.

- Square brackets ([ ]) indicate an optional element.

- Braces ({ }) indicate a required choice.

- Braces within brackets ([{ }]) indicate a required choice within an optional element.

Introduction

Of the many sources of information and documentation about Cisco Catalyst switches, few provide a quick and portable solution for networking professionals.

Cisco LAN Switching Configuration Handbook is designed to provide a quick and easy reference guide for all the features that can be configured on Cisco Catalyst switches. In essence, the subject matter from an entire bookshelf of Catalyst software documentation, along with other networking reference material, has been "squashed" into one handy volume that you can take with you.

The idea for this book began as a follow-on to the router configuration book. In larger switched network environments, it is common to see many different Catalyst platforms in use—each might have a different feature set. We have found it difficult to remember the configuration steps and commands when moving from one Catalyst platform to another. Perhaps you have. too.

As with router configuration, the commands for switch configuration went into a notebook of handwritten notes. This notebook began to travel with us into the field as a network consultant and engineer. When you're on the job and someone requires you to configure a feature that you're not too familiar with, it's nice to have your handy reference notebook in your bag! Hopefully, this book will be that handy reference for you as well.

Note   This book is based on the most current Cisco Catalyst software releases at press time—IOS switches according to the 12.2 major release. If you use an earlier version of either software, you might find that the configuration commands differ slightly.

Features

This book is meant to be used as a tool in your day-to-day tasks as a network administrator, engineer, consultant, or student. As such, we have avoided presenting a large amount of instructional information or theory on the operation of features or commands. That is better handled in other textbooks that are dedicated to a more limited subject matter.

Instead, the book is divided into chapters that present quick facts, configuration steps, and explanations of configuration options for each Cisco Catalyst switch feature. The chapters are as follows:

- **Chapter 1, "CLI Usage":** Describes the IOS environment and command-line interface

- **Chapter 2, "Switch Functionality":** Describes LAN switches and how to implement a switch campus network design

- **Chapter 3, "Supervisor Engine Configuration":** Explains how to configure switch prompts, IP addresses, passwords, switch modules, file management, and administrative protocols

- **Chapter 4, "Layer 2 Interface Configuration"**: Describes configuration of Ethernet, Fast Ethernet, Gigabit Ethernet, and EtherChannel interfaces

- **Chapter 5, "Layer 3 Interface Configuration"**: Explains how Layer 3 interfaces are used in a switch

- **Chapter 6, "VLANs and Trunking"**: Presents VLAN configuration, private VLANs, trunking, and VTP

- **Chapter 7, "Spanning Tree Protocol (STP)"**: Discusses STP operation, configuration, and tuning

- **Chapter 8, "Configuring High Availability Features"**: Explains how to configure and use Catalyst switch hardware for redundancy using multiple supervisors and hot standby routing protocol (HSRP)

- **Chapter 9, "Multicast"**: Explains how a switch handles multicast traffic and interacts with multicast routers

- **Chapter 10, "Server Load Balancing (SLB)"**: Presents Catalyst 6500 features that streamline access to server and firewall farms

- **Chapter 11, "Controlling Traffic and Switch Access"**: Discusses broadcast suppression, user authentication, port security, and VLAN access lists

- **Chapter 12, "Switch Management"**: Explains how to configure a switch for logging, SNMP and RMON management, port analysis (SPAN), power management, and connectivity testing

- **Chapter 13, "Quality of Service"**: Presents configuration of QoS theory and features in a switched network

- **Chapter 14, "Voice"**: Discusses specialized voice gateway modules, inline power, and QoS features needed to transport voice traffic

- **Appendix A, "Cabling Quick Reference," and Appendix B, :Well-Known Protocol, Port, and Other Numbers"**: Present a cabling quick reference and a table of well-known ports and addresses

How to Use This Book

All the information in this book has been designed to follow a quick-reference format. If you know what feature or technology you want to use, you can turn right to the section that deals with it. Sections are numbered with a quick-reference index, showing both chapter and section number (5-2, for example, is Chapter 5, section 2). You'll also find shaded index tabs on each page, listing the section number.

Facts About a Feature

Each section in a chapter begins with a bulleted list of quick facts about the feature, technology, or protocol. Refer to these lists to quickly learn or review how the feature works.

Configuration Steps

Each feature that is covered in a section includes the required and optional commands used for common configuration. The difference is that the configuration steps are presented in an outline format. If you follow the outline, you can configure a complex feature or technology. If you find that you don't need a certain feature option, skip over that level in the outline.

Example Configurations

Each section includes an example of how to implement the commands and their options. We tried to present the examples with the commands listed in the order you would actually enter them to follow the outline. Many times, it is more difficult to study and understand a configuration example from an actual switch because the commands are displayed in a predefined order—not in the order you entered them. The examples have also been trimmed down to show only the commands presented in the section (where possible).

Displaying Information About a Feature

Where applicable, each section concludes with a brief summary of the commands you can use to show information about the switch feature. You can use these command summaries as a quick reference when you are debugging or troubleshooting switch operation.

Further Reading

Most chapters conclude with a recommended reading list to help you find more in-depth sources of information for the topics discussed.

Chapter 1

CLI Usage

Refer to the following sections for information about these topics:

■ **1-1: Cisco Internetwork Operating System (IOS) Software:** Describes the use of Cisco IOS Software for switching configuration

■ **1-2: ROM Monitor:** Describes the use of the ROM monitor for recovery of a switch and configuration of boot parameters

1-1: Cisco Internetwork Operating System (IOS) Software

■ Cisco IOS Software supports user access by CLI or by a web browser.

■ The CLI can be accessed through the console port, Telnet, or through SSH.

■ Users can execute Cisco IOS Software commands from a *user level* or from a *privileged level*. User level offers basic system information and remote connectivity commands. Privileged level offers complete access to all switch information, configuration editing, and debugging commands.

■ Cisco IOS Software offers many levels of configuration modes, enabling you to change the configuration for a variety of switch resources.

■ Cisco IOS Software offers a VLAN database mode to configure and modify VLAN and VLAN Trunking Protocol (VTP) information.

■ A context-sensitive help system offers command syntax and command choices at any user prompt.

■ A history of Cisco IOS Software commands executed can be kept. As well, command lines can be edited and reused.

■   The output from a command can be searched and filtered so that useful information can be found quickly.

■   Parameters for the CLI connection to the switch can be set to preferred values.

Using Cisco IOS Software

Cisco IOS Software has two basic user modes for switch administration and a number of other modes that enable you to control the configuration of the switch. In addition to a variety of modes, Cisco IOS Software provides features such as help and command-line editing that enable you to interact with the switch for management purposes. The following items describe how to access these modes and use options to configure the switch.

1. User interface modes.

    a. User EXEC mode.

        `Switch>`

        Users can connect to a switch through the console port or Telnet session. By default, the initial access to a switch places the user in *user EXEC* mode and offers a limited set of commands. When connecting to the switch, a user-level *password* might be required.

    b. Privileged EXEC mode.

        `Switch>` **`enable`**

        `password: [password]`

        `Switch#`

        When a user gains access in user EXEC mode, the **enable** command can be used to enter *privileged EXEC* or *enable* mode. Full access to all commands is available. To leave privileged EXEC mode, use the **disable** or **exit** commands.

    c. Configuration mode.

        `Switch#` **`configure terminal`**

        From privileged EXEC mode, the configuration mode can be entered. Switch commands can be given to configure any switch feature that is available in the IOS software image. When you are in configuration mode, you manage the active memory of the switch. Anytime you enter a valid command in any configuration mode and press **Enter**, the memory is immediately changed. Configuration mode is organized in a hierarchical fashion. Global configuration mode enables commands that affect the switch as a whole. Interface configuration mode enables commands that configure switch interfaces. You can move in and out of many other configuration modes depending on what is configured. To move from a lower-level configuration mode to a higher level, type **exit**. To leave the global configuration mode and return to the privileged EXEC mode, type **exit** at the global configuration prompt. To leave any configuration mode and return to privileged EXEC mode, type **end** or **Ctrl-Z**.

2. User interface features.

    a. Entering commands:

```
Switch>, Switch#, Switch(config)#

Switch>, Switch#, Switch(config)#
```

Commands can be entered from any mode (EXEC, global config, interface config, subinterface config, vlan and so on). To enable a feature or parameter, type the command and its options normally, as in *command*. To disable a command that is in effect, begin the command with **no**, followed by the command. The commands that are in effect can be seen by using the **show running-config** command in privileged mode. Note that some commands and parameters are set by default and are not shown as literal command lines in the configuration listing.

Commands and their options can also be abbreviated with as few letters as possible without becoming ambiguous. To enter the interface configuration mode for Ethernet 0, for example, you can abbreviate the command **interface fastethernet 0** as **int fa 0**.

You can edit a command line using the Left and Right Arrow keys to move within the line. If additional characters are typed, the remainder of the line to the right is spaced over. You can use the Backspace and Delete keys to make corrections.

Note   If the switch displays a console informational or error message while you are typing a command line, you can press the **Ctrl-l** or **Ctrl-r** key to redisplay the line and continue editing. You can also configure the lines (console, vty, or aux) to use **logging synchronous**. This causes the switch to automatically refresh the lines after the switch output. You might have to wait for the switch to see output; if you issue **debug** commands with **logging synchronous** enabled, you might have to wait for the switch to finish the command (such as a ping) before you see the output.

    b. Context-sensitive help.

You can enter a question mark (**?**) anywhere in a command line to get additional information from the switch. If the question mark is typed alone, all available commands for that mode display. Question marks can also be typed at any place after a command, a keyword, or an option. If the question mark follows a space, all available keywords or options display. If the question mark follows another word without a space, a list of all available commands beginning with that substring displays. This can be helpful when an abbreviated command is ambiguous and flagged with an error.

An abbreviated command might also be typed, followed by the **Tab** key. The command name expands to its full form if it is not ambiguous.

If a command line is entered but doesn't have the correct syntax, an error "% Invalid input detected at '^' marker" is returned. A caret (^) appears below the command character where the syntax error was detected.

c. Command history.

(Optional) Set the number of commands to save (default 10). To set the history size for the current terminal session, enter the following:

```
Switch# terminal history [size lines]
```

To set the history size for all sessions on a line, enter the following:

```
Switch(config-line)# history [size lines]
```

Recalling commands to use again.

From any input mode, each press of the Up Arrow (q) key or **Ctrl-p** recalls the next older command. Each press of the Down Arrow (Q) key or **Ctrl-n** recalls the next most recent command. When commands are recalled from history, they can be edited as if you had just typed them. The **show history** command displays the recorded command history.

> **Note**   The Up and Down Arrow keys require the use of an ANSI-compatible terminal emulator (that is, VT100).

d. Searching and filtering command output.

Sift through output from a **show** command:

```
Switch# show command ... | {begin | include | exclude} reg-expression
```

contains more lines than the terminal session can display (set using the *length* parameter), it displays a screenful at a time with a More— prompt at the bottom. To see the next screen, press the Spacebar. To advance one line, press the **Return** key. To exit back out to the command line, press **Ctrl-c**, the **Q** key, or any key on the keyboard other than **Enter** or the Spacebar.

To search for a specific regular expression and start the output listing there, use the **begin** keyword. This can be useful if your switch has many interfaces in its configuration. Instead of using the Spacebar to eventually find a certain configuration line, you can use **begin** to jump right to the desired line. To display only the lines that include a regular expression, use the **include** keyword. To display all lines that don't include a regular expression, use the **exclude** keyword.

Sift through output from a **more** command:

```
Switch# more file-url | {begin | include | exclude} reg-expression
```

The **more** command displays the contents of a file on the switch. A typical use is to display the startup (**more nvram:startup-config**) or running (**more**

system:running-config) configuration file. By default the file displays one screen at a time with a —More— prompt at the bottom.

To search for a specific regular expression and start the output listing there, use the **begin** keyword. To display only the lines that include a regular expression, use the **include** keyword. To display all lines that don't include a regular expression, use the **exclude** keyword.

Search through output at a —More— prompt:

```
(—More—) {/ | + | -}regular-expression
```

At a —More— prompt, you can search the output by typing the slash (/) key followed by a regular expression. To display only lines that include the regular expression, press the plus (+) key. To display only lines that don't include the regular expression, press the minus (–) key.

What is a regular expression?

A regular expression can be used to match against lines of output. Regular expressions are made up of patterns, either simple text strings (that is, *ethernet* or *ospf*) or more complex matching patterns. Typically, regular expressions are regular text words that offer a hint to a location in the output of a **show** command.

A more complex regular expression is made up of patterns and operators. Table 1-1 shows the characters that are used as operators:

Table 1-1   *Operator Characters*

Character	Meaning
.	Matches a single character.
*	Matches 0 or more sequences of the preceding pattern.
+	Matches 1 or more sequences of the preceding pattern.
?	Matches 0 or 1 occurrences of the preceding pattern.
^	Matches at the beginning of the string.
$	Matches at the end of the string.
_	Matches a comma, braces, parentheses, beginning or end of a string, or a space.
[ ]	Defines a range of characters as a pattern.
( )	Groups characters as a pattern; if used around a pattern, the pattern can be recalled later in the expression by using the backslash (\) and the pattern occurrence number.

3. Terminal sessions.

   a. Start a new session:

   ```
   Switch# telnet host
   ```

   This initiates a Telnet connection to *host* (either an IP address or a hostname). Then from the switch CLI, you can continue to communicate with the remote host.

   b. Name a session:

   ```
   Switch# name-connection

   Switch# Connection number: number

   Switch# Enter logical name: name
   ```

   An active session can be assigned a text string name to make the session easier to identify with the **show sessions** or **where** command.

   c. Suspend a session to do something else.

   During an active Telnet session to a host, type the escape sequence **Ctrl-Shift-6** followed by an **x** (that is, press **Ctrl**, **Shift**, and **6** together, let up on all the keys; then press the letter **x**) to suspend the session. The suspend sequence is sometimes written as **Ctrl-^ x**. This suspends the Telnet session and returns you to the local switch command-line prompt.

Note   You can have nested Telnet sessions open. For example, from the local switch, you can Telnet to another switch A, and then Telnet on to another switch B, and so forth. To suspend one of these sessions, you must also nest your escape sequences. Typing a single **Ctrl-^x** suspends the session to switch A and returns you to the local switch. Typing **Ctrl-^ Ctrl-^x** suspends the session to switch B and returns you to switch A's prompt. (Only type the **x** at the final escape sequence.)

   d. Show all active sessions:

   ```
   Switch# show sessions
   ```

   All open sessions from your connection to the local switch are listed, along with connection numbers. You can also use the **where** command to get the same information.

   e. Return to a specific session.

   First, use the **show sessions** command to get the connection number of the desired session. Then just type the connection number by itself on the command line. The session will be reactivated. You can also just press **Return/Enter** at the command-line prompt, and the last active connection in the list will be reactivated. The last active connection in the list is denoted with the asterisk (*). This makes toggling between the local switch and a single remote session easier.

Note   When you resume the connection, you are prompted with the message "[Resuming connection 2 to Switch ...]." After you resume your connection, the message shown here does not change, and the switch does not display a prompt. To refresh the device prompt, press **Ctrl-r** or **Ctrl-l**.

    f.   End an active session:

```
Switch2#Ctrl-^ x
```

```
Switch1# disconnect connection-number
```

When the remote session is suspended, you can use the **disconnect** command to end the session and close the Telnet connection. Otherwise, your session remains open until the remote host times the connection out (if at all).

    g.   Terminal screen format.

Set the screen size for the current session only:

```
Switch#terminal length lines
```

```
Switch# terminal width characters
```

Set the screen size for all sessions:

```
Switch(config-line)# length lines
```

```
Switch(config-line)# width characters
```

The screen is formatted to *characters* wide by *lines* high. When the number of lines of output from a command exceeds *lines*, the —More— prompt is used. If you don't want the output displayed by page with —More—, use **length 0**. The default length for sessions is 24 lines, and the default width for settings is 80 characters.

    h.   Configure session timeout values.

Define an absolute timeout for a line:

```
Switch(config-line)# absolute-timeout minutes
```

All active sessions on the line are terminated after *minutes* have elapsed. (Default is 0 minutes, or an indefinite session timeout.)

Define an idle timeout for a line:

```
Switch(config-line)# session-timeout minutes [output]
```

All active sessions on the line are terminated only if they have been idle for *minutes*. (Default is 0 minutes, or an indefinite idle timeout.) The **output** keyword causes the idle timer to be reset by outbound traffic on the line, keeping the connection up.

Define an idle timeout for all EXEC mode sessions:

```
Switch(config-line)# exec-timeout minutes [seconds]
```

Active EXEC mode sessions are automatically closed after an idle time period of *minutes* and *seconds* (default 10 minutes). To disable idle EXEC timeouts on the line, use the **no exec-timeout** or **exec-timeout 0 0** command.

Enable session timeout warnings:

```
Switch(config-line)# logout-warning [seconds]
```

Users are warned of an impending logout *seconds* before it occurs. By default, no warning is given. If the *seconds* field is left off, it defaults to 20 seconds.

4.   Web browser interface.

   a.   Enable the web interface:

```
Switch(config)# ip http server
```

   The web interface server is started, enabling users to monitor or configure the switch through a web browser.

Note   The switch web interface should not be used for access from a public (Internet) network because of a major vulnerability with the HTTP server service. This vulnerability is documented as Cisco Bug ID CSCdt93862. To disable the HTTP server, use the **no ip http server** command. In addition to this bug, the default authentication uses clear-text passwords. If you must use the web interface, make sure to configure a stronger authentication method and limit access in Steps c and d that follow.

   b.   *(Optional)* Set the web browser port number:

```
Switch(config)# ip http port number
```

   HTTP traffic for the web interface can be set to use TCP port *number* (default 80).

   c.   *(Optional)* Limit access to the web interface:

```
Switch(config)# ip http access-class access-list
```

   A standard IP access list (specified by either number or name) can be used to limit the source IP addresses of hosts accessing the web interface. This should be used to narrow the range of potential users accessing the switch's web interface.

   d.   *(Optional)* Choose a method for user authentication:

```
Switch(config)# ip http authentication {aaa | enable | local | tacacs}
```

   Users attempting to access the switch's web interface can be challenged and authenticated with several different mechanisms. By default, the **enable** method (the clear-text **enable** password must be entered) is used for authentication. You should use one of the stronger authentication methods: **aaa**, **local** (authentication is performed locally on the switch, using usernames and passwords), and **tacacs** (standard or extended TACACS authentication).

e. View the switch's home page.

From a web browser, use the URL **http://***switch***/**, where *switch* can be the switch's IP address or hostname. The default switch home page is available to users with a privilege level of 15. Only IOS commands available to lesser-privilege levels are available to those users limited to a privilege level less than 15.

1-2: ROM Monitor

- The ROM monitor is a ROM-based program that is executed on power up or reset of the switch.

- The ROM monitor interface can be accessed if the user presses **Ctrl-Break** during the boot process.

- If the switch fails to load an operating system or if the value of 0 is specified in the BOOT field of the configuration register, the switch enters ROM monitor mode.

- If the switch encounters a fatal exception from which it cannot recover, it enters ROM monitor mode.

- Like the Cisco IOS Software interfaces, ROM monitor is a CLI.

- ROM monitor offers a limited number of commands associated with booting recovery of the switch.

- ROM monitor offers a limited help facility and basic history functions to aid users.

- ROM monitor allows for Xmodem asynchronous transfers to aid in the recovery of IOS.

Using the ROM Monitor Command Set

Many switches have a ROM monitor command set that enables the user to interact with the switch to recover operating systems or alter boot variables during the boot process. The ROM monitor has a basic set of commands and a help facility to aid the user. The following steps outline the use of the ROM monitor facility.

1. User interface modes:

```
rommon>
```

The **rommon** interface is a simple CLI that enables users to recover from fatal errors or change the boot parameters of the switch. It offers a single mode with a limited set of commands typically associated with booting the switch and managing environment parameters.

2. User interface features.

    a. Entering commands:

```
rommon> command
```

The rommon command line interprets input a line at a time like the Cisco IOS Software CLI.

    b. Help.

You can enter a question mark (**?**) at the beginning of a rommon> prompt to get a list of available commands for rommon.

    c. History.

The rommon interface keeps a history of the previous 16 commands a user typed. To view the history, use the command **history** or the letter **h** to view the list of commands in history. When the history is listed, users should see a numeric value to the left of each command. The user can recall the commands by using the **repeat** *value* or **r** *value*, where the *value* is the number to the left of the command shown during a history listing.

3. Viewing and changing configuration variables.

    a. Viewing the configuration variables.

```
rommon> set
```

The ROM monitor loads the configuration variables for the switch before giving the user access to the prompt. These variables include the location of the configuration file and the boot image that ROM monitor will look for. Use the command **set** with no options to view these variables.

    b. Setting the configuration variables:

```
rommon> PARAMETER=value
```

To set a configuration variable, use the parameter value *exactly* as it is shown in the **set** command (these are case-sensitive) followed by a value. To nullify a configuration variable, leave the value blank. For example, use the following command to clear the boot image that was specified for the switch:

```
rommon> BOOT=
```

Note   When you're in the ROM monitor, any variable or parameter you set should be in all uppercase, and any command that is typed should be in all lowercase. If you mistype the case, the ROM monitor cannot process the command.

    c. Saving the configuration variables:

```
rommon> sync
```

To save the configuration variables, use the command **sync**. This command saves the new variables to NVRAM to be used the next time the switch is reset.

    d. Loading the new configuration variables:

```
rommon> reset
```

    To load the configuration variables to the ROM monitor, you must power cycle or reset the switch. To reset the switch, use the command **reset**.

4. Booting a switch in rommon mode.

    a. Viewing the images on Flash devices:

```
rommon> dir [device:]
```

    ROM monitor is responsible for loading the Cisco IOS Software images for a device. To view an image, use the command **dir** followed by the device name such as **dir bootflash:** or **dir slot0:**. You can use the command **dev** to locate which devices are available.

    b. Booting an image from Flash.

```
rommon> boot [device:filename]
```

    To boot from ROM monitor, use the command **boot**. The command **boot** without any device or filename uses the BOOT field in the configuration variables. If the field is empty or the file is invalid, the user is returned to the rommon> prompt. If you specify the name of the file when using the **boot** command, the variable is ignored and the file is booted.

Caution   Boot variables and filenames are case-sensitive. If you specify an invalid name or miss a character or a case setting in the name, the file will not be found and the switch will return you to the rommon mode. It might be useful to view the Flash device and highlight and copy the filename into a buffer using the **edit** commands in the terminal application.

5. Xmodem transfers:

```
rommon> xmodem
```

    This command initiates an Xmodem receive for the ROM monitor. Using this command, you can boot a switch from a file located on a PC attached to the console port. Use the terminal software on your PC to start an asynchronous transfer using Xmodem and send a file from the PC hard drive to the Flash device. After the switch has booted the image that was transferred from the PC, the OS will be active, and a valid file can be copied into flash memory. This process can take a long time and should be considered a last resort to recovering a lost or damaged image.

Chapter 2

Switch Functionality

Refer to the following sections to configure and use these features:

- **2-1: Catalyst Switch Families:** Gives a brief summary of the Cisco Catalyst switch platforms, their capabilities, and the operating systems that are supported.

- **2-2: Switched Campus Network Designs:** Presents a quick reference checklist of guidelines and ideas you can use when designing your switched enterprise network.

2-1: Catalyst Switch Families

The family of Catalyst switches is an ever-expanding product offering.

One of the major challenges in choosing and deploying a switch in your network is understanding what functions that switch performs and how it functions within the network design. The purpose of this section is to give you a brief overview of the current Catalyst switch platforms and their basic functionalities.

Catalyst 2000 Series

The Catalyst 2000 series switches provide end user access ports for the wiring closet. The switches are available in several models such as the Catalyst 2940, 2960, and 2975. These access switches vary in port densities from 8 ports to 48 ports. The Catalyst 2940 series switch supports 8 10/100 interfaces along with several uplink options: 10/100/1000 UTP, 100Base-FX, and 1000Base-X SFP. The Catalyst 2960 series switch supports 8, 24, and 48 10/100 interfaces and 24- or 48-port 10/100/1000 interfaces in addition to a variety of dual-purpose uplinks interfaces. The Catalyst 2975 series switch supports 48 10/100/1000 interfaces along with four SFP 1000Base-X uplink interfaces. The Catalyst 2000 product families offer a wide variety of Cisco IOS feature sets such as Layer 2+ forwarding, enhanced integrated security, quality of service (QoS), and Power over Ethernet (PoE). Here is the performance for the Catalyst 29xx series switches:

- Catalyst 2940

    - 3.6 Gbps maximum forwarding bandwidth

    - 2.7 Mpps wire-speed forwarding rate (based on 64-byte packets)

- Catalyst 2960

    - 16-Gbps switching fabric (Cisco Catalyst 2960-8TC-S, Catalyst 2960-24-S, Catalyst 2960-24TC-S, Catalyst 2960-48TT-S, and Catalyst 2960-48TC-S)

    - Forwarding rate based on 64-byte packets:

        - Cisco Catalyst 2960-8TC-S: 2.7 Mpps

        - Cisco Catalyst 2960-24-S: 3.6 Mpps

        - Cisco Catalyst 2960-24TC-S: 6.5 Mpps

        - Cisco Catalyst 2960-48TT-S: 10.1 Mpps

        - Catalyst 2960-48TC-S: 10.1 Mpps

- Catalyst 2975:

    - 32-Gbps switching fabric

    - 38.7 Mpps forwarding rate based on 64-byte packets

Catalyst 3000 Series

The Catalyst 3000 series switches provide end user access ports for the wiring closet. The switches are available in several models such as the Catalyst 3560, 3560-E, 3750, 3750-E, and 3100. The Catalyst 3000 series is a midline switch that can offer Layer 2 services or both Layer 2 and Layer 3 services in the same device, depending on the software. The switch comes in different port densities and offers Fast Ethernet, Gigabit Ethernet, and Ten Gigabit Ethernet support. This switch series has ports that can be directly configured as Layer 3 interfaces or can use VLAN interfaces for Layer 3 switching. It also supports Layer 2 functionalities on a port-by-port basis for basic Layer 2 connectivity and enhanced features such as trunking, channeling, QoS classification and marking, in addition to access control for Layer 2 or Layer 3 ports. The Cisco Blade Switch 3100 series are used in the Data Center Access integrated into blade chassis. The Catalyst 3100, 3750, and 3750-E offer hardware stacking, high levels of resiliency, automation, and single point of management; with Cisco StackWise technology, customers can create a single, 64-Gbps switching unit with up to nine switches.

Here is the performance for the Catalyst 3xxx series switches:

- Catalyst 3560-E performance:

    - Switching fabric 128 Gbps

- Forwarding rate:
    - 3560E-24TD 65.5 Mpps
    - 3560E-24PD 65.5 Mpps
    - 3560E-48TD 101.2 Mpps
    - 3560E-48PD 101.2 Mpps
    - 3560E-48PD-F 101.2 Mpps
    - 3560E-12D 90 Mpps
    - 3560E-12SD 47.6 Mpps
- Catalyst 3750-E performance:
    - 160-Gbps switching fabric capacity
    - Stack-forwarding rate of 95 Mpps for 64-byte packets
    - Forwarding rate:
        - 3750E-24TD-65.5 Mpps
        - 3750E-24PD-65.5 Mpps
        - 3750E-48TD-101.2 Mpps
        - 3750E-48PD-101.2 Mpps
        - 3750E-48PD-F-101.2 Mpps

Because of its flexibility, the 3000 series makes an excellent switch in small to midsize campus environments and can be deployed as an access switch or a distribution switch. The 3000 series can run either the IP Base image for Layer 2 switching or the IP Services software image for Layer 2 and 3 switching. The IP Base image supports basic routing such as RIP, static, and EIGRP stub routing.

Catalyst 4500 Series

The Catalyst 4500 series switch is a midline switch that can act as a high-port-density access switch and distribution switch and a low-density core device. The 4500 series is also a modular switch that offers both Layer 2 and Layer 3 services. This switch offers Fast Ethernet, Gigabit Ethernet, and Ten Gigabit Ethernet connectivity. The Catalyst 4500 series offers a wide variety of supervisor engines—Supervisor II, IV, V, and VI. The Supervisor IV, V, and VI for the 4500 series have an integrated Layer 3 switching capability. These switches also perform Layer 2 trunking functions and provide support for EtherChannel, QoS, and PoE.

The Catalyst 4500 also offers a fixed form factor switch, which is based on the chassis Supervisor forwarding engine V and VI. The Catalyst 4948 is based on the Supervisor V, and the Catalyst 4900M and is based on the Supervisor VI forwarding engine. The

Catalyst 4948 offers 48 ports of 10/100/1000 and two X2 10 Gigabit Ethernet uplinks; the 4900M offers eight fixed wire-speed 10 Gigabit Ethernet ports, and two half-slots that you can fill with any combination of the following: (please remember that only the 8-port 10 Gigabit Ethernet expansion module supports the Cisco TwinGig converter):

- 20-port wire-speed 10/100/1000 (RJ-45) half-card

- 8-port (2:1) 10 Gigabit Ethernet (X2) half-card (Cisco TwinGig Converter Module-compatible)

- 4-port wire-speed 10 Gigabit Ethernet (X2) half-card

- The Catalyst 4500 also has a 7-slot and a 10-slot "R" chassis that allows for redundant supervisor modules.

Here is the performance for the Catalyst 45xx supervisor modules switches:

- **Supervisor 6-E 320:** Gbps/250 Mpps

- **Supervisor V-10GE:** 136 Gbps/102 Mpps

- **Supervisor V:** 96 Gbps/72 Mpps

- **Supervisor IV:** 64 Gbps/48 Mpps

- **Supervisor II-Plus-10GE:** 108 Gbps/81 Mpps

- **Supervisor II-Plus 64:** Gbps/48 Mpps

- **Supervisor II-Plus-TS:** 64 Gbps/48 Mpps

Catalyst 6500

The Catalyst 6500 series switch is the flagship of the Catalyst product lines. It is the most robust, has the highest backplane support, and is the most flexible of any of the Catalyst products. This modular switch can act as a high-port-density access switch, as a Layer 2 or Layer 3 distribution switch, and as a wire-speed Layer 2 or Layer 3 core switch. In addition to its high-speed Ethernet switching capabilities, it offers a variety of cards to support advanced features such as voice services, content switching, intrusion detection, network analysis, optical services, 10 Gigabit Ethernet, firewall support, and encryption services. All these features function at wire speeds. In addition to these services, the 6500 chassis supports connectivity for the fabric module (CEF256), Cross-Bar (CEF720) to interconnect the cards rather than the 32 classic Gbps bus. With this fabric module, a 6500-E chassis fully populated with fabric-enabled cards has a total of 720 Gbps of fabric connectivity. The switch also offers support for redundancy and high-availability features. The Catalyst 6500 series switches continue to evolve as new products provide more flexibility and functionality. For example, Cisco introduced Virtual Switching System (VSS) on the Catalyst 6500 with the announcement of the Supervisor 720-10GE-PFC3c. This allows for two Cisco Catalyst 6500 series switches with this supervisor engine to pool together into a VSS 1440. The two switches connect with 10 GbE links called Virtual Switch Links (VSL). When a VSS 1440 is created, it acts as a single virtual Catalyst switch.

Note The Catalyst 6500 chassis was classified as end of sale and was replaced with the Catalyst 6500-E chassis. The E chassis supports all existing line cards but was enhanced to provide a better power bus for PoE and power supplies. The E chassis also provides the following benefits from the non-E chassis: support for 80 Gbps per slot, increase cooling capacity per slot to accommodate high-performance line cards, and adds a redundant control channel to improve high availability (HA) capabilities of the switch.

2-2: Switched Campus Network Designs

When you design a switched network, you must consider many things. Adding to or redesigning a large enterprise or campus network can seem complex or overwhelming. An accepted, organized approach to switched network design can simplify the design process and make the network more efficient and scalable.

This section is organized as a quick reference "checklist" of guidelines, rules of thumb, and ideas to help you think through the overall network architecture and configuration. Many of the checklist items include a reference to the appropriate sections of this book that deal with the switch features.

1. Segment LANs into the smallest collision domains possible by using LAN switches.

2. Organize your enterprise network into a hierarchical structure.

    A network designed around a layered structure gives the foundation for predictable behavior, consistent latency (number of switch hops) from anywhere in the network, and scalability. If the network needs to be expanded, you can add more switch blocks into the existing structure.

    Figure 2-1 shows the basic network hierarchy divided into three distinct layers:

    ■   Access layer: Consists of switches that connect to the end users

    ■   Distribution layer: Consists of switches that aggregate traffic from the access layer

    ■   Core layer: Consists of switches that aggregate traffic from the distribution layers

Tip In small- to medium-sized enterprise networks, the distribution layer can be omitted. The access layer switches uplink directly into the core layer, which is referred to as a *collapsed core* design.

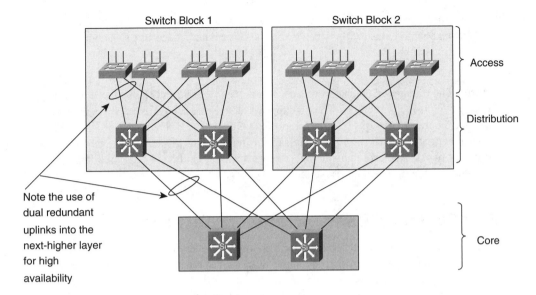

Note the use of
dual redundant
uplinks into the
next-higher layer
for high
availability

Figure 2-1 *Layers of a Hierarchical Network Design*

To provide high availability, each switch in a network layer needs to have dual or redundant uplinks to two switches in the next higher layer. If a link failure or the failure of an entire switch occurs, the extra uplink can be quickly used. The uplink failover is handled by the *Spanning Tree Protocol (STP)* at Layer 2 or by routing protocols at Layer 3.

3. Place switching functionality at each layer of the hierarchy.

   ■ **Access:** Switches at this layer generally have a high port density, lower cost, features that address user access or security, and several high-speed uplink ports. Usually, Layer 2 switching is sufficient, although Layer 3 switching can provide higher availability for applications such as IP telephony.

   ■ **Distribution:** Distribution switches have a port density consisting of high-speed ports and offer higher switching performance, ideally at Layer 3.

   ■ **Core:** The core layer should be built from the highest performance switches in the network, aggregating traffic from the distribution switches. Layer 2 switches can be used effectively, although switching at Layer 3 adds higher availability and enhanced QoS. Usually a dual-switch core layer is sufficient to support an entire enterprise.

4. Identify resources in your network that serve common functions. These become the modules or building blocks of your network design. Figure 2-2 shows some examples of these blocks and how they fit within the network hierarchy.

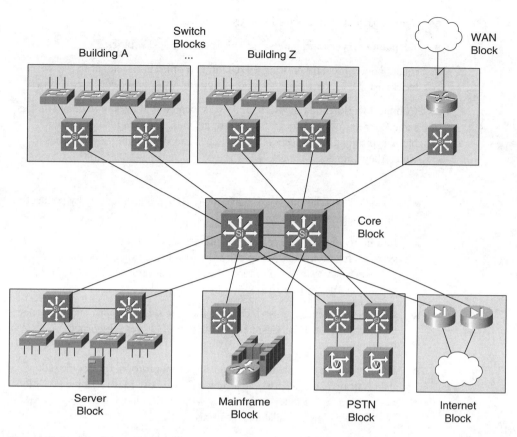

Figure 2-2 *Modular Approach to a Campus Network Design Consider High Availability or Redundancy Features That Can Be Used in Each Network Building Block*

Tip The network in Figure 2-2 is shown with single uplinks to higher layers for simplicity. In a real network, you need to always add dual redundant uplinks to two switches in the next higher network layer for the highest network availability.

In this case, each access layer switch would have two uplinks to the two nearest distribution switches. In addition, each distribution switch in each block of the diagram would have two uplinks to the two core layer switches. In other words, the basic principles of Figure 2-1 need to be applied to the enterprise layout of Figure 2-2.

- **Server farms and mainframes:** These are called server blocks and mainframe blocks, respectively.

- **Internet access, e-commerce or extranet server farms, and firewall farms:** These are called an Internet block.

- **Remote access:** This is called a WAN block.

- **Telephony servers and gateways:** This is called a PSTN block.

- **Legacy networks (Token Ring, FDDI, and so on):** This is similar to the WAN block, using a router to provide connectivity to various network media types.

- **Common workgroups of users:** End users located in the same building, on the same floor, or in the same area of a floor are called *switch blocks*. A switch block typically groups access layer switches and the distribution switches to which they connect.

a. Core

  - If Layer 2 switches are used, don't create a spanning-tree loop by connecting the two core switches.

  - Be sure to identify and configure both primary and secondary root bridge switches for each VLAN. Typically, the root bridge should be placed close to the core layer. Refer to section "7-2: STP Configuration," in Chapter 7, "Spanning Tree Protocol (STP)."

  - If Layer 3 switches are used, connect the core switches with multiple links. See section "4-4: EtherChannel," in Chapter 4, "Layer 2 Interface Configuration."

  - In a Layer 3 core, make use of Layer 3 routing protocol to provide redundant routing paths, as possible leverage Equal Cost Multi Pathing (ECMP). See section "8-3: Router Redundancy with HSRP," in Chapter 8, "Configuring High Availability Features."

  - Each core switch should connect to each distribution switch for full redundancy. If Layer 3 is not used in the core or distribution layers, use STP BackboneFast to reduce STP convergence time. See section "7-2: STP Configuration," in Chapter 7.

b. Server block

  - Use redundant uplinks into the distribution or core layer. Utilize STP UplinkFast (section "7-2: STP Configuration" in Chapter 7) or HSRP (section "8-6: Router Redundancy with HSRP" in Chapter 8) for fast failover.

  - Consider using dual network interface cards (NIC) in servers for redundancy. Connect the NICs into different switch cards or modules.

c. Internet block

  - Use Server Load Balancing to distribute traffic across multiple servers in a server farm. See section "10-1: SLB," in Chapter 10, "Server Load Balancing (SLB)."

  - Use Firewall Load Balancing to distribute traffic across multiple firewalls in a firewall farm. See section "10-2: SLB Firewall Load Balancing," in Chapter 10.

  d. Switch blocks

- ■ Each access layer switch has dual uplinks to two separate distribution switches.

- ■ Use STP UplinkFast on access layer switches to reduce uplink failover time.

- ■ Use STP PortFast on access layer ports to reduce startup time for end users.

- ■ To load balance across the access layer uplinks, adjust the STP parameters so that one access VLAN travels over one uplink while another VLAN travels over the other uplink (Layer 2 distribution layer). Otherwise, adjust the HSRP priorities in a Layer 3 distribution so that one distribution switch supports one access VLAN and the other distribution switch supports another VLAN.

- ■ If Layer 3 is used in the distribution layer, use passive interfaces toward the access layer where no other routers reside.

5. Other considerations

  a. For each VLAN, configure an STP root bridge and a secondary root bridge as close to the core layer as possible. See section "7-2: STP Configuration," in Chapter 7.

  b. Broadcast domains

- ■ Limit the size of broadcast domains by controlling the size of VLANs. It is permissible to extend VLANs anywhere in the network, but broadcast traffic will follow it.

- ■ Consider using broadcast suppression on switch ports. See section "11-1: Broadcast Suppression," in Chapter 11, "Controlling Traffic and Switch Access."

  c. VLAN Trunking Protocol (VTP)

- ■ VTP Transparent mode is recommended as the best practice instead of VTP client/server modes.

- ■ Use VTP manual pruning specific VLANs to be transported on trunks. This reduces the unnecessary broadcast traffic on the trunks.

  d. Scaling trunks

- ■ Bundle multiple trunk links together into an EtherChannel. For fault tolerance, divide the EtherChannel across switch modules. See section "4-4: EtherChannel," in Chapter 4.

- ■ Do not configure trunk negotiation; use the "On" mode. See section "6-3: Trunking," in Chapter 6, "VLANs and Trunking."

e. QoS

■ Configure QoS on every switch in your network. QoS must be properly supported end-to-end. See section "13-2: QoS Configuration," in Chapter 13, "Quality of Service."

■ Extend the QoS trust boundary to edge devices (IP phones, for example) that can provide trust.

■ Use policers to control nonmission-critical traffic flows.

f. Redundant switch modules

■ Consider using redundant supervisors in server farm switches where hosts are single-attached (one NIC).

■ If redundant uplinks are provided at each network layer, two physically separate switches will always provide redundancy. Use redundant supervisors in distribution or core layer switches where only single uplinks are available.

■ Use high-availability redundancy between supervisors in a chassis. Enable versioning so that the OS can be upgraded without a switch downtime. See section "3-6: Redundant Supervisors," in Chapter 3, "Supervisor Engine Configuration."

g. Port security, authentication

■ You can control the end-user MAC address or the number of users connected to an access layer switch port with port security. See section "11-3: Port Security," in Chapter 11.

■ Authenticate users at the access layer switch ports. Section "11-8: 802.1X Port Authentication," in Chapter 11 describes how to configure a port to require a login or certificate for user authentication before granting access to the network.

■ Control access to VLANs with VLAN ACLs. See section "11-4: VLAN Access Control Lists," in Chapter 11.

■ Dynamic ARP Inspection (DAI) is a security feature that validates ARP packets in a network. See section "11-9: Layer 2 Security," in Chapter 11.

■ DHCP Snooping provides the security against the Denial-of-Service (DoS) attacks. See section "11-9: Layer 2 Security," in Chapter 11.

■ IP Source Guard prevents IP spoofing by allowing only the IP addresses that are obtained through DHCP Snooping on a particular port. See section "11-9: Layer 2 Security," in Chapter 11.

   h. End station discovery

- LLDP is a neighbor discovery protocol that is used for network devices to support non-Cisco devices and to allow for interoperability between other devices; the switch supports the IEEE 802.1AB.

- LLDP-Med for Media Endpoint Devices (LLDP-MED) is an extension to LLDP that operates between endpoint devices, such as IP phones, and network devices, such as switches.

- CDP is a device discovery protocol that runs over Layer 2 (the data link layer) on all Cisco-manufactured devices (routers, bridges, access servers, and switches).

Further Reading

Refer to the following recommended sources for further information about the topics covered in this chapter.

Catalyst Switch Families

Cisco Product Quick Reference Guide (CPQRG) at http://www.cisco.com/en/US/prod/qrg/index.html.

For Catalyst LAN switches, go to http://www.cisco.com/en/US/products/hw/switches/index.html#~hide_v3~+.

Software Advisor: A tool to compare and match Catalyst COS and IOS features, releases, and hardware platforms. Go to http://tools.cisco.com/Support/Fusion/FusionHome.do (CCO login required).

Cisco Validated Designs: Campus

Enterprise Campus 3.0 Architecture: Overview and Framework (CCO login required): http://www.cisco.com/en/US/partner/docs/solutions/Enterprise/Campus/campover.html#wp7 08798.

Enterprise QoS Solution Reference Network Design Guide: http://www.tinyurl.com/ancser.

High Availability Campus Recovery Analysis Design Guide: http://www.tinyurl.com/d5vz3c.

High Availability Campus Network Design—Routed Access Layer using EIGRP or OSPF: http://www.tinyurl.com/cqwwzq.

Campus Network for High Availability Design Guide: http://www.tinyurl.com/d3e6dj.

Froom, Richard, Balaji Sivasubramanian, and Erum Frahim. *Building Cisco Multilayer Switched Networks (BCMSN)*, Fourth Edition. Cisco Press, ISBN-10: 1-58705-273-3.

Hucaby, Dave. *CCNP BCMSN Official Exam Certification Guide*, Fourth Edition. Cisco Press, ISBN 1-58720-171-2.

Chapter 3

Supervisor Engine Configuration

See the following sections for configuration information about these topics:

- **3-1: Prompts and Banners:** Describes the method for configuring prompts and banners for switch identification

- **3-2: IP Addressing and Services:** Explains how to configure IP addressing and services for switch management using the TCP/IP protocol

- **3-3: Passwords and Password Recovery:** Covers the processes that set passwords for switches and the methods that recover lost and unknown passwords

- **3-4: Managing Modules:** Describes how to control power to a module, reset a module, and manage the configuration of individual modules for modular switches

- **3-5: File Management and Boot Parameters:** Explains the process for management of configuration and system files and how to control the boot process

- **3-6: Redundant Supervisors:** Explains the feature by which redundant Supervisor modules synchronize their configurations and how to manage this feature

- **3-7: Cisco Discovery Protocol:** Describes the interaction of the *Cisco Discovery Protocol (CDP)* with other Cisco devices and how to control CDP functions for switch ports

- **3-8: Time and Calendar:** Presents the basic steps needed to configure date and time information on the switch using both manual configuration techniques and *Network Time Protocol* (NTP)

3-1: Prompts and Banners

- Switch prompts help users identify the device they are managing by providing a useful name at each command-line entry point.

- System banners both identify switches and provide information about security policies and monitoring procedures.

- The configuration of prompts and banners is optional.

Configuration of Prompt

1. *(Optional)* Configure the prompt.

   a. Configure a prompt by setting a device name:

   (global) **hostname** *string*

   By default, the hostname for an IOS device is Switch or Router, depending on the function (Layer 2 or Layer 3) of the switch.

   b. Specifically configure a prompt:

   (global) **prompt** *string*

   By default, the hostname for an IOS device is Switch or Router, depending on the function (Layer 2 or Layer 3) of the switch.

Configuration of Banner

1. *(Optional)* Configure a *Message of the Day (MOTD)* banner.

   MOTD banners are not required to make any system operational; however, they are extremely useful for identifying any security policies pertaining to accessing network devices.

   a. Configure an MOTD banner:

   (global) **banner motd &** *string* **&**

   The banner text is typed in between delimiting characters (in the table, the ampersand [&]). The delimiting character is typed at the beginning and end of the banner, which can include multiple lines, line breaks, and words. The delimiting character can be any character that is not part of the banner text.

Note   Banners are limited in size by device and operating system. There is no consistent number or limitation.

Feature Example

This example shows a typical configuration for setting the system name, prompt, and banner.

An example of the Supervisor IOS configuration follows:

```
Switch(config)# hostname Core_Switch1
Core_Switch1(config)# banner motd *
```

```
This is Core_Switch1 for the XYZ corporation.
You have accessed a restricted device, unauthorized logins are prohibited.
*
```

Core_Switch1(config)# **end**
Core_Switch1# **copy running-config startup-config**

3-2: IP Addressing and Services

- Switches use IP addresses and services for management purposes.

- IP addresses can be set or obtained using *Dynamic Host Configuration Protocol (DHCP), BOOTstrap Protocol (BOOTP)*, or *Reverse Address Resolution Protocol (RARP)*.

- Gateways, routes to networks, and default routes are established to allow communications with devices that are not local to the management network.

- Static entries or DNS servers can be used to resolve computer names.

- HTTP services are available for some switches to provide a configuration interface.

- *Simple Network Management Protocol (SNMP)* service allows for switch configuration and management.

Configuring an IP Management Address

IP addresses are used in Layer 2 switches for management purposes only. This step is not required to make the switch operational. If you do not configure an IP address, however, the only way to manage the switch is by using the console connection.

1. (*Optional; recommended*) Configure the IP address.

    a. Configure the IP address manually:

        ```
        (global) interface vlan vlannumber
        (interface or subinterface) ip address address mask
        (interface or subinterface) management
        ```

        Catalyst switches can have an active management address in only one VLAN. The management command on the Layer 2 IOS switches specifies which VLAN is active. VLAN 1 is the default management VLAN for IOS. On a Layer 2 IOS switch, if VLAN 1 is not the management VLAN, the prompt reads "subinterface."

        To view the IP configuration, use the **show interface vlan** n (where *n* is your VLAN number) command.

Note   This addressing section deals exclusively with Layer 2 management addresses and interfaces only. Layer 3 interfaces are discussed in Chapter 5, "Layer 3 Interface Configuration."

b. (*Not recommended*) Automatically obtain an IP address.

You can have the switch request an address from a service, such as RARP, BOOTP, or DHCP. This is not recommended because it is conceivable that the address could change for DHCP unless the lease is permanent or static (meaning that the lease never expires or a specific IP address is reserved for the switch MAC). This also means that a change of hardware could create a problem with BOOTP and the static DHCP address.

For Layer 2 switches, you can obtain an address via DHCP/BOOTP if you have configured the device for autoconfig. The command **service config** enables auto-config. If automatic configuration is enabled, the switch ignores any manual IP configuration parameters:

```
(global) service config
(privileged exec)reload
```

Note   Service configuration loads a complete configuration for the switch automatically. It is referred to as *autoinstall* in the router community. Autoconfig also requires that a configuration file be available on a TFTP server for a full configuration. For more details on autoconfig, consult the Cisco website at http://www.tinyurl.com/akvdx8.

Configuring a Default Gateway

To access the switch from IP subnets other than the subnet in the management address, you need to configure a default gateway. This provides the switch with the minimum information that it needs to provide remote connectivity.

1.   (*Optional; recommended*) Configure the default gateway:

```
(global) ip default-gateway gatewayaddress
```

The gateway address is the IP address of the Layer 3 interface that acts as a router for traffic generated by the switch. To view your default gateways, use the **show ip route default** command.

Setting Up DNS Services or Host Tables

Each Catalyst switch can resolve common names, such as URLs or fully qualified domain names, into IP addresses if the proper IP service is configured. This service is a *Domain Name System (DNS)* server or a local host table. By default, DNS services are enabled on Catalyst switches, but the server is not specified. To configure the switch for DNS operation, use the following guidelines.

1.   (*Optional*) Enable the DNS service on the switch:

```
(global) ip domain-lookup
```

This command enables the switch to use DNS for name lookups. The default is for **ip domain-lookup** to be enabled.

> **Tip**   If you are not going to use DNS, it is recommended that you disable DNS lookups with the global configuration command **no ip domain-lookup**. This command prevents the switch from trying to resolve mistyped commands.

2. *(Optional)* Define the address of the DNS server:

```
(global) ip name-server serveraddress1 [serveraddress2. . . serveraddress6]
```

Use this command to specify the addresses of one or more DNS servers. You can specify up to six addresses on a single command-line entry. In IOS switches, the first address configured is the first address DNS queries are sent for resolution. Subsequent addresses are used only if the first address times out or returns a negative acknowledgment.

-or-

(Optional) Specify host entries for name resolution:

```
(global) ip host name address
```

By specifying the name and address of the device on the switch, the name is resolved in the local table. DNS can be enabled or disabled when using local hostnames; locally configured hosts are searched before a request is sent to DNS.

Configuring HTTP Services

You can enable an HTTP server so that the switch can be managed using a web browser. The web-based GUI is a straightforward management option that gives users another configuration option.

1. *(Optional)* Configure HTTP service for switch configuration:

```
(global) [no] ip http server
```

The command **ip http server** is enabled by default. You can choose to disable it with the **no** command.

Feature Example

This example shows a typical configuration for setting the IP address, gateway, and DNS servers for a switch in an administrative VLAN 986. This example disables the HTTP server service:

```
Switch(config)# interface vlan 986
Switch(config-subif)# ip address 10.1.1.5 255.255.255.0
Switch(config-subif)# management
Switch(config-subif)# ip default-gateway 10.1.1.1
Switch(config)# ip name-server 10.1.1.254
Switch(config)# no ip http server

Switch(config)# end
Switch# copy running-config startup-config
```

Section 3-2

3-3: Passwords and Password Recovery

- Passwords provide a layer of protection for the switch to prevent unauthorized use.

- Catalyst switches have two levels of password protection (user level and privileged level).

- Privileged passwords are encrypted for tighter security.

- If a password is lost, IOS offers a password recovery process to gain access to the device.

Configuration of Passwords

1. *(Optional; highly recommended)* Configure a user-level password:

    ```
    (line) login
    (line) password password
    ```

    The user-level password prevents anyone who is not authorized from accessing the *command-line interface (CLI)* from Telnet or console sessions. The command **login** and a **password** must be configured on each line (**con0** or **vty**). To enable password checking at login, use the **login** command. The vty lines are often referred to as Telnet. You can SSH into vty lines.

    > **Note**   On a switch, you can configure a different user-level password for any line, such as Telnet or console connections.

2. *(Optional; highly recommended)* Configure a privileged-level password:

    ```
    (global) enable secret password
    ```

    The privileged password prevents anyone who is not authorized from gaining access to privileged level, where configuration changes can be made to the switch and other features. The **enable secret** command followed by the password is used to configure the password.

    > **Note**   Only the secret, privileged password is encrypted by default. You can use the **service password-encryption** command to prevent the console and vty passwords from being stored in clear text.

Feature Example

This example shows a typical configuration for setting the user and privileged passwords:

```
Switch(config)# enable secret san-fran
Switch(config)# line vty 0 4
Switch(config-line)# password cisco
```

```
Switch(config-line)# line con 0
Switch(config-line)# login
Switch(config-line)# password cisco
Switch(config-line)# end
Switch1# copy running-config startup-config
```

Password Recovery: Procedure 1

Password recovery procedure 1 covers the Cisco Catalyst Layer 2 fixed configuration switches 2900XL/3500XL, 2940, 2950/2955, 2960, and 2970 Series, and the Cisco Catalyst Layer 3 fixed configuration switches 3550, 3560, and 3750 series. If you have lost or forgotten your passwords, or if you want to bypass the configuration file, you can use this recovery process to gain access to the device.

To recover from a lost password, you have to stop the boot process and then direct the switch to not use the configuration file. When the switch loads without a file, you have no passwords and can enter into privileged mode. From there, you can copy the configuration file into active memory and then change and save the passwords. To complete the recovery process, follow these steps:

1. Attach a device to the console of the switch. Make sure you have connectivity and then unplug the power cord from the switch.

2. Press and hold down the mode button while plugging the switch back in. Release the mode button after the LED above port 1x has been on for at least two seconds.

3. You receive some information indicating that the Flash initialization has been interrupted. After you receive this information, at the prompt type the command **flash_init**.

4. Next type the command **load_helper**.

5. You need to get a listing of the Flash image with the command **dir flash:** (the colon [:] is required).

6. Rename the file to config.text with the command rename **flash:config.text flash:config.old**.

7. Continue the boot process with the command **boot**.

8. Answer **n** to the question about entering the setup mode.

9. Press **Enter** to access the user mode and enter into privileged mode with the command **enable**.

10. Rename the configuration file back to **config.text** with the command **rename flash:config.old flash:config.text**.

11. Copy the configuration file into active memory with the command **copy flash:config.text system:running-config**.

12. Enter configuration mode with the command **configure terminal**.

13. Change the line and secret passwords as covered previously in this section.

14. Save the configuration.

Section 3-3

32 Cisco LAN Switching Configuration Handbook

> **Tip** You can find additional information about the password recovery procedure for Cisco Catalyst Layer 2 fixed configuration switches at http://www.tinyurl.com/4jmw4.

Feature Example

This example shows a typical password recovery procedure 1 for IOS switches.

The system has been interrupted prior to initializing the Flash file system. The following commands initialize the Flash file system and finish loading the operating system software:

```
switch: flash_init
Initializing Flash...
flashfs[0]: 143 files, 4 directories
flashfs[0]: 0 orphaned files, 0 orphaned directories
flashfs[0]: Total bytes: 3612672
flashfs[0]: Bytes used: 2729472
flashfs[0]: Bytes available: 883200
flashfs[0]: flashfs fsck took 86 seconds
....done Initializing Flash.
Boot Sector Filesystem (bs:) installed, fsid: 3
Parameter Block Filesystem (pb:) installed, fsid: 4
switch: load_helper
switch: dir flash:
 Directory of flash:
2  -rwx 843947 Mar 01 1993 00:02:18 C2900XL-ms-12.2.8.bin
4 drwx   3776 Mar 01 1993 01:23:24 html
66 -rwx    130 Jan 01 1970 00:01:19 env_vars
68 -rwx 1296   Mar 01 1993 06:55:51 config.text
1728000 bytes total (456704 bytes free)
rename flash:config.text flash:config.old
boot
Continue with the configuration dialog? [yes/no] : N
Switch>enable
Switch# rename flash:config.old flash:config.text
Switch# copy flash:config.text system:running-config
Switch# configure terminal
Switch(config)# enable secret newpassword
Switch(config)# line vty 0 4
Switch(config-line)# password newpassword
Switch(config)# line con 0
Switch(config-line)# password newpassword
Switch#(config-line)# end
Switch# copy running-config startup-config
```

Password Recovery on IOS Devices: Procedure 2

Password recovery procedure 2 covers the 6000 series switch. If you have lost or forgotten your passwords, or if you want to bypass the configuration file, you can use this recovery process.

To recover from a lost password, you must stop the boot process of the route processor and then direct the switch to not use the configuration file. When the switch loads without a file, you have no passwords and can enter into privileged mode. From there you can copy the configuration file into active memory and then change and save the passwords. To complete the recovery process, follow these steps:

1. Attach a device to the console of the switch and power cycle the device.

2. Watch the console output. When you see the message "%OIR-6-CONSOLE: Changing console ownership to route processor," initiate the break sequence from your terminal emulator (typically **Ctrl-Break**).

3. You should see a rommon1> prompt. At this prompt, type **confreg 0x2142** to tell the switch to ignore the current configuration.

4. Now type **reset** at the rommon2> prompt to reset the switch and restart to boot process.

5. Answer **no** to the question about entering setup.

6. Press **Enter** to gain access to the Router> prompt and enter the command **enable** to access privileged mode.

7. At the Router# prompt, copy the startup configuration into the running configuration with the command **copy startup-config running-config**.

8. Enter global configuration mode with the command **configure terminal**.

9. Change the line and secret passwords as covered previously in this section.

10. Reset the configuration register with the command **config-register 0x2102**.

11. Exit setup mode with the command **end**.

12. Save the configuration with the command **copy running-config startup-config**.

Feature Example

This example shows a typical password-recovery procedure 2 for switches:

```
%OIR-6-CONSOLE: Changing console ownership to route processor
issue break
rommon>confreg 0x2142
rommon>reset
! switch output omitted
Continue with the configuration dialog? [yes/no] : N
Router>enable
Router# copy startup-config running-config
Router# configure terminal
Router(config)# enable secret newpassword
```

```
Router(config)# line vty 0 4
Router(config-line)# password newpassword
Router(config)# line con 0
Router(config-line)# password newpassword
Router# config-register 0x2102
Router#(config-line)# end
Router# copy running-config startup-config
```

3-4: Managing Modules

- Many devices have multiple blades or modules used for switching services.

- Some of these modules have their own operating systems and can be accessed directly for configuration.

- Most modules can be power-cycled or reset individually.

- For some switches, it is possible to power down a module.

Viewing Modules

You can use modular switches to effect a more flexible switch configuration. To view the modules installed on a switch, use one of the following commands:

Supervisor IOS   (privileged) **show module all**

L2 IOS   (privileged) **show hardware** or **show version**

These commands show the hardware or module information for the switches.

Accessing Modules

Most modules and ports are configured through the main CLI for the switch. However, a handful of modules, such as the services modules that are placed in the Catalyst 6500, contain their own independent operating system and CLI. To access these interfaces, use the **session** command:

(privileged)**session** *slot#*

The *slot#* or *mod#* indicates in which slot or module that the switch card occupies.

Resetting Modules

You can reset modules on an individual basis. Therefore, you can jumpstart a group of ports without having to reset the entire switch:

(privileged) **power cycle module** *slot*

The **reset** command causes an entire module to be powered down and then back up and forces the module to go through *Power-On Self-Test (POST)* as it reloads. Some switches do not offer this option. For those switches, you can reset a port with the **shutdown** and **no shutdown** commands.

Powering Modules Up and Down

For modular switches, you can power down a module. Powering down disables the module and all its ports. If the switch is reset or power-cycled, the module remains in a powered-down state. This state can be useful for troubleshooting a boot problem or if the power supply cannot handle the complete switch power load:

```
(global) no power enable module slot
```

This command disables the modules. None of the module's configuration are saved, and if the switch is reset, all the configuration entries for that module are lost. To reenable the modules, use the following command:

```
(global)power enable module slot
```

3-5: File Management and Boot Parameters

- Cisco operating systems have many files and file systems that require management.

- File management consists of managing configuration files and operating system files.

- File system commands replace many older file management commands.

- File system commands enable you to view and classify all files, including files on remote servers.

- File system commands enable you to copy files with complete path information to eliminate the need for system prompting.

- Cisco platforms support various Flash and ATA file system types.

- When copying various files into Flash memory, it is important to configure the switch to boot the proper file with boot parameters.

Note   Switches have a set of file system commands that facilitate file management. Cisco refers to the file system as the *IFS* or *IOS file system*. This file system provides an extremely powerful way to manage files within the switch devices and on remote systems. To provide backward compatibility, many aliases map to older commands for file management. See Table 3-3 at the end of this section for a listing of the older commands and the IFS equivalent.

Section 3-5

Navigating File Systems

1. View the available file system devices:

    (privileged) **show file systems**

    This command gives a listing of the file systems available on the device and the total size and the amount of free space on the file system in bytes, the type of file system, the flags for the file system, and the alias name used to access the file system. File system types include Flash, *nonvolatile random-access memory (NVRAM)*, and network (and some others, such as ROM file systems, that contain microcode). Table 3-1 lists some of the available file systems. Note that not all file systems are available on all platforms.

Table 3-1   *Cisco File Systems*

Prefix	File System
system:	Contains the system memory, including the running configuration.
nvram:	Nonvolatile RAM. This contains the startup configuration.
flash:	Flash memory. Typically the location of the IOS image. This is the default or starting file system for file system navigation. The prefix *flash*: is available on all platforms. For platforms that do not have a device named *flash*:, the prefix *flash*: is aliased to *slot0*:. Therefore, you can use the prefix *flash*: to refer to the main Flash memory storage area on all platforms.
bootflash:	Boot flash memory. Typical location for Rxboot IOS image.
Sup-boot-flash:	The boot flash for the Supervisor module is the *switch processor (SP)*. This is where IOS is loaded.
Slot0:	First PCMCIA Flash memory card.
Disk0:	Available for CompactFlash Type II cards that provide additional storage.
Disk1:	Available for CompactFlash Type II cards that provide additional storage.
Tftp:	Trivial File Transfer Protocol network server.
ftp:	FTP network server.
slave-nvram:	NVRAM on a redundant Supervisor module running native IOS.
slave-sup-bootflash:	The boot flash for the Supervisor SP on a redundant Supervisor module.
slave-boot-flash:	Internal Flash memory on a redundant MSFC running native IOS.
slave-slot0:	First PCMCIA card on a redundant Supervisor module.

Table 3-1   *Cisco File Systems*

Prefix	File System
null:	Null destination for copies. You can copy a remote file to null to determine its size.
rcp:	*Remote Copy Protocol (RCP)* network server.

2. Change the default file system directory:

   `(privileged)` **cd** `[filesystem:]`

   Use this command to move to a specific file system or directory within that file system. By moving to a specific file location, you can use file system commands without having to specify the *file system:* option. If you do a **dir** command without specifying the *file system:*, for example, it uses the directory that has been specified by the default directory or the **cd** command. The default file system directory is Flash.

3. List the current directory:

   `(privileged)` **pwd**

   This command prints or displays the name of the working directory to the screen and enables you to determine the default file system directory. Use this command to verify that you have moved into the appropriate directory when using **cd** command.

4. Display information about the files:

   `(privileged)` **dir** `[/`**all**`]` `[filesystem:][path/filename]`

   This command displays a directory of the default directory structure as specified by the **cd** command. The option **/all** enables you to see all files, including those that have been deleted but not permanently removed from a file system. You can also specify a file system by using the *filesystem:* or *device:* option. If you want to view a single file, provide the path and filename, too. You can use an asterisk (*) as a wildcard to display a group of files with common starting characters. Use this command to get a list of files off of any available local file system:

   `(privileged)` **show** `filesystem:`

   This command displays the contents of a file system. It is similar to the **dir** command, but the output is formatted differently. This command does not enable you to display individual files or remote file systems.

   > **Note**   With ATA disk devices you no longer need to use the **squeeze** command because it deletes the file upon entering the **delete** keyword; **squeeze** was only relevant in flash devices.

5. View the information about a local or remote file:

(privileged) **show file information** *filesystem:path*

This command enables you to view information about a file on a remote or local file system. The output displays the image type and size.

6. View the contents of a local or remote file:

(privileged) **more [/ascii | /binary | /ebcdic]** *filesystem:path*

Use this command to view the contents of a remote or local file. The options **ascii**, **binary**, and **ebcdic** enable you to specify the type of format in which you want to have the file presented. If you specify **dump**, it shows the file in binary format. The *filesystem:path* options enable you to specify a particular file on a valid file system. For example, **more /ascii flash:myconfig.txt** displays the file myconfig.txt in ASCII format located in the current Flash device.

Deleting Files from Flash

Cisco switch platforms have three different classifications of file systems. Each of these file systems deals differently with deleting and permanently removing files from the Flash file system. Table 3-2 shows the three types of file systems and the platforms that use these file systems.

Table 3-2   *Switch File System Types*

File System Type	Platforms
Class A	Catalyst 6500, 4500, 4848, 4900M
Class B	Catalyst 3560-E, 3750-E
Class C	Catalyst 2940, 2960

1. Delete a file from Flash memory:

(privileged) **delete** *[filesystem:]filename*

This command deletes a file from Flash on any of the three classifications of file systems. For Class A and B file systems, the file is marked as deleted and shows up only if the command **dir /all** is used. You can restore files that are marked as deleted by using the **undelete** command. For Class C file systems, the **delete** command permanently removes the file from the system. The file system must be a Flash file system.

2. Restore a deleted file:

(privileged) **undelete** *index [filesystem:]*

For a Class A file system, if a file has been deleted, you can restore the file by using the **undelete** command. You must provide the *index* number of the file listed by using the **dir /all** command. If the file is not located in your working directory, determined by the **pwd** command, you can specify the *filesystem:* option.

3. Permanently remove a file from Class A Flash memory:

    (privileged) **squeeze** *filesystem*

    If you want to permanently remove a file that has been deleted from a Class A file system, you must **squeeze** the file system. This command permanently removes any file on the file system that has been marked as deleted.

4. Remove a file from Class B Flash memory or NVRAM:

    (privileged) **delete** [**flash:**/*filename* | **bootflash:**/*filename* | **nvram:**/*filename*]

    To remove a file on a Class B Flash device, use the **delete** command. When you delete a file from a Class B Flash device, it remains in Flash memory and retains the memory space used. To permanently remove a file from a Class B file system, you must reformat the file system. Because this removes all files, you should save OS files and copy them back to memory after you reformat the device:

    (privileged) **format** *filesystem:*

    For Class A and Class C devices, you can also remove all the files and reformat the device by using the **format** command.

Copying System Files

Like on most computer systems, it is important to move the files from one location to another. To move system files, you can use the **copy** command. This command, along with path parameters, moves the system files. The results of some file system moves are unique; for example, when a file is copied into the system:running-configuration file, the result is a file merge. This section discusses some common **copy** commands and the results. On the whole, however, you can move files into file systems that enable you to write to the system. The command structure for **copy** commands is **copy** [**/erase**] *source-location destination-location*. The source location and destination location can be any writeable file system and path. By using the **/erase** option, you can always erase the destination of a writeable file system. The source location can be any file system that contains files that need to be moved. With all these commands, you can specify the address and filename, or you can leave them out and the system will prompt you for information.

1. Save the active configuration file to be used for startup:

    (privileged) **copy system:running-config nvram:startup-config**

    This command copies the system's current active configuration into the startup configuration file. When anything is copied into the location nvram:startup-configuration, it is a complete overwrite; that is, any information that was in that file is completely lost and overwritten with the source file. The startup configuration file is loaded at startup.

2. Copy a file into active configuration:

    (privileged) **copy** *source* **system:running-config**

Section 3-5

This command copies a file into the current running configuration. The source or device can be any location that contains a text file that has configuration parameters framed in the appropriate syntax. When files are copied into the running configuration, they are merged with the current configuration. That is, if a configuration parameter (such as an address) exists in both places, such as the running configuration and the source configuration, the running configuration will be changed by the parameter that is copied from the source location. If the configuration parameter exists only in the source location, it is added to the running configuration. In the case that a parameter exists in the running configuration, but is not modified in the source configuration, there is no change to the running configuration. The source location can be a file in any location, including a file on a TFTP server, FTP server, or a text file that has been written to Flash memory.

3. Save a file to a TFTP server:

    (privileged) **copy** *source* **tftp:**//*address*/*filename*

    This command enables you to save any readable file from an IFS source location to a TFTP server specified in the address of the destination parameter. If you do not supply a filename and address, the system prompts for this information.

4. Save a file to Flash memory:

    (privileged) **copy** *source* **flash-filesystem:**//*path*/*filename*

    You can copy a file into any Flash file system of a router with the **copy** commands. Some writeable file systems, such as a Class A file system, enable you to create and write to directories and files. This **copy** command enables you to move files into a Flash file system. Files that are moved into Flash are usually IOS files; however, you can use Flash to store any file if you have room to place the file. If fact, after a file has been placed into Flash memory, the router can be configured as a TFTP server and can then serve that file to other devices. Refer to the related commands portion of section "1-1: Cisco Internetwork Operating System (IOS) Software," in Chapter 1, "CLI Usage," for more information about configuring your router to act as a TFTP server.

File System Boot Parameters

1. Specify an OS image to boot from in a Flash file system:

    (global) **boot system flash** *flash-filesystem:*/*directory*/*filename*

    By default, switches boot the first valid image in the default Flash location. If you have more than one file in Flash memory and you do not want to boot the first file, you must specify which file is to be used as the IOS image.

2. Change the configuration file environmental parameter for Class A file systems:

    (global) **boot config** *device:directory*/*filename*

    For a Class A file system, you can copy configuration files to the Flash file system. You can also specify that some switches need to load a configuration from Flash instead of the startup configuration file located in NVRAM. To do this, you must first copy the active configuration into the Flash file system, and then in global configuration, use the **boot config** parameter followed by the file system name and file location and name. After you save this configuration, the router attempts to load the configuration from the specified location.

Alias Commands

Because the new file system functionality is the third generation of file management systems for Cisco IOS, alias commands have been established to provide backward compatibility for commands that existed in previous operating systems. This backward compatibility enables you to use file management commands that you might have learned in previous releases without having to relearn the new command structure. Table 3-3 shows the alias commands and the IFS equivalent command.

Table 3-3   *File Management Alias Commands*

Cisco IOS Software Release 10.2 and Earlier Command	Cisco IOS Software Release 10.3 to 11.3 Command	Cisco IOS Software Release 12.0 and Later (IFS) Command
write terminal	show running-config	show system:running-config or more system:running-config
show config	show startup-config	show system:startup-config or more system:startup-config
write memory	copy running-config startup-config	copy system:running-config nvram:startup-config
write erase	erase startup-config	erase nvram:
write network	copy running-config tftp:	copy system:running-config tftp://address/filename
config memory	copy startup-config running-config	copy nvram:startup-config system:running-config
config network	copy tftp running-config	copy tftp://address/filename system:running-config
config overwrite	copy tftp startup-config	copy tftp://address/filename nvram:startup-config

Section 3-5

3-6: Redundant Supervisors

- When identical Supervisor hardware is placed in slots 5 and 5 of a Catalyst 6500 series switches, one Supervisor is active, and the other is in standby mode.

- If a failure occurs, the redundant Supervisor takes over switch functionality.

- Configuration files and operating system files are synchronized between switches.

- Layer 2 tables are synchronized between the supervisors for quick transitions between modules.

- Parameters such as the Layer 2 synchronization and operating system synchronization can be managed for the modules.

- Catalyst 6500 series switches provide both Layer 2 and Layer 3 synchronization within the same operating system and configuration.

By placing identical Supervisor hardware and software in slots 5 and 5 of a Catalyst 6500 series switch, you have activated system redundancy. No parameters enable you to activate this feature. The first Supervisor to come online is active, and the second one is in standby mode. The standby Supervisor has an orange system light, and the console port is not active. However, the interfaces on the module are active.

You can remove or insert Supervisor cards while the switch is powered on. If a second Supervisor is added or a standby Supervisor is replaced, the card inserted into the switch goes through the power-on diagnostics but does not test the backplane (because this would interrupt traffic flow) and then goes into standby mode. The standby Supervisor becomes active if there is a failure in the primary Supervisor or if you force a change by resetting the primary Supervisor.

The Supervisor and MSFC are each responsible for different functions and protocols (Layer 2 versus Layer 3). However, the system is dependent on both engines being available for proper operation. Failure of either the Supervisor or the MSFC in RPR/RPR+/SSO mode causes a switchover from the active Supervisor to the standby Supervisor/MSFC.

- **RPR:** The first redundancy mode of operation introduced in Cisco IOS Software. In RPR mode, the startup configuration and boot registers are synchronized between the active and standby supervisors; the standby is not fully initialized; and images between the active and standby supervisors do not need to be the same. Upon switchover, the standby Supervisor becomes active automatically, but it must complete the boot process. In addition, all line cards are reloaded, and the hardware is reprogrammed. The RPR switchover time is two or more minutes.

- **RPR+:** An enhancement to RPR in which the standby Supervisor is completely booted and line cards do not reload upon switchover. The running configuration is synchronized between the active and the standby supervisors. All synchronization activities inherited from RPR are also performed. The synchronization is done before the switchover, and the information synchronized to the standby is used when the stand-by becomes active to minimize the downtime. No link layer or control-plane information is synchronized between the active and the standby Supervisors. Interfaces can bounce after switchover, and the hardware contents need to be reprogrammed. The RPR+ switchover time is 30 or more seconds. The actual failover time is dependent on the size and complexity of the configuration.

■ **NSF/SSO:** Cisco IOS Software supports NSF with SSO. The key differentiators apply in where and how these features are applied with the more advanced forms of these features deployed first in Cisco IOS. SSO expands the RPR+ capabilities to provide transparent failover of Layer 2 protocols when a supervisor failure occurs. SSO is stateful for Layer 2 protocols. The PFC and Distributed Forwarding Card (DFC) hardware tables are maintained across a switchover. This allows for transparent failover at Layer 2 and Layer 4. NSF works in conjunction with SSO to ensure Layer 3 integrity after a switchover. It allows a router that experiences the failure of an active Supervisor to continue forwarding data packets along known routes, while the routing protocol information is recovered and validated. This forwarding can continue to take place by the leverage of restart mechanisms that allow peering arrangements to recover upon failover. This avoids unnecessary route flaps and network instability. The failover time is 0 to 3 seconds with NSF/SSO.

■ **SRM/SSO:** When the switch is powered on, SRM with SSO runs between the two Supervisor engines. The Supervisor engine that boots first becomes the active Supervisor engine. The MSFC and PFC become fully operational. The configuration of the redundant Supervisor engine and MSFC is exactly the same as the active Supervisor engine and MSFC. Processes, such as routing protocols, are created on both the active MSFC and the redundant MSFC. The redundant Supervisor engine is fully initialized and configured, which shortens the switchover time. The active Supervisor engine checks the image version of the redundant Supervisor engine when the redundant Supervisor engine comes online. If the image on the redundant Supervisor engine does not match the image on the active Supervisor ENGINE, RPR mode is used. If the active Supervisor engine or MSFC fails, the redundant Supervisor engine and MSFC become active. SRM with SSO supports a switchover time of 0 to 3 seconds for Layer 2 unicast traffic.

Note   SRM with SSO is supported only on Supervisor Engine 720 and Supervisor Engine 32.

Forcing a Change to the Standby Supervisor

To reset the active Supervisor engine, enter the following command:

```
(privileged)reload
```

Note   The **reload** command reloads the switch. If you want to have Supervisor redundancy, use the **redundancy force-switchover** command, which conducts a manual switchover to the redundant Supervisor engine. The redundant Supervisor engine becomes the new active Supervisor engine running the new Cisco IOS image.

Catalyst 6500 native IOS switches do not automatically synchronize images. Therefore, to have redundancy operational, you must have the same images on both the active and redundant Supervisor modules. To manually synchronize the images, make sure you have IOS on both Supervisor modules and then copy the image from the active Supervisor to the "slave" Supervisor.

Synchronizing IOS Images

To manually synchronize the images for IOS Supervisor modules, the required command is as follows:

```
(privileged) # copy source_device:source_filename
destination_device:target_filename
```

The destination device can be one of the following:

- **slaveslot0:** The PCMCIA card on the redundant Supervisor

- **slave-supbootflash:** The Supervisor boot flash on the redundant Supervisor

- **slave-bootflash:** The MSFC boot flash on the redundant Supervisor

- **Disk0:** Available for CompactFlash Type II cards that provide additional storage

- **Disk1:** Available for CompactFlash Type II cards that provide additional storage

As each Supervisor boots, it checks the configuration register to determine how the device is to boot and where to look for the image. Typically the image is specified in a flash location using boot variable parameters. For Cisco IOS devices, the configuration registers are synchronized by default, but the boot variables are not automatically synchronized.

It is important that both modules have configuration parameters that enable them to automatically boot the same image before redundancy actually takes place. By default the configuration registers of both operating systems use boot system commands to load the OS. Therefore, they are correctly configured. The IOS devices synchronize the configuration register by default. If you change the boot parameters, however, saving the configuration on the active Supervisor will not change to boot variables on the standby Supervisor.

Synchronizing Boot Parameters

1. Synchronization of the configuration register is automatic and requires no further configuration.

2. *(Required)* Synchronize the location of the boot image:

```
(global) redundancy
(redundancy) main-cpu
(redundancy-maincpu) auto-sync bootvar
(redundancy-maincpu) end
(privileged) copy running-config startup-config
```

After you have redundant Supervisors operational, you can check the status with the command **show module all** to verify that one Supervisor is active and the other in standby mode.

Catalyst 6500 Series switches allow a redundant Supervisor engine to take over if the primary Supervisor engine fails to support fault resistance. Redundant Supervisor engines must be of the same type with the same model feature card to support redundancy. When you install two Supervisor engines, the first one to come online becomes the active module. The second Supervisor engine goes into standby mode. All administrative and network management functions, such as Simple Network Management Protocol (SNMP), command-line interface (CLI) console, Telnet, Spanning Tree Protocol (STP), Cisco Discovery Protocol (CDP), and VLAN Trunking Protocol (VTP) are processed on the active Supervisor engine. On the standby Supervisor engine, the console port is inactive. Redundant Supervisor engines are not swappable. The system continues to operate with the same configuration after it switches over to the redundant Supervisor engine.

> **Note** Redundancy is always enabled and cannot be disabled. Redundancy is enabled any time the switch has two Supervisor engines installed on it and the switch decides which specific redundancy mode to use in accordance to the type of images it has.

Cisco IOS Software on the Catalyst 6500 supports RPR, also known as Enhanced High System Availability (EHSA), RPR+, NSF/SSO, and single router mode with stateful switchover (SRM/SSO). In this operational model, one Supervisor/MSFC pair is fully operational, and the other pair is in standby mode. The **show module** command lists the active and standby Supervisors. There are heartbeat messages between two pairs to ensure rapid failure detection. There is no stateful protocol redundancy between Supervisor engines with RPR or RPR+. The SSO redundancy mode provides the stateful protocol redundancy between Supervisor engines.

Section 3-6

3-7: Cisco Discovery Protocol

- CDP identifies directly connected Cisco devices.

- CDP is enabled on all Cisco devices.

- CDP identifies neighbor address, operating system, VLAN, *VLAN Trunking Protocol (VTP)* domain, and duplex information between Cisco switches.

- CDP can be disabled globally or on a per-port (interface) basis.

Configuration of CDP

1. *(Default)* Enable CDP globally:

   (global) **cdp run**

   CDP is enabled by default. To disable CDP for the entire device, use the command **no cdp run.**

2. *(Optional)* Set the update time for CDP advertisements:

   (global) **cdp timer** *interval*

   CDP sends advertisements every 60 seconds by default. Use these commands to change the update interval in seconds. Keep in mind that the update interval must be less than the holdtime.

3. *(Optional)* Specify the holdtime of CDP information:

   (global) **cdp holdtime** *interval*

   If CDP does not hear an update for the specified amount of time in the holdtime interval in seconds, that information is purged from the CDP table. Use these commands to change the holdtime. The holdtime should be greater than the advertisement (usually three times the value of the update timer).

4. *(Default)* Set the CDP version send parameters for the switch:

   (global) **cdp {advertise-v2 | advertise-v1}**

   CDP has two versions (v1 and v2). These versions are compatible, but version 2 has enhanced *type-length-values* (TLV) that support VTP domain name, native VLAN, and duplex information. This information is important in the operation of switch ports. If you receive CDP mismatch messages, the errors are not fatal, but they can indicate a problem.

5. *(Optional)* Disable CDP on an interface or port:

   (interface)**no cdp enable**

   CDP is enabled by default on every port. For ports that are not connected to Cisco devices, it makes no sense to have CDP running. Use the commands in Step 2 to disable CDP on a port-by-port basis. To reenable CDP, use the command **cdp enable.**

   The command **show cdp** displays global information about CDP configuration on both operating systems. Use the commands **show cdp neighbors** for both operating systems to view neighbor information. The command **show cdp interface** *type mod/port* or **show cdp port** *mod/port* displays port-specific information about CDP.

Feature Example

This example shows a switch with the CDP timers altered so that the holdtime is 480 seconds and the update time is 120 seconds. It also shows Fast Ethernet ports 1 to 12 on an IOS switch:

```
Switch(config)# cdp timer 120
Switch(config)# cdp holdtime 480
Switch(config)# interface fastethernet 0/1
Switch(config)# no cdp enable
Switch(config)# interface fastethernet 0/2
Switch(config)# no cdp enable
Switch(config)# interface fastethernet 0/3
Switch(config)# no cdp enable
Switch(config)# interface fastethernet 0/4
Switch(config)# no cdp enable
Switch(config)# interface fastethernet 0/5
Switch(config)# no cdp enable
Switch(config)# interface fastethernet 0/6
Switch(config)# no cdp enable
Switch(config)# end
Switch# copy running-config startup-config
```

3-8: Time and Calendar

- System time is maintained by the software. When a switch is initialized, the system time is set from a hardware time clock (system calendar) in the switch.

- An accurate system clock is important to maintain, especially when you need to compare the output of logging and debugging features. A switch timestamps these messages, giving you a frame of reference.

- System time is maintained as *coordinated universal time* (UTC, also known as *Greenwich mean time*, or GMT). The format of time as it is displayed can be configured with operating system commands.

- System time can be set manually or by *Network Time Protocol (NTP)*. In addition, the hardware time clock in a switch can be updated by NTP if desired.

- NTP uses a concept of *stratum* to determine how close an NTP speaker is to an authoritative time source (an atomic or radio clock). Stratum 1 means that an NTP server is directly connected to an authoritative time source. NTP also compares the times reported from all configured NTP peers and will not listen to a peer that has a significantly different time.

- NTP associations with other NTP peers can be protected through an encrypted authentication.

NTP version 3 is based on RFC 1305 and uses UDP port 123. You can find information about public NTP servers and other NTP subjects at http://www.ntp.org/htdig/search.html or http://www.eecis.udel.edu/~mills/database/rfc/rfc1769.txt.

> **Note**   Catalyst 4500 and 6500 series switches running native IOS switches can also be configured as NTP authoritative time sources. For configuration information on these devices, check out the Cisco Network Time Protocol: Best Practices White Paper at http://www.tinyurl.com/4r3ow or refer to Cisco Field Manual: Router Configuration by David Hucaby and Steve McQuerry, Cisco Press, ISBN 1-58705-024-2.

System Time Configuration

You can set the system time using two different ways:

- Manually

- Using the NTP

For manual configuration, you set the time and date on the router along with the time zone and whether to observe summer hours. With manual configuration, the router has no way to preserve the time settings and cannot ensure that time remains accurate. NTP is defined by RFC 1305 and provides a mechanism for the devices in the network to get their time from an NTP server. With NTP, all the devices would be synchronized and keep accurate time.

Setting the System Time Manually

1. Set the time zone:

   ```
   (global) clock timezone zone hrs-offset min-offset
   ```

   The time zone is set to the abbreviated name *zone* (that is, EST, PST, CET). This name is used only for display purposes and can be any common zone name. The actual displayed time is defined by an offset in hours (*hrs-offset*) and minutes (*min-offset*) from UTC.

2. *(Optional)* Configure daylight savings time (DST):

   ```
   (global) clock summer-time zone recurring [week day month hh:mm week day month
   hh:mm [offset]]
   (global) clock summer-time zone date [date month|month date] year hh:mm [date
   month|month date] year hh:mm [offset]
   ```

   If DST begins and ends on a certain day and week of a month, use the command with the **recurring** keyword. To start and stop DST, you can give the *week* number (including the words "first" and "last"), the name of the *day*, the name of the *month*, and time *hh:mm* in a 24-hour format. If no arguments are given, the U.S. standard of beginning at 2:00 a.m. on the first Sunday in April, and ending at 2:00 a.m. on the last Sunday in October is used. The *offset* value can be given to set the number of minutes that are added during DST (default 60 minutes).

Otherwise, you can use the **date** keyword to specify the exact date and time that DST begins and ends in a given year.

3. *(Optional)* Set the system clock (IOS clock):

    `(exec) clock set hh:mm:ss [day month | month day]  year`

    The clock is set when this command is executed. The time is given in a 24-hour format; *day* is the day number, *month* is the name of the month, and *year* is the full four-digit year.

4. *(Optional)* Set the system calendar (hardware clock):

    `(exec) calendar set hh:mm:ss [day month | month day] year`

    The hardware clock is set to the given time (24-hour format) and date. The *month* is the name of the month, *day* is the day number, and *year* is the full four-digit year. As an alternative, you can set the system calendar from the system clock using the (EXEC) **clock update-calendar** command.

Setting the System Time Through NTP

1. Define one or more NTP peer associations:

    `(global) ntp peer ip-address [version number] [key keyid] [source interface] [prefer]`

    The NTP peer is identified at *ip-address*. The NTP version can be given with the **version** keyword (1 to 3, default is version 3). If NTP authentication is used, the **key** keyword identifies the authentication key to use (see Step 3b in this section). If desired, you can take the source address used in NTP packets from an interface by using the **source** keyword. Otherwise, the router uses the source address from the outbound interface. The **preferred** keyword forces the local router to provide time synchronization if contention exists between peers.

2. *(Optional)* Configure the NTP broadcast service:

    `(global) ntp broadcast client`
    `(global) ntp broadcastdelay microseconds`

    By default, NTP sends and receives unicast packets with peers. Broadcasts can be used instead if several NTP peers are located on a common network. The **ntp broadcast** command enables sending broadcast packets. The **ntp broadcast client** command enables the reception of broadcast packets. The **ntp broadcastdelay** command sets the round-trip delay for receiving client broadcasts (1 to 999,999 microseconds; default is 3000 microseconds).

3. *(Optional)* Restrict access to NTP using authentication.

    a. Enable NTP authentication:

        (global) `ntp authenticate`

    b. Define an authentication key:

        (global) `ntp authentication-key` *key-number* `md5` *value*

        An MD5 authentication key numbered *key-number* is created. The key is given a text-string *value* of up to eight clear-text characters. After the configuration has been written to NVRAM, the key value displays in its encrypted form.

    c. Apply one or more key numbers to NTP:

        (global) `ntp trusted-key` *key-number*

    Remote NTP peers must authenticate themselves using the authentication key numbered *key-number*. You can use this command multiple times to apply all desired keys to NTP.

Example

This example shows a switch that is configured for the U.S. eastern time zone and daylight savings time. The time is manually set.

```
Switch(config)# clock timezone EST -5
Switch(config)# clock summer-time EST recurring 1 sunday april 2:00
  last sunday october 2:00
Switch(config)# end
Switch# clock set 15:30:00 August 11 1990
Switch# copy running-config startup-config
```

In the configuration that follows, NTP is enabled, and NTP is configured for authentication:

```
Switch(config)# ntp authenticate
Switch(config)# ntp authentication-key 1 md5 sourceA
Switch(config)# ntp authentication-key 2 md5 sourceB
Switch(config)# ntp trusted-key 1
Switch(config)# ntp trusted-key 2
Switch(config)# ntp peer 172.17.76.247 key 1
Switch(config)# ntp peer 172.31.31.1 key 2
```

One key, source1key, authenticates a peer at 172.17.76.247, whereas another key, source2key, authenticates a peer at 172.31.31.1.

Further Reading

Refer to the following recommended sources for further information about the topics covered in this chapter.

Hucaby, Dave. *CCNP BCMSN Official Exam Certification Guide*, Fourth Edition. Cisco Press, ISBN 1-58720-171-2.

Hucaby, Dave and Steve McQuerry. *Cisco Field Manual: Router Configuration*. Cisco Press, ISBN 1-58705-024-2.

Section 3-8

Chapter 4

Layer 2 Interface Configuration

See the following sections to configure and use these features:

- **4-1: Switching Table:** Explains how to view and add entries to the switching table of *Media Access Control (MAC)* addresses

- **4-2: Port Selection:** Discusses the various ways you can select switch ports to be configured

- **4-3: Ethernet:** Presents the steps needed to configure Ethernet, Fast Ethernet, Gigabit Ethernet, and 10 Gigabit Ethernet switch ports

- **4-4: EtherChannel:** Covers the configuration steps necessary to bundle several switch ports into a single logical link

4-1: Switching Table

- The switching table contains MAC addresses and the switch ports on which they were learned or statically configured.

- Packets or frames are forwarded by looking up the destination MAC address in the switching table. The frame is sent out the corresponding switch port.

- The switching table entries are normally dynamically learned as packets flow. Entries can also be statically defined.

Configuration

1. *(Optional)* Assign a static switching table entry:

   ```
   (global) mac-address-table {dynamic | static | secure} mac-addr {vlan
     vlan-id} {interface int1 [int2 ... int15] [protocol {ip | ipx | assigned}]
   ```

An entry for the destination MAC address *mac-addr* (dotted-triplet format) is made to point to one or more switch interfaces. If the destination port is a trunk, you must also specify the destination VLAN number *vlan-id*.

Switching table entries can be **static** (not subject to aging), **dynamic** (entries are aged), or **secure.**

> **Note**   You can use the port security feature to restrict input to an interface by limiting and identifying MAC addresses of the workstations that are allowed to access the port. When you assign secure MAC addresses to a secure port, the port does not forward packets with source addresses outside the group of defined addresses. If you limit the number of secure MAC addresses to one and assign a single secure MAC address, the workstation attached to that port is assured the full bandwidth of the port.

2.   *(Optional)* Set the switching table aging time:

```
(global) mac-address-table aging-time seconds [vlan vlan-id]
```

For VLAN number *vlan-id* (2 to 1001), entries are aged out of the switching table after *seconds* (0, 10 to 1,000,000 seconds; default 300 seconds). A value of 0 disables the aging process. The VLAN number is optional. If not specified, the aging time is modified for all VLANs.

3.   *(Optional)* Remove a switching table entry:

```
(global) no mac-address-table static mac-addr {vlan vlan-id} [interface int1
    [int2 ... int15] [protocol {ip | ipx | assigned}]
```

You can remove an entry by referencing its MAC address *mac-addr*. If it is defined on more than one VLAN, the *vlan-id* must also be given. Switches allow the specific destination interfaces to be given, along with a specific protocol.

Displaying Information About the Switching Table

Table 4-1 lists some switch commands that you can use to display helpful information about the Layer 2 switching table contents.

Switching Table Example

Suppose you need to locate the switch port where a specific PC is connected. The PC's MAC address is 00-b0-d0-f5-45-0e:

```
(exec) show mac-address-table address 00b0.d0f5.450e
```

An IOS switch can have this output:

```
switch-ios# show mac-address-table address 00b0.d0f5.450e
Non-static Address Table:
Destination Address   Address Type   VLAN   Destination Port
- - - - - - - - - -   - - - - - -    - -    - - - - - - - - -
00d0.b7e5.4dc3        Dynamic        534    FastEthernet0/2
```

Table 4-1 *Switch Commands to Display Layer 2 Switching Table Content Information*

Display Function	Command
Display dynamically learned addresses based on a port or VLAN number	(exec) `show mac-address-table dynamic`
Display statically defined addresses based on a port or VLAN number	(exec) `show mac-address-table static` `[address` *mac-addr* `| detail | interface` *interface interface-number* `| protocol` *protocol* `| vlan` *vlan-id*`]`
Display the port or VLAN associated with a MAC address	(exec) `show mac-address-table address` *mac-addr* `[detail | {interface` *interface interface-number*`} | {protocol` *protocol*`} |` `{vlan` *vlan-id*`} | all]`
Display the switching table aging time	(exec) `show mac-address-table aging-time` `[vlan` *vlan-id*`]`
Display the switching table address count and size	(exec) `show mac-address-table count [vlan` *vlan-id*`] [slot slot-num]`

If you need to find a list of all the MAC addresses that have been learned on a specific switch port, you would enter the following command (for example):

(exec) `show mac-address-table dynamic interface gigabit 0/1`

The switch produces output like this:

```
switch-ios# show mac-address-table dynamic interface gig 0/1
Non-static Address Table:
Destination Address  Address Type   VLAN  Destination Port
———————————          ——————         ——    ——————————

0000.0c45.2100       Dynamic        999   GigabitEthernet0/1
0000.1b04.2f76       Dynamic        64    GigabitEthernet0/1
0000.489a.3b0b       Dynamic        57    GigabitEthernet0/1
```

Tip If you need to locate a specific MAC address within a large network and you have no idea where to start, begin looking on a core layer switch near the center of the network. Look for the MAC address in the switching table there. After finding it, move to the neighboring switch that connects to the destination port.

Keep looking for the address in the switching tables and then move to the next neighboring switch. Repeat this process until you reach the edge of the network, where the device is physically connected.

4-2: Port Selection

- When configuring a Layer 2 port or interface, the port must first be selected or identified.

- Cisco IOS switches allow a range of interfaces to be defined by using the **interface range** EXEC command.

Configuration

1. Select a port:

    `(global)` **`interface`** `type mod/num`

    A switch port is called an interface and is identified by its type (**fastethernet**, **gigabitethernet**, and so on), module number *mod*, and port number *num*.

2. Select a range of ports:

    `(global)` **`interface range`** `port-range`

    OR

    `(global)` **`define interface-range`** `macro-name port-range`

    `(global)` **`interface range macro`** `macro-name`

    The Cisco IOS switches allow lists or ranges of interfaces to be given once so that subsequent commands are applied to each of the interfaces. A *port-range* is defined as the interface type (**ethernet**, **fastethernet**, **gigabitethernet**, **tengigabitethernet**, or **vlan**) followed by the module number, a slash (/), and the starting port number. The end of the range is given by a space, a hyphen, another space, and the ending port number. If additional ranges are given, the ranges must be separated by a comma.

    The basic range format is *type slot/first-port - last-port* [,*type slot/first-port - last-port* ...], where up to five different ranges can be listed. Following the **interface range** command, you are placed into interface configuration mode.

    If you need to make several configuration changes to a range of interfaces, you can define a macro that contains a list of interface ranges. Use the **define interface-range** command, with a *macro-name* (arbitrary text name) and a *port-range* (list of interface ranges as defined earlier). You can save this macro in the switch configuration so that you can reference it in the future. To invoke the interface range macro, use the **interface range macro** command with the *macro-name*.

Port Selection Example

Module 1 ports 1 and 2 with module 6 ports 1 through 4 need their port speed set to autonegotiate mode. (You can use any port configuration function; port speed is shown here only as a demonstration of port selection.) Cisco IOS switches enable the ports to be identified as two ranges and their speeds to be set with a single interface configuration command:

```
(global) interface range gig 1/1 - 2, gig 6/1
(interface) speed auto

(global) interface gig 6/2 - 4
(interface) speed auto
```

4-3: Ethernet

- Autonegotiation of link speed and duplex mode for 10/100/1000BASE-T is possible through the functions standardized in IEEE 802.3u and 802.3ab. The two endpoints of a connection exchange capability information and choose the highest common speed and duplex supported by both.

- Ethernet ports are referenced by interface type and number (**interface** and one of **ethernet**, **fastethernet**, **gigabitethernet**, or **tengigabitethernet**).

- If certain problems are detected on a port, the switch automatically moves that port into the *errDisable* or error disabled state. This minimizes the effect that the problem port could have on the rest of the network.

- Ports in errDisable can be automatically reenabled or recovered after a timeout period, or they can be manually recovered. In either case, determine and correct the problem condition before attempting to recover errDisable ports.

Configuration

1. *(Optional)* Assign a descriptive name to the port:

   ```
   (interface) description port-name
   ```

   The description *port-name* (text string) is assigned to the port for human use. Usually the description includes a reference to the location, function, or user of the port.

2. *(Optional)* Set the port speed:

   ```
   (interface) speed {10 | 100 | 1000 | auto | nonegotiate}
   ```

   You can set the port speed to one of the following: **10** (10 mbps for 10, 10/100, and 10/100/1000BASE-T ports); **100** (100 mbps for 10/100 and 10/100/1000BASE-T ports); **1000** (1000 mbps for 10/100/1000BASE-T ports); **auto** (autonegotiate the speed for 10/100 and 10/100/1000BASE-T ports; the default); or **nonegotiate** (don't autonegotiate the speed). The speeds of 10BASE-T, 100FX, *Gigabit Interface Converter* (GBIC), and Small Form-factor Pluggable (SFP) ports are fixed and cannot be set with this command.

> **Tip**   Choosing the **auto** speed for a port (the default) enables the port to participate in a negotiation with the far end of the link. The two endpoints exchange information about their capabilities and choose the best speed and duplex mode supported by both. If one endpoint of a link has autonegotiation disabled, however, the other endpoint can only sense the link speed from the electrical signals. The duplex mode can't be determined and is left to the current default mode.
>
> If you need to set the speed and duplex mode of the switch port to something other than **auto**, be sure to set the device at the far end of the link to the same values.
>
> Generally, if a 10/100/1000BASE-T switch port connects to another similar switch port or to a mission-critical device such as a server, router, or firewall, you should set the speed and duplex to a fixed value. By so doing, you eliminate any possibility of autonegotiation forcing the port to a lower speed in the future.

   3. *(Optional)* Set the port duplex mode:

```
(interface) duplex {full | half | auto}
```

You can set the duplex mode to one of **full**. The **auto** option is not available on the Catalyst 6500 IOS; if the speed is set to **auto**, the duplex follows suit.

> **Tip**   The duplex mode can be autonegotiated only if the port speed is also set to **auto** (or autonegotiate). The 10/100 Ethernet ports can be set to either full- or half-duplex. Beware of a port that has a duplex mismatch, in which one end is full- and the other is half-duplex. This condition can cause a poor response and a high error rate. Make sure that both ends of a link are set to autonegotiate or the same duplex setting. Although Cisco devices support only full-duplex, the IEEE 802.3z standard does have support for half-duplex GigabitEthernet. Because of this, duplex is negotiated between GigabitEthernet devices.

   4. *(Optional)* Set the port traffic flow control:

```
(interface) flowcontrol {send | receive} {desired | off | on}
```

A switch port can receive *pause* frames, causing transmission to stop for a short time while buffers at the far end are full. By default, **receive** processing is **off** for all switch port types (except 10 Gigabit Ethernet). A port can also send pause frames if its buffers are full. By default, **send** is **on** for Fast Ethernet, **desired** for Gigabit, and **off** for all other port types. The **desired** keyword is available for Gigabit ports only, where autonegotiation is inherent.

   5. *(Optional)* Control port negotiation:

```
(interface) [no] negotiation auto
```

By default, link negotiation (flow control, duplex, fault information) is enabled on Gigabit Ethernet ports. To disable negotiation, use the **disable** or **no** keyword.

6.   (Optional; Catalyst 6500 only) Enable the port debounce timer:

`(interface)` **link debounce** [**time** *debounce_time*]

By default, the line cards wait 300 milliseconds (10 milliseconds for fiber Gigabit ports) before announcing to the main processor that a port has changed state. This "debounces" the up/down state change so that quick changes do not trigger *Spanning Tree Protocol (STP)*, *Port Aggregation Protocol* (PAgP), *Simple Network Management Protocol* (SNMP) traps, and so on. This debounce gives a port the chance to settle down to a stable state. If you find that this period is too short, you can enable an extended port debounce for specific ports. When enabled, the debounce period becomes 3.1 seconds (100 milliseconds for fiber Gigabit ports).

Note   When link debounce is enabled, port up/down detection is delayed. The normal STP state progression, along with PAgP negotiation, can cause a long delay before a port can become usable. Use this with caution.

7.   *(Optional)* Optimize the port as a connection to a single host:

`(interface)` **switchport host**

Several options are set for the port: STP PortFast is enabled, trunk mode is disabled, EtherChannel is disabled, and no dot1q trunking is allowed. This optimizes the link startup time when the port is attached to only one host.

8.   *(Optional)* Use inline power where an IP Phone is connected:

`(interface)` **power inline** {**auto** | **never**}

On ports or line cards that can support inline power to IP phones, power is supplied if an IP Phone is detected on the port by default (**auto**). If power should never be supplied to a connected device, choose the **off** or **never** keyword. See Chapter 14, "Voice," for more configuration information.

9.   *(Optional)* Allow large or *jumbo* frames:

`(interface)` **mtu** *bytes*

By default, the maximum frame size or *maximum transmission unit* (MTU) that can be switched is 1548. Sometimes you might need to switch larger packets to improve performance from server to server. To allow switching of packets up to 9216 bytes, set an MTU size of bytes (1500 to 9216 bytes).

Tip   Enabling jumbo frame support allows large frames to be switched. If they also need to be routed, make sure that the MTU on the respective router interfaces is set to the same size. Jumbo frame support is available on an MSFC2 or higher with the **mtu** interface command but is not available on the *Multilayer Switch Feature Card (MSFC)*.

10. *(Optional)* Automatically reenable ports from the errDisable state.

    a. Set the timeout period before ports are automatically reenabled:

```
(global) errdisable recovery {interval interval}
```

If ports in errDisable are automatically reenabled, the ports remain in the errDisable state for *interval* (30 to 86400 seconds, default 300 seconds).

    b. Choose the causes that will automatically reenable ports:

```
(global) [no] errdisable recovery cause reason
```

By default, ports in the errDisable state are not automatically recovered or reenabled. If automatic recovery is desired for an errDisable condition, use the **errdisable recovery cause** command. The ports will be recovered after the errDisable timeout period has expired. Choose one of the following reasons:

- **BPDU Port Guard:** A bridge protocol data unit (BPDU) is received on a port in the STP PortFast state; use **bpduguard**.

- **UDLD:** A unidirectional link is detected; use reason **udld**.

- **STP Root Guard:** Use reason **rootguard**.

- **EtherChannel misconfiguration:** The EtherChannel ports no longer have consistent configurations; use reason **pagp-flap**.

- **Trunk negotiation flapping:** Dynamic Trunking Protocol (DTP) is detecting changes from one trunk encapsulation to another; use reason **dtp-flap**.

- **Port is going up and down:** Use reason **link-flap**.

- **All known errDisable causes:** Ports are put into errDisable if any problem from this list is detected; use reason **all**.

11. Enable or disable the port:

```
(interface) shutdown
```

OR

```
(interface) no shutdown
```

By default, a port is enabled (**enable** or **no shutdown**). To disable the port, use the **disable** or **shutdown** keywords.

Ethernet Example

A 10/100/1000 switch port connects a mail server. The port is set to 100 mbps, full duplex. The port is also tuned for a single host so that there are no port startup delays because of PAgP, STP, or trunk negotiations:

```
(interface) description Mail server
(interface) speed 100
(interface) duplex full
```

```
(interface) spanning-tree portfast
(interface) switchport mode access
(interface) no channel-group
(interface) no shutdown
```

Displaying Information About Layer 2 Interfaces

Table 4-2 lists some switch commands that you can use to display helpful information about Layer 2 interfaces.

Table 4-2   *Switch Commands to Display Layer 2 Interface Information*

Display Function	Command
Port status	(exec) **show interfaces** [*type num*]
Port error counters	**show interfaces counters** [**broadcast** | errors | {module *mod-num*} | {**trunk** [**module** *mod-num*]}]
Port MAC address used by the switch	(exec) **show interfaces** [*type num*] OR **show catalyst6500 chassis-mac-address**
Port flow control	**show interfaces** [*interface* [*mod*]] **flowcontrol**
Port negotiation	**show port negotiation** [*mod*[*/port*]]
Port debounce	**show port debounce** [*mod*[*/port*]]
Port inline power	**show power inline** [*interface-id*] [**actual** | configured]
Jumbo frame support	(exec) **show interfaces** [*type num*]
errDisable recovery and port status	(exec) **show errdisable recovery**

You can generate and view reports of utilization, traffic volume, and errors on each port in the switch. These *TopN* reports can prove useful if you don't have network management applications that can generate statistical reports about the switch ports.

1. Enable TopN report:

   (exec) **collect top** [*number_of_ports*] **counters interface** {*type[1]* \| **all** \| **layer-2** \| **layer-3**} [**sort-by** *statistic_type[2]*] [**interval** *seconds*]

   TopN reports enable you to collect and analyze data for each physical port on a switch. When Top-N reports start, they obtain statistics from the appropriate hardware counters and then go into sleep mode for a user-specified interval. When the interval ends, the reports obtain the current statistics from the same hardware counters, compare the current statistics from the earlier statistics, and store the difference. The statistics for each port are sorted by one of the following statistic types:

- **Broadcast:** Number of input/output broadcast packets.

- **Bytes:** Number of input/output bytes.

- **Errors:** Number of input errors.

- **Multicast:** Number of input/output multicast packets.

- **Overflow:** Number of buffer overflows.

- **Packets:** Number of input/output packets.

- **Utilization:** When calculating the port utilization, TopN reports bundle the Tx and Rx lines into the same counter and also look at the full-duplex bandwidth when calculating the percentage of utilization. For example, a Gigabit Ethernet port would be 2000-Mbps full duplex.

2. Display stored TopN report:

```
show top counters interface report [report_num]
```

You can view a specific TopN report numbered *report-num*. To see a list of all the stored TopN reports, omit the report number. Reports are stored in switch memory and remain there until the switch is rebooted or loses power. To clear TopN reports from memory, use the **clear top** [**all** | *report-num*] command.

4-4: EtherChannel

- You can aggregate several individual switch ports into a single logical port or EtherChannel.

- Fast Ethernet ports, when bundled together, form a *Fast EtherChannel (FEC)*. Gigabit ports form a *Gigabit EtherChannel (GEC)*.

- You can manually configure EtherChannels or aggregate them through the use of dynamic protocols. PAgP is a Cisco proprietary protocol, whereas *Link Aggregation Control Protocol (LACP)* is a standards-based protocol defined in IEEE 802.3ad (also known as IEEE 802.3 Clause 43, "Link Aggregation").

- Frames are distributed onto the individual ports that make up an EtherChannel by using a hashing algorithm. The algorithm can use source, destination, or a combination of source and destination IP addresses, source and destination MAC addresses, or TCP/UDP port numbers, depending on the hardware platform and configuration.

- Frame distribution is deterministic; that is, the same combination of addresses or port numbers always points to the same port within the EtherChannel.

- The frame distribution hashing algorithm performs an *exclusive-OR (XOR)* operation on one or more low-order bits of the addresses or TCP/UDP port numbers to select on which link a frame will be forwarded. For a two-port bundle, the last bit is used; a four-port bundle uses the last two bits; and an eight-port bundle uses the last three bits. (With XOR, if two bits are identical, a 0 bit results; if two bits are different, a 1 bit results.)

- If a link within an EtherChannel fails, the traffic that normally crosses the failed link is moved to the remaining links.

- EtherChannel links can be static access ports or trunk ports. However, all links to be bundled must have consistent configurations before an EtherChannel can form.

Note PAgP sends frames to destination address 01:00:0C:CC:CC:CC, as an 802.2 Subnetwork Access Protocol (SNAP) protocol 0x000C0104. LACP sends frames to destination address 01-80-c2-00-00-02 using protocol 0x8809.

Configuration

1. (*Optional*) Select an EtherChannel protocol under the physical interface you are assigning to the port-channel:

   ```
   channel-protocol {pagp | lacp}
   ```

   By default, each module uses the PAgP protocol (**pagp**) for dynamic EtherChannel control.

Tip PAgP and LACP are not interoperable. Therefore, use the same protocol on the modules and ports at both ends of a potential EtherChannel.

2. *(Optional)* Adjust the STP costs for an EtherChannel.

   a. Set the STP port cost:

      ```
      interface [mod[/port]]
      ```

      ```
      spanning-tree cost cost
      ```

      By default, the STP port cost for an EtherChannel is based on the port cost of the aggregate bandwidth. For example, a single 100 mbps port has a port cost of 19. When two 100 mbps ports are bundled as an FEC, the port cost for 200 mbps is 12. A bundle of four 100 mbps ports gives a port cost of 8 for the 400 mbps bandwidth. Refer to Table 7-1 in Chapter 7, "Spanning Tree Protocol (STP)," for STP port cost values.

      You can change the port cost for all EtherChannels by using the **all** keyword or a single EtherChannel by giving its *channel-id* number. To find this index, use the **show channel group** (PAgP) or **show lacp-channel group** (LACP) command. The *channel-id* is a unique number that is automatically assigned to the EtherChannel.

      The STP port cost is given as *cost* (1-65535 in 16-bit "short mode" or 1-4294967296 in 32-bit "long mode"). Refer to section "7-1: STP Operation," in Chapter 7 for more cost information.

Section 4-4

b. Set the STP port cost per VLAN:

```
interface [mod[/port]]

spanning-tree cost cost
```

Use the **set spantree channelvlancost** command to enable the port cost per VLAN to be configured for the EtherChannel with *channel-id*. The STP port cost is set to *cost* for all VLANs that will be carried over the EtherChannel. Then you should adjust the port cost for specific VLANs by using the **set spantree portvlancost** command. Refer to section "7-1: STP Operation," in Chapter 7 for more cost information.

3. *(Optional)* Use PAgP on an EtherChannel:

> **Tip**   When you make configuration changes to add or remove ports from an EtherChannel, be aware of the effects this has on the STP. This is especially important in a live production network where you might cause an interruption of service.
>
> STP operates on an EtherChannel as if it were a normal switch port. After ports have been assigned to an EtherChannel, STP moves through its various states to guarantee a loop-free topology. Switch ports within the EtherChannel administrative group can be enabled and disabled without triggering an STP topology change. As a result, the other links in the EtherChannel remain in the STP "forwarding" state.
>
> If you attempt to add a new port into an active EtherChannel administrative group, however, an STP topology change is triggered. The same result occurs if you change the administrative group number on an active EtherChannel. You have now reconfigured the logical link, so STP moves the EtherChannel (and all its ports) back through the "listening" and "learning" states. This interrupts traffic on the EtherChannel for up to 50 seconds.

a. Assign interfaces to the EtherChannel:

```
interface [mod[/port]]

channel-group {channel group number} mode {active | auto | desirable | on |
passive}
```

One or more ports, given by *mod/port*, are assigned as an EtherChannel. A specific administrative group number *admin-group* can be given if desired. If this is omitted, the switch automatically assigns these ports a new unique group number. If you do specify a group number and that number is already in use, the new EtherChannel receives the group number, and the ports that were previously assigned are moved to a different unique group number.

Ports are assigned to an EtherChannel group at the same time as the PAgP mode is set. This is done in Step 3b.

Tip You must list all the ports that belong to the EtherChannel in this one command. To add or delete individual ports from the bundle, reissue this command with an updated list of all the desired ports.

b. Set the PAgP mode:

```
interface) channel-group number mode {on | auto [non-silent] | desirable
   [non-silent]}
```

The channel is referenced by one of its ports by selecting the interface and the group *number*. You can configure PAgP in one of these modes: **on** (EtherChannel is used, but no PAgP packets are sent), **off** (EtherChannel is disabled), **desirable** (switch is actively willing to form an EtherChannel; PAgP packets are sent), or **auto** (switch is passively willing to form an EtherChannel; no PAgP packets are sent; the default).

When in **auto** or **desirable** mode, PAgP packets are required before an EtherChannel can be negotiated and brought up. However, there might be times when one end of the EtherChannel (a server or network analyzer) doesn't generate PAgP packets or is "silent." You can use the **silent** keyword (the default) to enable a port to become an EtherChannel with a silent partner after a 15-second delay. Use the **non-silent** keyword to require PAgP negotiation before bringing the EtherChannel active.

c. *(Optional)* Choose a load-balancing algorithm:

```
(global) port-channel load-balance method
```

Choose a load-balancing *method*:

- **dst-ip:** Dst IP Addr

- **dst-mac:** Dst Mac Addr

- **dst-mixed-ip-port:** Dst IP Addr and TCP/UDP Port

- **dst-port:** Dst TCP/UDP Port

- **mpls:** Load Balancing for MPLS packets

- **src-dst-ip:** Src XOR Dst IP Addr

- **src-dst-mac:** Src XOR Dst Mac Addr

- **src-dst-mixed-ip-port:** Src XOR Dst IP Addr and TCP/UDP Port

- **src-dst-port:** Src XOR Dst TCP/UDP Port

- **src-ip:** Src IP Addr

- **src-mac:** Src Mac Addr

- **src-mixed-ip-port:** Src IP Addr and TCP/UDP Port

- **src-port:** Src TCP/UDP Port

Section 4-4

> **Note**   Depending on your hardware switching platform, the hashing option can vary. See the following link for additional information: http://www.tinyurl.com/2o44ew.

4. *(Optional)* Use LACP on an EtherChannel.

    a.   Set the system priority:

        `(global)` **`lacp system-priority`** `{value}`

        Specifies the priority of the system for LACP. The higher the number, the lower the priority.

        The valid range for *value* is from 1 to 65535. The default is 32768. A LACP system priority is configured on each router running LACP. The system priority can be configured automatically or through the CLI. LACP uses the system priority with the router MAC address to form the system ID and also during negotiation with other systems. The LACP system ID is the combination of the LACP system priority value and the MAC address of the router.

    b.   Set the port priority for individual ports:

        `(interface)` **`lacp port-priority`** `{value}`

        This command specifies the priority for the physical interface. The valid range for value is from 1 to 65535. The higher the number, the lower the priority. A LACP port priority is configured on each port using LACP. The port priority can be configured automatically or through the CLI. LACP uses the port priority with the port number to form the port identifier. The port priority determines which ports should be put in standby mode when a hardware limitation prevents all compatible ports from aggregating.

    c.   Group ports by setting their administrative keys (automated).

        Ports that have the potential to become an EtherChannel should have their administrative key, *admin-key* (1 to 65535), set to the same value. Up to eight ports can be assigned the same administrative key value. Ports that have a unique value are considered to be individual ports and do not become part of an EtherChannel.

        By default, each group of four consecutive ports in a module has the same unique key value. Key values are only locally significant. However, ports with the same key value on one switch can potentially form an EtherChannel with ports sharing another common key value on another switch.

        If the *admin-key* value is not specified, the switch selects an unused, unique value for the ports listed. If you do specify a key value and that value is already in use, the ports already assigned are moved to another unique key value.

LACP automatically configures an administrative key value equal to the channel group identification number on each port configured to use LACP. The administrative key defines the capability of a port to aggregate with other ports, which is determined by the following configuration restrictions that you establish:

- Port physical characteristics such as data rate

- Duplex capability

- Point-to-point or shared medium

d. Set the EtherChannel mode:

interface [*mod*[*/port*]]

channel-group *number* **mode {active** | **on** | {**auto** [**non-silent**]} | {**desirable** [**non-silent**]} | **passive**}

LACP can be configured in one of these modes: **on** (EtherChannel is used, but no LACP packets are sent), **off** (EtherChannel is disabled), **active** (switch is actively willing to form an EtherChannel; LACP packets are sent), or **passive** (switch is passively willing to form an EtherChannel; no LACP packets are sent; the default).

> **Tip**   Although PAgP and LACP are not compatible or interoperable, you can form an EtherChannel between one switch that uses PAgP on a module and another switch that uses LACP on its module. In this case, set the PAgP switch to the **on** mode and the LACP switch to the **on** mode. Neither protocol will be used to negotiate an EtherChannel, but the EtherChannel will be formed.

EtherChannel Example

Figure 4-1 shows a network diagram for this example. A switch has three line cards with Ethernet ports. Modules 4 and 5 use PAgP to aggregate ports, whereas module 6 uses LACP. One EtherChannel is made up of ports 4/1, 4/2, 5/1, and 5/2, demonstrating that an EtherChannel can be split across multiple line cards. This EtherChannel uses PAgP in the desirable mode to dynamically bundle the ports together. The nonsilent mode requires a PAgP speaker on the far end before the EtherChannel will be built. Both source and destination IP addresses distribute traffic across the bundled ports.

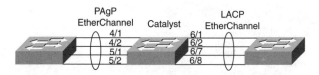

Figure 4-1   *Network Diagram for the EtherChannel Example*

A second EtherChannel is configured to use LACP. The LACP system priority is set to 8192 so that this switch will become the higher-priority decision maker. Ports 6/1, 6/2, 6/7, and 6/8 all belong to LACP administrative key 101, forming a common aggregate link. Ports 6/1 and 6/2 are given a port priority of 100, which is less than the default 128. These ports are used in the LACP bundle first. If for some reason ports 6/7 or 6/8 cannot be used in the EtherChannel, they are placed in a "standby" state and used if another port fails. Each of the bundled ports is put into the active LACP mode and is willing to initiate an EtherChannel with the far-end switch:

```
(global) interface fastethernet 4/1
(interface) channel-group 100 mode desirable non-silent
(global) interface fastethernet 4/2
(interface) channel-group 100 mode desirable non-silent
(global) interface fastethernet 5/1
(interface) channel-group 100 mode desirable non-silent
(global) interface fastethernet 5/2
(interface) channel-group 100 mode desirable non-silent
(global) port-channel load-balance src-dst-ip
```

Displaying Information About EtherChannels

Table 4-3 lists some switch commands that you can use to display helpful information about EtherChannel links.

Tip   If you are debugging an EtherChannel that will not form, remember that all ports with the bundle must have the same attributes. For example, all the ports should have the same allowed VLAN range, and so on.

The commands listed in Table 4-3 provide a great deal of information about EtherChannels that are already formed. To be sure that the ports are all configured consistently, use other **show** commands that display the port attributes. Beyond that, you sometimes have to resort to looking through the switch configuration to spot port configurations that are not identical or viewing the switch's log file.

Table 4-3   *Switch Commands to Display EtherChannel Link Information*

EtherChannel protocol used on each module	`show lacp` [`channel-group-number`] | {`counters` | `internal` [`detail`] | `neighbor` [`detail`]} | [`sys-id`]
EtherChannel capabilities on a module	(`exec`) `show interfaces capabilities`
EtherChannel ID numbers	(`exec`) `show etherchannel summary`
EtherChannel load balancing	(`exec`) `show etherchannel` [`channel-group`] `load-balance`
EtherChannel traffic utilization	(`exec`) `show pagp` [`group-number`] `counters`
	(`exec`) `show etherchannel` [`channel-group`] {`port-channel` | `brief` | `detail` | `summary`/`port` | `load-balance` | `protocol`}

Further Reading

Refer to the following recommended sources for further information about the topics covered in this chapter.

Ethernet

Charles Spurgeon's Ethernet website: http://www.ethermanage.com/ethernet/ethernet.html.

Spurgeon, Charles. *Ethernet: The Definitive Guide*. O'Reilly and Associates, ISBN 1-56592-660-9.

Gigabit Ethernet

The Gigabit Ethernet Alliance at http://www.gigabit-ethernet.org.

The 10 Gigabit Ethernet Alliance: http://www.10gea.org.

IEEE P802.3ae 10Gb/s Ethernet Task Force: http://grouper.ieee.org/groups/802/3/index.html.

EtherChannel

Understanding EtherChannel Load Balancing and Redundancy on Catalyst Switches: http://www.tinyurl.com/yw2lw.

Campus Network for High Availability Design Guide: http://www.tinyurl.com/d3e6dj.

IEEE P802.3ad Link Aggregation Task Force: http://www.ieee802.org/3/ad/index.html.

Chapter 5

Layer 3 Interface Configuration

See the following sections for configuration information about these topics:

- **5-1: Layer 3 Switching:** Describes the process involved with Layer 3 switching and the switching elements needed to perform Layer 3 switching

- **5-2: Layer 3 Ethernet Interfaces:** Explains the steps needed to configure Ethernet interfaces for Layer 3 processing

- **5-3: Layer 3 EtherChannels:** Covers the method for configuring multiple interfaces into a single logical channel that can be configured for Layer 3 processing

- **5-4: WAN Interfaces:** Describes how to configure Layer 3 WAN interfaces installed in Catalyst 6500 switches

- **5-5: Layer 3 Virtual Interfaces:** Explains how to configure a logical VLAN or BVI to perform Layer 3 processing for members of a VLAN or bridge group

- **5-6: Routing Tables:** Explains the basic process for populating and viewing the Layer 3 routing tables

5-1: Layer 3 Switching

- Layer 3 switching is the movement of data between devices using tables or pathways containing Layer 3 network addressing.

- To perform Layer 3 switching, the device must have a Layer 3 switching processor that can be a separate module or card.

- A Layer 3 switching processor uses Layer 3 IOS to configure the Layer 3 switching components.

- To allow Layer 3 switching, the switch must have the routing function enabled for a given protocol.

■   To provide connectivity between the different networks, the switch must have knowl-
    edge of available pathways for these networks.

5-2: Layer 3 Ethernet Interfaces

■   Layer 3 switching requires an interface on the switch that can forward packets based
    on Layer 3 addressing.

■   Each Layer 3 interface defines a separate broadcast domain and, therefore, a separate
    network.

■   After a Layer 3 interface has been configured with a protocol, it can act as a gateway
    for other devices in the same broadcast domain.

■   On some switches, you can configure an Ethernet port (interface) as a Layer 3 inter-
    face.

Configuration

A Layer 3 interface is a direct routed interface that is designed to provide Layer 3 processing of packets entering and exiting the interface. Not every physical interface on
every switch is designed to be a Layer 3 interface; however, on some switches, each port
is, or can be, configured to be a direct routed port. To configure these interfaces for
Layer 3 processing, use the following steps.

1.   Select the physical Layer 3 interface:

`(global) `**`interface`**` type mod/port`

Access global configuration mode and use this command to specify the interface and
move to interface configuration mode in the device. You must specify the type of
interfaces: **ethernet**, **fastethernet**, **gigabitethernet**, or **tengigabitethernet**. The
mod/port specifies the module and port number of the interface. Fixed-configura-
tion switches, such as the 2960, have no module option, and for switches like these,
the module (or slot) is always **0**. However, when leveraging the Cisco StackWise
technology in 3750 and 3750-E series switches, there is a member switch number
that distinguishes a switch number for interface numbering *switch/port*.

2.   Configure the interface for Layer 3 operation:

`(interface)`**`no switchport`**

For multilayer switches, such as the 4500 or 6500 running IOS or the 3560/3750
series, you can configure ports to act as Layer 2 (switchport) ports or Layer 3 (routed) ports. To configure a port to act as a Layer 3 port, use the **no switchport** command to disable Layer 2 operation and enable Layer 3 operation.

Note   When the **switchport** or **no switchport** command is issued, the port might be disabled and then reenabled.

> **Note**   The default port operation for the 4500 and 6500 series switches running IOS is routed mode; the Catalyst 2900, 3500, and 3700 defaults to switchport mode. Also, on the Catalyst 4500 and 6500, the interfaces are shutdown by default.

3. Assign an IP address:

```
(interface) ip address address netmask
```

When an interface begins acting as a Layer 3 interface, you must configure it with information about the network connected to the broadcast domain. For IP networks, this means the interface must be given an IP address. This address becomes the gateway address used by clients in the broadcast domain to which the interface is connected.

> **Note**   The information presented here for configuring protocol information on a Layer 3 interface is the minimal requirements. You can find more detailed information concerning protocol configuration in Cisco Field Manual: Router Configuration, published by Cisco Press.

4. Enable the interface:

```
(interface) no shutdown
```

The default status of many Layer 3 interfaces is **shutdown**, which is a disabled state. To ensure that the interface is operational, enable the interface with the command **no shutdown**.

Verifying the Configuration

After you configure a protocol on an interface, use the following command to verify the configuration:

```
(privileged) show ip interface type mod/port
```

Feature Example

The following example shows the configuration of interface Gigabit Ethernet 1/1 on Distribution_Switch_A for Layer 3 processing. This interface acts as the gateway for all the clients connected to Access_Switch_A. Figure 5-1 shows the network topology for this example.

An example of the configuration for Distribution_Switch_A follows:

```
Distribution_Switch_A(config)# interface gigabitethernet 1/1
Distribution_Switch_A (config-if)# no switchport
Distribution_Switch_A (config-if)# ip address 192.168.10.1 255.255.255.0
Distribution_Switch_A (config-if)# no shut
```

Section 5-2

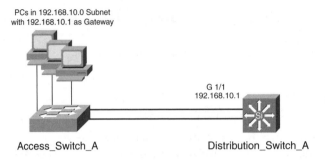

PCs in 192.168.10.0 Subnet
with 192.168.10.1 as Gateway

G 1/1
192.168.10.1

Access_Switch_A   Distribution_Switch_A

Figure 5-1   *Network Topology for Layer 3 Interface*
Configuration

```
Distribution_Switch_A (config-if)# end
Distribution_Switch_A # copy running-config startup-config
```

5-3: Layer 3 EtherChannels

- An *EtherChannel* is the aggregation of multiple physical channels into a single logical connection.

- The single logical connection is referred to as a *port channel*.

- You can configure the port channel to operate as a Layer 3 interface on some switches.

- When assigned with an IP address, the port channel becomes the logical Layer 3 interface.

- If any single link of the channel fails, the port channel interface is still accessible through the other links.

- Layer 3 EtherChannel operation is the same as Layer 2 EtherChannels for traffic distribution and channel establishment.

Configuration

An EtherChannel offers the capability to bond multiple physical connections for greater throughput for links that carry traffic for multiple hosts. Because EtherChannel operates at an almost physical layer, multiple Layer 3 interfaces can be bonded into a single channel. After the channel has been formed, a virtual interface known as a *port channel* interface acts as the Layer 3 conduit for all the members of the channel. To configure a Layer 3 EtherChannel, use the following steps:

1. Create a logical port channel:

```
(global) interface port-channel number
```

In global configuration mode, use this command to create the logical port channel interface. This acts as the Layer 3 interface for all the members of the channel. The *number* option specifies the channel group number with which each channel member will be configured.

2. Configure protocol information on the port channel:

    ```
    (interface) ip address address netmask
    ```

    Use the appropriate command to configure the Layer 3 interface with network addressing. The example here shows the configuration of an IP address.

> **Caution**   If you create a channel that uses an address that is currently configured on the interface, you must first remove that address before assigning it to the port channel interface. Step 3b describes how to remove a protocol address.

3. Assign physical Layer 3 interfaces to the channel group.

    a. Select an interface:

    ```
    (global) interface type mod/port
    ```

    Select a Layer 3 interface to assign to the channel group. Because you are creating a Layer 3 channel, the interface must be a Layer 3 interface. For switches that enable an interface to act as a Layer 2 or Layer 3 interface, issue the command **no switchport** to ensure the interface operates at Layer 3.

    b. Remove any protocol addressing:

    ```
    (interface) no ip address
    ```

    If the interface has been configured with any protocol addressing, such as IP, you must remove the protocol address with the **no** form of the command that established the addressing. For example, the **no ip address** command removes an IP address from the interface.

    c. Assign the interface to the channel group:

    ```
    (interface) channel-group number mode {auto | desirable | on}
    ```

    For a physical Layer 3 interface that you want to be part of the channel, specify the **channel-group** command. The *number* option specifies with which port channel interface the physical interface is associated. The modes specify how the channel communicates to the other side of the link. (Refer to the section "4-4: EtherChannel" in Chapter 4 for more details on the channel modes.)

    d. Verify that the interface is enabled:

    ```
    (interface) no shutdown
    ```

    The default status of many Layer 3 interfaces is **shutdown**, which is a disabled state. To ensure that the interface is operational, you need to enable the interface with the command **no shutdown**.

    e. Repeat Steps 4a through 4d for each same-speed interface that will be a member of the channel.

Verifying the Channel

After you configure a channel, you can verify the operation with the following commands:

```
(privileged) show etherchannel number port-channel
(privileged) show interfaces port-channel channel-id
```

Consider the following output examples for both of these commands:

```
Router# show etherchannel 1 port-channel
Port-channels in the group:

Port-channel: Po1

Age of the Port-channel = 01h:56m:20s

Logical slot/port = 10/1 Number of ports in agport = 2
GC = 0x00010001 HotStandBy port = null
Passive port list = Fa3/1 Fa3/2
Port state = Port-channel L3-Ag Ag-Inuse
Ports in the Port-channel:
Index Load  Port

0 55 Fa3/1
1 AA Fa3/2
Time since last port bundled: 01h:55m:44s Fa3/2
Router#
```

```
Router# show interfaces port-channel 1
Port-channel1 is up, line protocol is up
Hardware is FastEtherChannel, address is 00e0.1476.7600 (bia 0000.0000.0000)
Internet address is 11.1.1.1/24
MTU 1500 bytes, BW 400000 Kbit, DLY 100 usec, rely 255/255, load 62/255
Encapsulation ARPA, loopback not set, keepalive set (10 sec), hdx
ARP type: ARPA, ARP Timeout 04:00:00
No. of members in this fechannel: 2
Member 0 : FastEthernet0/0
Member 1 : FastEthernet0/1
Last input never, output never, output hang never
Last clearing of "show interface" counters 10:51:55
Queueing strategy: fifo
Output queue 0/40, 0 drops; input queue 0/300, 0 drops
5 minute input rate 0 bits/sec, 0 packets/sec
5 minute output rate 98281000 bits/sec, 8762 packets/sec
4545 packets input, 539950 bytes, 0 no buffer
Received 0 broadcasts, 0 runts, 0 giants
0 input errors, 0 CRC, 0 frame, 0 overrun, 0 ignored, 0 abort
```

```
0 watchdog, 0 multicast
0 input packets with dribble condition detected
342251216 packets output, 3093422680 bytes, 0 underruns
0 output errors, 0 collisions, 0 interface resets
0 babbles, 0 late collision, 0 deferred
0 lost carrier, 0 no carrier
0 output buffer failures, 0 output buffers swapped out
```

When using the **show etherchannel** command, the *number* option specifies the port channel or channel group number of the channel you want to view. The **show interfaces** command enables you to specify individual members of the channel and view the EtherChannel parameters for those interfaces.

Feature Example

The following example shows the configuration of interfaces Gigabit Ethernet 1/1 and Gigabit Ethernet 2/1 on Distribution_Switch_A as a Layer 3 channel. This interface acts as the gateway for all the clients connected to Access_Switch_A. Figure 5-2 shows the network topology for this configuration example.

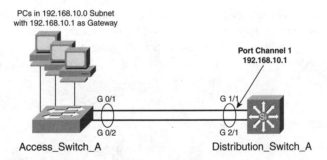

Figure 5-2   *Network Topology for Layer 3 Channel Configuration Example*

An example of the configuration for Distribution_Switch_A follows:

```
Distribution_Switch_A(config)# interface port-channel 1
Distribution_Switch_A (config-if)# ip address 192.168.10.1 255.255.255.0
Distribution_Switch_A (config-if)# interface gigabitethernet 1/1
Distribution_Switch_A (config-if)# no switchport
Distribution_Switch_A (config-if)# no ip address
Distribution_Switch_A (config-if)# channel-group 1 mode on
Distribution_Switch_A (config-if)# no shut
Distribution_Switch_A(config-if)# interface gigabitethernet 2/1
Distribution_Switch_A (config-if)# no switchport
Distribution_Switch_A (config-if)# no ip address
Distribution_Switch_A (config-if)# channel-group 1 mode on
```

```
Distribution_Switch_A (config-if)# no shut
Distribution_Switch_A (config-if)# end
Distribution_Switch_A # copy running-config startup-config
```

An example of the configuration for Access_Switch_A (a 3560) follows:

```
Access_Switch_A (config)# interface gigabitethernet 0/1
Access_Switch_A (config-if)# channel-group 1 mode on
Access_Switch_A (config)# interface gigabitethernet 0/2
Access_Switch_A (config-if)# channel-group 1 mode on
Access_Switch_A (config-if)# end
Access_Switch_A # copy running-config startup-config
```

5-4: WAN Interfaces

The Catalyst 6500/7600 series switches offer support for WAN interfaces to be added to the switch chassis. WAN interfaces are only known to the Layer 3 switching processor and must be configured from an interface. The 6500 series switch supports the enhanced FlexWAN card, which provides support for a variety of WAN Port Adapters for WAN connectivity.

In addition to the enhanced FlexWAN module, the 6500 series switch offers SPA Interface Processor modules (SIP) that provide support for the shared port adapters. Recommended practice dictates the use of SIP/SPA Modules instead of FlexWan or enhanced FlexWan because new features and solutions are being developed on these platforms.

Configuration

WAN interfaces enable users to connect to remote services from the Catalyst switch chassis.

> **Note**   This section offers an abbreviated look at configuring some basic parameters for Layer 3 switching using these interfaces. For a more detailed look at these interfaces and WAN connectivity, see the "Further Reading" section at the end of this chapter.

Each of the following sections details the steps to configure the different WAN interfaces for basic network connectivity.

Configuring an Enhanced FlexWAN Interface

The Enhanced FlexWAN module for the 6500 series is similar to the modular router series. This module allows for the installation of a limited number of WAN port adapters to be used by the Layer 3 switching processor for WAN connectivity. The Enhanced

FlexWAN module can accept up to two Cisco 7200 or Cisco 7500 WAN port adapters, which deliver WAN consolidation and extend QoS and traffic management capabilities over WAN segments. The Enhanced FlexWAN module supports ATM and Packet over SONET (POS) OC-3 links and channelized, multichannel, and clear channel port adapters at speeds from T1/E1 to T3/E3. The Enhanced FlexWAN does require that an MSFC be installed into the switch before it can operate. The following steps describe the process for configuring the Enhanced FlexWAN interfaces.

Note   You can find a list of supported port adapters for the Enhanced Flexwan module at the following site (Cisco.com login required):

http://www.cisco.com/en/US/partner/products/hw/modules/ps4835/products_data_sheet0 9186a00801df1d9.html

1.   Configure the WAN interface:

    (global) **interface** *type slot/bay/number*

    In global configuration mode, use this command to access the WAN interface. The *type* option specifies the type of WAN interface (for example, **serial, hssi, pos,** or **atm**). The *slot* indicates the slot in the switch chassis, the *bay* is the bay number on the enhanced FlexWAN card (bays are numbered 0 to 1 from left to right), and interface is the *number* on the port adapter (interface numbers start at 0).

2.   Assign a protocol address to the interface:

    (interface) **ip address** *address netmask*

    Use the appropriate command to configure the Layer 3 interface with network addressing. The example here shows configuration of an IP address.

3.   Enable the interface:

    (interface) **no shutdown**

    The default status of many Layer 3 interfaces is **shutdown**, which is a disabled state. To ensure that the interface is operational, enable the interface with the command **no shutdown**.

Configuring a SPA Interface Processor (SIP) / Shared Port Adapter (SPA) WAN Interface

The SIP module is a carrier card that inserts into a switch slot like a line card. It provides no network connectivity on its own. A SIP contains one or more subslots, which contain one or more SPAs. The SPA provides interface ports for network connectivity. SIPs and SPAs requires a 6500 series switch with a Supervisor 720 or Supervisor 32. Each port on this blade acts as a Layer 3 port and can be configured with an IP address only, with a variety of traffic-control features. To provide basic configuration for these interfaces, use the following steps:

Section 5-4

> **Note**   SIP / SPA Compatibility Matrix:
>
> http://www.cisco.com/univercd/cc/td/doc/product/core/cis7600/76sipspa/sipspahw/76intr o.htm#wp1131939

1. Access the interface:

    ```
    (global)interface fastethernet slot/subslot/port[.subinterface-number]
    ```

    In global configuration mode, use this command to access the interface. The *type* is a **ge-wan**, the *slot* is the chassis slot, and the *number* is the port number.

2. Assign an IP address:

    ```
    (interface) ip address address netmask
    ```

    Use this command to enable IP processing for the port. The Gigabit Ethernet WAN ports support only IP processing.

3. Enable the interface:

    ```
    (interface) no shutdown
    ```

    The default status of many Layer 3 interfaces is **shutdown,** which is a disabled state. To ensure that the interface is operational, you need to enable the interface with the command **no shutdown.**

Configuring a Packet-over-SONET Interface

The *packet-over-SONET* (POS) interfaces offer another method for connecting the 6500 series switches to high-speed metropolitan area networks. Use the following steps to provide basic configuration for POS interfaces:

1. Access the POS interface:

    ```
    (global) interface pos slot/port
    ```

    In global configuration mode, use this command to access the POS interface. The *slot* option designates the slot in the switch chassis, and the *port* option indicates which POS port you configure.

2. Specify an encapsulation:

    ```
    (interface) encapsulation {hdlc | ppp}
    ```

    You need to ensure that the Layer 2 encapsulation between the devices is compatible. *High-level data link control (HDLC)* is typically used if attaching to another Cisco device; if not, use PPP.

3. *(Optional)* Specify a clocking:

    ```
    (interface) clock source {line | internal}
    ```

    If you connect two switches back-to-back using dark fiber, you need to configure one of the switches with the option **clock source internal;** otherwise, the default is **line.**

4. Assign an IP address to the interface:

```
(interface) ip address address netmask
```

Use this command to enable IP processing for the port.

5. Enable the interface:

```
(interface) no shutdown
```

The default status of many Layer 3 interfaces is **shutdown**, which is a disabled state. To ensure that the interface is operational, enable the interface with the command **no shutdown.**

Verifying Configurations

After you configure your WAN interfaces, use the following command to verify configuration:

```
(privileged) show interface type number
```

Feature Example

This configuration shows an example of a Catalyst 5500 (Core_switch_1) using a VIP2 with a serial interface connecting to a 6500 (Core_switch_2) using a FlexWAN interface across a Frame Relay network. The *data-link connection identifier (DLCI)* number for the Catalyst 6500 is 110, and the DLCI for the 6500 is 120. Figure 5-3 shows the network topology associated with this configuration example.

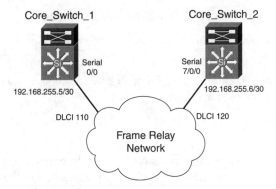

Figure 5-3 *Network Topology for WAN Interface Configuration Example*

An example of the Core_switch_1 configuration follows:

```
Core_switch # config t
Core_switch (config)# interface serial 0/0
Core_switch (config-if)# encapsulation frame-relay
Core_switch (config)# interface serial 0/0.110
```

```
Core_switch (config-if)# frame-relay interface-dlci 110
Core_switch (config-if)# ip address 192.168.255.5 255.255.255.252
Core_switch (config-if)# no shutdown
Core_switch (config-if)# end
Core_switch # copy running-config startup-config
Core_switch # quit
```

An example of the Core_switch_2 configuration running IOS follows:

```
Core_switch_2>enable
Core_switch_2# config t
Core_switch_2(config)# interface serial 7/0/0
Core_switch_2(config-if)# encapsulation frame-relay
Core_switch_2(config)# interface serial 7/0/0.120
Core_switch_2(config-if)# frame-relay interface-dlci 120
Core_switch_2(config-if)# ip address 192.168.255.6 255.255.255.252
Core_switch_2(config-if)# no shutdown
Core_switch_2(config-if)# end
Core_switch_2# copy running-config startup-config
```

5-5: Layer 3 Virtual Interfaces

- Virtual interfaces exist for configuration where there is no single physical attachment to a broadcast domain.

- For switches with Layer 2 interfaces, VLANs define broadcast domains.

- The VLAN interface is a Layer 3 interface for any member of the given VLAN.

- For switches or routers with Layer 3 interfaces, broadcast domains are defined as bridge groups.

- To route between bridge groups and other broadcast domains, a *bridged virtual interface (BVI)* is used as a Layer 3 interface.

- In some instances, a physical Layer 3 interface can support traffic from multiple VLANs.

- To provide Layer 3 interfaces for each VLAN on the physical connection, a subinterface is configured as the Layer 3 interface for the members of the VLAN.

Configuring a VLAN Interface

1. Configure a VLAN switched virtual interface (SVI):

   (global) **interface vlan** *number*

   In global configuration mode, use this command to create and access a VLAN interface. This interface is in the same broadcast domain as the members of the VLAN number. For this interface to be active, it must first exist in the VLAN database of the switch. (See the section "6-1: VLAN Configuration." in Chapter 6, "VLANs and Trunking.")

2. Assign a protocol address to the interface:

`(interface)` **ip address** `address netmask`

Use the appropriate command to configure the Layer 3 interface with network addressing. The example here shows configuration of an IP address. See Step 3 of section "5-2: Layer 3 Ethernet Interfaces" for other protocol options.

3. Enable the interface:

`(interface)` **no shutdown**

The default status of many Layer 3 interfaces is **shutdown**, which is a disabled state. To ensure that the interface is operational, you need to enable the interface with the command **no shutdown**.

Configuring Subinterfaces

1. Create and access the subinterfaces:

`(global)` **interface** `type number.subnumber`

In global configuration mode, use this command to create and access a subinterface. The *type* is the controller type of the interface (for example, **fastethernet** or **gigabitethernet**). The *type* can also be **port-channel** for a channeled connection. The *number* specifies the location or logical number of the interface, and the *subnumber* creates a logical Layer 3 subinterface off the main connection.

2. Specify an encapsulation and VLAN:

`(sub-interface)` **encapsulation** {**dot1q** | **isl**} `vlannumber` [**native**]

In subinterface mode, you specify which VLAN is associated with a given subinterface using the encapsulation command. The type (**dot1q** or **isl**) depends on the type of trunk connected to the router interface. The *vlannumber* option specifies which VLAN is associated with the subinterface, that is, in which broadcast domain this subinterface acts as a Layer 3 interface.

For dot1q trunks only, the option **native** specifies which one of the VLANs is the native VLAN. This is important because native VLAN packets are not tagged as per the 802.1Q specification.

> **Note** Subinterfaces are used in configurations for routers or interfaces connected to a trunk link. Layer 3 interfaces do not run the *Dynamic Trunking Protocol (DTP)*, and any switch connected to these interfaces must be configured in trunk on mode.

3. Assign a protocol address to the subinterface:

`(sub-interface)` **ip address** `address netmask`

Use the appropriate command to configure the Layer 3 subinterface with network addressing. The example here shows the configuration of an IP address. See Step 3 of section "5-2: Layer 3 Ethernet Interfaces" for other protocol options.

4.   Enable the interface:

```
(interface) no shutdown
```

The default status of many Layer 3 interfaces is **shutdown**, which is a disabled state. To ensure that the interface is operational, enable the interface with the command **no shutdown**.

Verifying Configurations

After configuring your subinterfaces, use the following commands to verify configuration:

```
(privileged) show interface type number.subnumber
(privileged) show vlan [number]
```

Feature Example

This example shows the configuration of a 3750 connected to a 3560 through an 802.1Q trunk link between ports G49 on the 3560 and G0/1 on the 3550. A virtual interface for VLAN 10 has been configured on both switches. Figure 5-4 shows the network topology for this example.

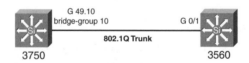

Figure 5-4   *Network Topology for Virtual Interface Configuration Example*

An example of the 3750 configuration follows:

```
3750 (config)# interface gigabitethernet 49.10
3750 (config-subif)# encapsulation dot1q 10
3750 (config-subif)# no shutdown
3750 (config-subif)# interface vlan 10
3750 (config-if)# ip address 192.168.10.1 255.255.255.0
3750 (config-if)# no shutdown
3750 (config-if)# end
3750 # copy running-config startup-config
```

```
3560# conf t
```

```
3560 (config)# vlan 10
3560 (config-vlan)# exit
3560 (config)# interface gigabitethernet 0/1
3560 (config-if)# switchport mode trunk
3560 (config-if)# switchport mode on
3560 (config-if)# switchport trunk encapsulation dot1q
3560 (config-if)# interface vlan 10
3560 (config-if)# ip address 192.168.10.2 255.255.255.0
3560 (config-if)# no shutdown
3560 (config-if)# end
3560 # copy running-config startup-config
```

5-6: Routing Tables

- To move packets between separate networks, the switching processor must have knowledge of the destination network.

- Networks that are connected to a physical or virtual interface are connected routes and are automatically known by the switching processor.

- You can configure the Layer 3 switching processor with statically defined routes by entering the routes into the configuration file.

- One of the most common ways to learn and maintain routes is to use a dynamic routing protocol, such as *Open Shortest Path First (OSPF) Protocol* or *Enhanced Interior Gateway Routing Protocol (EIGRP)*.

Configuration

1. Establish connected routes:

   (interface) **ip address** *address mask*

   By specifying a network address on an interface, you have also established an entry for that network in the routing table. This step shows the configuration for an IP address, but the same would hold true for other protocols (as shown in the section "5-2: Layer 3 Ethernet Interfaces").

2. Establish static routes:

   (global) **ip route** *network netmask {nexthop | interface} [admin-distance]*

   This command specifies a static route for the network using the mask specified. The *nexthop* address or *interface* shows how to get to the network configured.

3. Enable dynamic routes:

   (global) **router** *protocol*

   (router)**network** *network*

   The **router** command along with a protocol such as *Routing Information Protocol* (RIP), OSPF, or EIGRP places you in router configuration mode. In this mode, you specify the networks for which you want to run the protocol.

Section 5-6

> **Note**   This section is an abbreviated look at establishing and maintaining routes. It is intended as a reminder and not as a comprehensive configuration of routing protocols. A Layer 3 switch works exactly like a router for maintaining routes. Refer to *Cisco Field Manual: Router Configuration* by Cisco Press for more detailed configuration information. For more general information on routing and routing technologies, see the "Further Reading" section at the end of the chapter.

Verifying Routes

After you have configured a port for routing, use the following command to verify the VLAN port assignments:

```
(privileged) show protocol route
```

The *protocol* option enables you to look at the routing table for a given protocol, such as IP, IPX, or AppleTalk.

Further Reading

Refer to the following recommended sources for further information about the topics covered in this chapter.

Layer 3 Switching (Routing) and Routing Updates

McQuerry, Stephen. *Interconnecting Cisco Network Devices, Part 1 (ICND1): CCNA Exam 640-802 and ICND1 Exam 640-822, Adobe Reader*, Second Edition. ISBN-10: 1-58705-589-9.

McQuerry, Stephen. *Interconnecting Cisco Network Devices, Part 2 (ICND2): (CCNA Exam 640-802 and ICND exam 640-816), Adobe Reader*, Third Edition. ISBN-10: 1-58705-564-3.

Doyle, Jeff. *Routing TCP/IP, Volume 1*, Second Edition. Cisco Press, ISBN-10: 1-58705-202-4.

Doyle, Jeff and Jennifer DeHaven Carroll. *Routing TCP/IP, Volume II*. Cisco Press, ISBN 1-57870-089-2.

Hucaby, David and Steve McQuerry. *Cisco Field Manual: Router Configuration*. Cisco Press, ISBN 1-58705-024-2.

WAN Interfaces

Route Switch Module Catalyst VIP2-15 and VIP2-40 Installation and Configuration Note: http://www.tinyurl.com/7wasde.

Enhanced FlexWAN Catalyst Installation Guide: http://www.tinyurl.com/7nyg5k.

Enhanced FlexWAN Module Performance and Configuration Guide: http://www.tinyurl.com/7ub6uk.

SPA Interface Processors: http://www.tinyurl.com/9d2lm5.

Chapter 6

VLANs and Trunking

See the following sections for configuration information about these topics:

- **6-1: VLAN Configuration:** Describes the method for configuring, creating, and configuring VLANs on a switch

- **6-2: VLAN Port Assignments:** Explains how to assign a port to a VLAN using static or dynamic methods

- **6-3: Trunking:** Covers the method for extending a VLAN beyond the boundaries of a single switch through tagging mechanisms

- **6-4: VLAN Trunking Protocol:** Describes the Cisco proprietary protocol for maintaining a forwarding path between switches that are trunking and how to prune for unused VLANs

- **6-5: Private VLANs:** Explains the feature that allows for more granular traffic control within the VLAN using the private VLAN structure

6-1: VLAN Configuration

- *VLANs* are broadcast domains defined within switches to enable control of broadcast, multicast, unicast, and unknown unicast within a Layer 2 device.

- VLANs are defined on a switch in an internal database known as the *VLAN Trunking Protocol (VTP) database*. After a VLAN has been created, ports are assigned to the VLAN.

- VLANs are assigned numbers for identification within and between switches. Cisco switches have two ranges of VLANs, the *normal range* and *extended range*.

- VLANs have a variety of configurable parameters, including name, type, and state.

- Several VLANs are reserved, and some can be used for internal purposes within the switch.

Creation of an Ethernet VLAN

VLANs are created on Layer 2 switches to control broadcasts and enforce the use of a Layer 3 device for communications. Each VLAN is created in the local switch's database for use. If a VLAN is not known to a switch, that switch cannot transfer traffic across any of its ports for that VLAN. VLANs are created by number, and there are two ranges of usable VLAN numbers (normal range 1 to 1000 and extended range 1025 to 4096). When a VLAN is created, you can also give it certain attributes such as a VLAN name, VLAN type, and its operational state. To create a VLAN, use the following steps.

1. Configure VTP.

    VTP is a protocol used by Cisco switches to maintain a consistent database between switches for trunking purposes. VTP is not required to create VLANs; however, Cisco has set it up to act as a conduit for VLAN configuration between switches as a default to make administration of VLANs easier. Because of this, you must first either configure a VTP with a domain name or disable VTP on the switch. VTP is explained in detail in section "6-4: VLAN Trunking Protocol."

    ■ Specify a VTP name:

    ```
    (global) vtp domain domain-name
    ```

    By default, the VTP is in server mode and must be configured with a domain name before any VLANs can be created. These commands specify the VTP domain name.

    OR

    ■ Disable VTP synchronization:

    ```
    (global) vtp mode transparent
    ```

    Another option is to disable VTP synchronization of the databases. Disabling it enables you to manage your local VTP database without configuring and relying on VTP. You can configure the VTP parameters in global configuration mode as well.

2. Create the VLAN.

    VLANs are created by number. The two ranges of VLANs are as follows:

    ■ The standard range consists of VLANs 1 to 1000.

    ■ The extended range consists of VLANs 1025 to 4096.

    Extended VLANs are supported in switches running IOS software. When you create a VLAN, you have many options to consider, several of which are valid only for FDDI and Token Ring VLANs. Some of the items configured deal with options, such as private VLANs, which are discussed in other sections in this book. VLANs are created using the **vlan** command in global mode. For Ethernet VLANs, you can also configure the standard parameters, as shown in Table 6-1.

Table 6-1 *Configurable VLAN Parameters*

Parameter	Description
`name`	A description of the VLAN up to 32 characters. If none is given, it defaults to VLAN00XXX, where XXX is the VLAN number.
`mtu`	The maximum transmission unit (packet size in bytes) that the VLAN can use; valid values are from **576** to **18190**. The MTU can extend up to 1500 for Ethernet, but beyond for Token Ring or FDDI. The default is **1500**.
`state`	Used to specify whether the state of the VLAN is active or suspended. All ports in a suspended VLAN will be suspended and not allowed to forward traffic. The default state is **active**.

a. Create a VLAN in the standard range:

```
(global) vlan vlan-id [name vlan-name] [state {suspend | active}] [mtu
    mtu-size]
```

The **vlan-id** specifies the VLAN by number. You can create VLANs in global configuration mode if the switch is in VTP transparent mode. To do this, enter the **vlan** *vlan-id* command to move to vlan-config mode. From vlan-config mode, you can manage the parameters of the VLANs.

Note You cannot modify any of the parameters for VLAN 1.

b. Create a VLAN in the extended range.

Extended VLANs support VLANs up to 4096 in accordance with the 802.1Q standard.

3. Enable spanning-tree MAC reduction:

```
(global) vlan internal allocation policy descending
```

You can instruct the Catalyst 6500 series switch to start to borrow VLANs from the top, and descend from 4096, or from bottom, and ascend from 1006, with the use the global config mode **vlan allocation policy** command.

Note   After you create a VLAN in the extended range, you cannot disable this feature unless you first delete the VLAN.

4.   Create a VLAN in the extended range:

```
(global) vlan vlan-id [name vlan-name] [state {suspend | active}] [mtu
    mtu-size]
```

Here the *vlan-id* would be a number from 1025 to 4096. Numbers 1001 to 1024 are reserved by Cisco and cannot be configured.

Caution   For Catalyst 6000 series switches with FlexWAN cards, the system identifies these ports internally with VLAN numbers starting with 1025. If you have any FlexWAN modules, be sure to reserve enough VLAN numbers (starting with VLAN 1025) for all the FlexWAN ports you want to install. You cannot use these extended VLANs if you install FlexWAN ports.

Feature Example

In this example, the switches Access_1 and Distribution_1 are going to be configured with VLANs 5, 8, and 10 with the names Cameron, Logan, and Katie, respectively. Also the distribution switch will be configured with VLAN 2112 with the name Rush.

An example of the configuration for Distribution 1 follows:

```
Distribution_1# conf t
Distribution_1 (config)# vtp mode transparent
Distribution_1 (config)# vlan 5
Distribution_1 ((config-vlan)# name Cameron
Distribution_1 ((config-vlan)# vlan 8
Distribution_1 ((config-vlan)# name Logan
Distribution_1 ((config-vlan)# vlan 10
Distribution_1 ((config-vlan)# name Katie
Distribution_1 ((config-vlan)# vlan 2112
Distribution_1 ((config-vlan)# name Rush
Distribution_1 ((config-vlan)# end
Distribution_1 # copy running-config startup-config
```

An example of the Layer 2 configuration for Access 1 follows: •

```
Access_1(config)# vlan 5
Access_1(config-vlan)# name Cameron
Access_1(config-vlan)# vlan 8
Access_1(config-vlan)# name Logan
Access_1(config-vlan)# vlan 10
Access_1(config-vlan)# name Katie
```

```
Access_1(config-vlan)# end
Access_1 #copy running-config startup-config
```

6-2: VLAN Port Assignments

■ VLANs are assigned to individual switch ports.

■ Ports can be statically assigned to a single VLAN or dynamically assigned to a single VLAN.

■ All ports are assigned to VLAN 1 by default.

■ Ports are active only if they are assigned to VLANs that exist on the switch.

■ Static port assignments are performed by the administrator and do not change unless modified by the administrator, whether the VLAN exists on the switch.

■ Dynamic VLANs are assigned to a port based on the MAC address of the device plugged into a port.

■ Dynamic VLAN configuration requires a *VLAN Membership Policy Server* (VMPS) client, server, and database to operate properly.

Configuring Static VLANs

On a Cisco switch, ports are assigned to a single VLAN. These ports are referred to as *access ports* and provide a connection for end users or node devices, such as a router or server. By default all devices are assigned to VLAN 1, known as the *default VLAN*. After creating a VLAN, you can manually assign a port to that VLAN, and it can communicate only with or through other devices in the VLAN. Configure the switch port for membership in a given VLAN as follows:

1. Statically assign a VLAN:

```
(global) interface type mod/port

(interface) switchport access vlan number
```

For the device, you must first select the port or port range and then use the **switchport access vlan** command followed by the VLAN *number*.

> **Caution**   If the VLAN that the port is assigned to does not exist in the database, the port is disabled until the VLAN is created.

Configuring Dynamic VLANs

Although static VLANs are the most common form of port VLAN assignments, it is possible to have the switch dynamically allocate a VLAN based on the authentication. The IEEE 802.1X standard defines a client and server-based access control and authentication protocol that restricts unauthorized clients from connecting to a LAN through publicly accessible ports. The authentication server authenticates each client connected to a switch port and assigns the port to a VLAN before making available any services offered by the switch or the LAN. Until the client is authenticated, 802.1X access control enables only Extensible Authentication Protocol over LAN (EAPOL) traffic through the port to which the client is connected. After authentication is successful, normal traffic can pass through the port. Use the following steps to configure dynamic VLANs using 802.1x with VLAN assignment:

1. Enable AAA authorization by using the **network** keyword to allow interface configuration from the RADIUS server.

   (global) **RADIUS configuration**

   (global) **radius-server host** *ip_address*

   (global) **radius-server key** *key*

   (global) **aaa new-model**

   (global) **aaa authentication dot1x default group radius**

   (global) **aaa authorization default group radius**

   (global) **aaa authorization config-commands**

2. Enable 802.1x authentication:

   (global) **dot1x system-auth-control**

   (global) **dot1x max-req**

   (global) **dot1x timeout quiet-period**

   (global) **dot1x timeout tx-period**

   (global) **dot1x timeout re-authperiod**

   (global) **dot1x re-authentication**

Note   The VLAN assignment feature is automatically enabled when you configure 802.1X authentication on an access port.

3. Assign vendor-specific tunnel attributes in the RADIUS server. The RADIUS server must return these attributes to the switch: [64] Tunnel-Type = VLAN [65] Tunnel-Medium-Type = 802 [81] Tunnel-Private-Group-ID = VLAN name or VLAN ID.

Note   The dynamic VLAN mechanism:

■   RADIUS AV-Pairs used to send back VLAN configuration information to authenticator.

- AV-Pair usage for VLANs is IEEE specified in the 802.1x standard.

- AV-Pairs used (all are IETF standard):

  - [64] **Tunnel-Type:** "VLAN" (13)

  - [65] **Tunnel-Medium-Type:** "802" (6)

  - [81] **Tunnel-Private-Group-ID:** *<VLAN name>*

Using VLAN names to assign VLANs allows independence between separate L2 or VTP domains.

4. IOS Per-port configuration:

```
(interface) dot1x port-control auto
```

Verifying VLAN Assignments

To display the system dot1x capabilities, protocol version, and timer values, enter the following command:

```
(exec) show dot1x
```

6-3: Trunking

- VLANs are local to each switch's database, and VLAN information is not passed between switches.

- Trunk links provide VLAN identification for frames traveling between switches.

- Cisco switches have two Ethernet trunking mechanisms: ISL and IEEE 802.1Q.

- Certain types of switches can negotiate trunk links.

- Trunks carry traffic from all VLANs to and from the switch by default but can be configured to carry only specified VLAN traffic.

- Trunk links must be configured to allow trunking on each end of the link.

Enabling Trunking

Trunk links are required to pass VLAN information between switches. A port on a Cisco switch is either an access port or a trunk port. Access ports belong to a single VLAN and do not provide any identifying marks on the frames that pass between switches. Access ports also carry traffic that comes from only the VLAN assigned to the port. A trunk port is by default a member of *all* the VLANs that exist on the switch and carry traffic for all those VLANs between the switches. To distinguish between the traffic flows, a trunk port must mark the frames with special tags as they pass between the switches.

Section 6-3

Trunking is a function that must be enabled on both sides of a link. If two switches connect together, for example, both switch ports must be configured for trunking, and they must both be configured with the same tagging mechanism (ISL or 802.1Q).

To enable trunking between the switches, use the following steps:

1. Enable trunking on a port.

   a. Enable the trunk:

      (global) **interface** *type mod/port*

      (interface) **switchport mode dynamic** [**auto** | **desirable**]

      (interface) **switchport mode trunk**

      (interface) **switchport nonegotiate**

      The most basic way to configure a trunk link is to use the option **on**. This option enables the trunk and requires that you also specify a tagging mechanism for the trunk. For IOS devices, the command **switchport mode trunk** is equivalent to the **set trunk** *mod/port* **on** command. When specifying the option **on**, you must also choose a tagging mechanism (see Step 1b).

Note   Some switches do not support Dynamic Trunking Protocol. For these switches, the only command that you can use to configure trunking is **switchport mode trunk**, which essentially turns trunking on.

Many Cisco switches employ an automatic trunking mechanism known as the *Dynamic Trunking Protocol (DTP)*, which enables a trunk to be dynamically established between two switches. All integrated switches can use DTP to form a trunk link. The options of **dynamic auto**, **dynamic desirable**, and **trunk** configure a trunk link using DTP. If one side of the link is configured to trunk and sends DTP signals, the other side of the link dynamically begins to trunk if the options match correctly.

If you want to enable trunking and not send any DTP signaling, use the option **nonegotiate** for switches that support that function. If you want to disable trunking completely, use the **no switchport mode trunk** command.

Tip   Remember that not all switches support DTP and might not establish a trunk without intervention. Also remember that DTP offers no benefit when you are trunking with a non-Cisco switch. To eliminate any overhead associated with DTP, it is useful to use the **nonegotiate** option when DTP is not supported.

Note   When enabling trunking, you cannot specify a range of ports.

Table 6-2 shows the DTP signaling and the characteristics of each mode.

Table 6-2 *Trunking Mode Characteristics*

Trunking Mode	Characteristics
mode trunk	Trunking is on for these links. They will also send DTP signals that attempt to initiate a trunk with the other side. This forms a trunk with other ports in the states **on, auto,** or **desirable** that are running DTP. A port that is in **on** mode always tags frames sent out the port.
mode dynamic desirable	These links would like to become trunk links and send DTP signals that attempt to initiate a trunk. They only become trunk links if the other side responds to the DTP signal. This forms a trunk with other ports in the states **on, auto,** or **desirable** that are running DTP. This is the default mode for the 6000 running Supervisor IOS.
mode dynamic auto	These links only become trunk links if they receive a DTP signal from a link that is already trunking or wants to trunk. This only forms a trunk with other ports in the states **on** or **desirable.**
mode nonegotiate	Sets trunking on and disables DTP. These only become trunks with ports in **on** or **nonegotiate** mode.
no switchport mode trunk	This option sets trunking and DTP capabilities off. This is the recommended setting for any access port because it prevents any dynamic establishments of trunk links.

Note Cisco 2950 and 3500XL switches do not support DTP and are always in a mode similar to **nonegotiate.** If you turn trunking on for one of these devices, it will not negotiate with the other end of the link and requires that the other link be configured to **on** or **nonegotiate.**

b. Specify the encapsulation method:

```
(global) interface type mod/port

(interface) switchport trunk encapsulation [negotiate | isl | dot1Q]
```

Section 6-3

The other option when choosing a trunk link is the encapsulation method. For Layer 2 IOS switches, such as the 2900XL or the 3500XL, the default encapsulation method is **isl**. You can change from the default with the **switchport trunk encapsulation** command. For integrated IOS switches, the default encapsulation is **negotiate**. This method signals between the trunked ports to choose an encapsulation method. (ISL is preferred over 802.1Q.) The **negotiate** option is valid for **auto** or **desirable** trunking modes only. If you choose **on** as the mode or if you want to force a particular method or if the other side of the trunk cannot negotiate the trunking type, you must choose the option **isl** or **dot1Q** to specify the encapsulation method.

Note   Not all switches enable you to negotiate a trunk encapsulation setting. The 2900XL and 3500XL trunks default to **isl**, and you must use the **switchport trunk encapsulation** command to change the encapsulation type. The 2950 and some 4000 switches support only 802.1Q trunking and provide no options for changing the trunk type.

c. *(Optional)* Specify the native VLAN:

```
(global) interface type mod/port

(interface) switchport trunk native vlan number
```

For switches running 802.1Q as the trunking mechanism, the native VLAN of each port on the trunk must match. The native VLAN on IOS devices is configured for VLAN 1, so the native VLAN does match. If you choose to change the native VLAN, use the **switchport trunk native vlan** command to specify the native VLAN. Remember that the native VLAN *must* match on both sides of the trunk link for 802.1Q; otherwise the link will not work. If there is a native VLAN mismatch, *Spanning Tree Protocol (STP)* places the port in a *port VLAN ID (PVID)* inconsistent state and will not forward on the link.

Note   *Cisco Discovery Protocol (CDP)* version 2 passes native VLAN information between Cisco switches. If you have a native VLAN mismatch, you see CDP error messages on the console output.

Specifying VLANs to Trunk

By default a trunk link carries all the VLANs that exist on the switch. This is because all VLANs are active on a trunk link; and as long as the VLAN is in the switch's local database, traffic for that VLAN is carried across the trunks. You can elect to selectively remove and add VLANs from a trunk link. To specify which VLANs to add or remove from a trunk link, use the following commands.

1. *(Optional)* Manually remove VLANs from a trunk link:

```
(global) interface type mod/port

(interface) switchport trunk allowed vlan remove vlanlist
```

By specifying VLANs in the *vlanlist* field of this command, the VLANs will not be allowed to travel across the trunk link until they are added back to the trunk using the command **set trunk** *mod/port vlanlist* or **switchport trunk allowed vlan add** *vlanlist*.

Verifying Trunks

After configuring a port for trunking, use the following command to verify the VLAN port assignments:

```
Router# show interfaces trunk
```

Feature Example

In this example the switches Access_1, Distribution_1, and Core_1 are connected as shown in Figure 6-1. 802.1Q trunking is configured in the on mode between Access_1 and Distribution_1 switches. ISL is configured in desirable mode on the Distribution_1 switch to the link connecting to the core. The core is configured for autotrunking mode and encapsulation negotiate. The trunk connected between the access switch is configured to only trunk for VLANs 5, 8, and 10. The trunk between the Distribution_1 and Core_1 is configured to carry only VLAN 1 and VLAN 10.

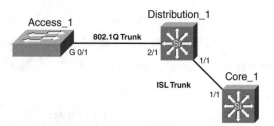

Figure 6-1 *Network Diagram for Trunk Configuration on Access_1, Distribution_1, and Core_1*

An example of the Catalyst IOS configuration for Distribution_1 follows:

```
Distribution_1 (config#) interface gigabitethernet 2/1
Distribution_1 (config-if)# switchport mode trunk
Distribution_1 (config-if)# switchport trunk encapsulation dot1q
Distribution_1 (config-if)# switchport trunk allowed vlan allowed 5,8,10
Distribution_1 (config-if)# end
Distribution_1# copy running-config startup-config
```

An example of IOS configuration for Core_1 follows:

```
Core_1(config)# interface gigabitethernet 1/1
```

```
Core_1(config-if)# switchport encapsulation negotiate
Core_1(config-if)# switchport mode dynamic auto
Core_1(config-if)# switchport trunk allowed vlan allowed 1,10
Core_1 (config-if)# end
Core_1# copy running-config startup-config
```

An example of the Layer 2 IOS configuration for Access_1 follows:

```
Access_1 (config)# interface gigabitethernet 0/1
Access_1 (config-if)# switchport mode trunk
Access_1 (config-if)# switchport trunk encapsulation dot1q
Access_1 (config-if)# switchport trunk allowed vlan allowed 5,8,10
Access_1 (config-if)# end
Access_1# copy running-config startup-config
```

6-4: VLAN Trunking Protocol

- VTP sends messages between trunked switches to maintain VLANs on these switches to properly trunk.

- VTP is a Cisco proprietary method of managing VLANs between switches and runs across any type of trunking mechanism.

- VTP messages are exchanged between switches within a common VTP domain.

- VTP domains must be defined or VTP disabled before a VLAN can be created.

- Exchanges of VTP information can be controlled by passwords.

- VTP manages only VLANs 2 through 1002.

- VTP allows switches to synchronize their VLANs based on a configuration revision number.

- Switches can operate in one of three VTP modes: server, transparent, or client.

- VTP can prune unneeded VLANs from trunk links.

Enabling VTP for Operation

VTP exists to ensure that VLANs exist on the local VLAN database of switches in a trunked path. In addition to making sure the VLANs exist, VTP can further synchronize name settings and can be used to prune VLANs from trunk links that are destined for switches that do not have any ports active in that particular VLAN.

To manage and configure VTP, use the following steps.

1.   Activate VTP on a switch.

    a. Specify a VTP domain name:

        `(privileged)` **`vlan database`**

        `(vlan_database)` **`vtp domain`** *`name`*

        OR

        `(global)` **`vtp domain`** *`name`*

By default VTP is in server mode, which is an operational mode that enables you to manage VLANs on the local switch's database and use the information in the database to synchronize with other switches. To configure VTP for operation, you must specify a name. After you enable trunking, this name propagates to switches that have not been configured with a name. If you choose to configure names on your switches, however, remember that VTP names are case-sensitive and must match exactly. Switches that have different VTP names will not exchange VLAN information.

Note   The global configuration command **vtp domain** is not supported on all switches that run the IOS.

Note   VTP names are used only in the context of synchronizing VTP databases. VTP domain names do not separate broadcast domains. If VLAN 20 exists on two switches trunked together with different VTP domain names, VLAN 20 is still the same broadcast domain!

Section 6-4

    b. Enable the trunk:

        `(global)` **`interface`** *`type mod/port`*

        `(interface)` **`switchport mode dynamic`** [**`auto`** | **`desirable`**]

        `(interface)` **`switchport mode trunk`**

        `(interface)` **`switchport nonegotiate`**

VTP information is passed only across trunk links. If you do not enable a trunk, VLAN information is not exchanged between the switches. See section "6-3: Trunking" for more details on trunking.

Note   Some IOS switches do not support DTP. For these switches, the only command that you can use to configure trunking is **switchport mode trunk**, which essentially turns trunking on.

Setting VTP Passwords

By default, there are no passwords in VTP informational updates, and any switch that has no VTP domain name will join the VTP domain when trunking is enabled. Also any switch that has the same VTP domain name configured will join and exchange VTP information. This could enable an unwanted switch in your network to manage the VLAN database on each of the switches. To prevent this from occurring, set a VTP password on the switches you want to exchange information.

1. *(Optional)* Set the VTP password:

    (privileged) **vlan database**

    (vlan_database) **vtp password** *password*

    OR

    (global)**vtp password** *password*

    The password is entered on each switch that participates in the VTP domain. The passwords are case-sensitive and must match exactly. If you want to remove the passwords, use the command **no vtp password** in VLAN database mode.

Note   If you choose to set a password for VTP, it must be between 8 and 32 characters in length.

Note   The global configuration command **vtp password** is not supported on all switches that run the IOS.

Changing VTP Modes

VTP operates in one of three modes: server, client, and transparent. The modes determine how VTP passes information, how VLAN databases are synchronized, and whether VLANs can be managed for a given switch.

To set the VTP mode, enter the following commands:

(privileged) **vlan database**
(vlan_database) **vtp** [**server** | **client** | **transparent**]

OR

(global)**vtp mode** [**server** | **client** | **transparent**]

By default, Cisco switches are in VTP server mode. For a VTP server, you can create, delete, or modify a VLAN in the local VLAN database. After you make this change, the VLAN database changes are propagated out to all other switches in server or client mode in the VTP domain. A server also accepts changes to the VLAN database from other switches in the domain. You can also run the VTP in client mode. Switches in client mode cannot create, modify, or delete VLANs in the local VLAN database. Instead, they rely on other switches in the domain to update them about new VLANs. Clients synchronize their databases, but they do not save the VLAN information and lose this information if they are powered off. Clients also advertise information about their database and forward VTP information to other switches. VTP transparent mode works much like server mode in that you can create, delete, or modify VLANs in the local VLAN database. The difference is that these changes are not propagated to other switches. In addition, the local VLAN database does not accept modifications from other switches. VTP transparent mode switches forward or relay information between other server or client switches. A VTP transparent mode switch does not require a VTP domain name.

Note   The global configuration command **vtp mode** is not supported on all switches that run the IOS.

Enabling VTP Pruning

By default all the VLANs that exist on a switch are active on a trunk link. As noted in section "6-3: Trunking," you can manually remove VLANs from a trunk link and then add them later. VTP pruning allows the switch to not forward user traffic for VLANs that are not active on a remote switch. This feature dynamically prunes unneeded traffic across trunk links. If the VLAN traffic is needed at a later date, VTP dynamically adds the VLAN back to the trunk.

Note   Dynamic pruning removes only unneeded user traffic from the link. It does not prevent any management frames such as STP from crossing the link.

1. *(Optional)* Enable VTP pruning.

    a. Enable pruning:

        ```
        (privileged) vlan database
        ```

        ```
        (vlan_database) vtp pruning
        ```

        After VTP pruning is enabled on one VTP server in the domain, all other switches in that domain also enable VTP pruning. VTP pruning can only be enabled on switches that are VTP version 2-capable, so all switches in the domain must be version 2-capable before you enable pruning.

Note   The switch must be VTP version 2-capable but does not need to have version 2 enabled to turn on pruning.

    b. *(Optional)* Specify VLANs that are eligible for pruning:

        ```
        (global) interface type mod/port
        ```

        ```
        (interface) switchport trunk pruning vlan remove vlanlist
        ```

        By default all the VLANs on the trunk are eligible for pruning. You can remove VLANs from the list of eligible VLANs using these commands. After a VLAN has been removed from the eligible list, it cannot be pruned by VTP. To add the

VLANs back, use the command **set vtp pruneeligible** *vlanlist* for IOS switches or **switchport trunk pruning vlan add** *vlanlist* for IOS.

Changing VTP Versions

VTP supports two versions. By default all switches are in VTP version 1 mode, but most switches can support version 2 mode.

To enable VTP version 2, which is optional, enter the following commands:

```
(privileged) vlan database
(vlan_database)vtp v2-mode
```

OR

```
(global)vtp version 2
```

VTP version 2 is disabled by default. After you have enabled version 2 on one switch, all other switches in the domain also begin to operate in version 2 mode.

> **Note**   The global configuration command **vtp version 2** is not supported on all switches that run the IOS.

VTP version 2 offers the following support options not available with version 1:

- **Unrecognized type-length-value (TLV) support:** A VTP server or client propagates configuration changes to its other trunks, even for TLVs it cannot parse. The unrecognized TLV is saved in NVRAM.

- **Version-dependent transparent mode:** In VTP version 1, a VTP transparent switch inspects VTP messages for the domain name and version and forwards a message only if the version and domain name match. Because only one domain is supported in the Supervisor engine software, VTP version 2 forwards VTP messages in transparent mode without checking the version.

- **Consistency checks:** In VTP version 2, VLAN consistency checks (such as VLAN names and values) are performed only when you enter new information through the command-line interface (CLI) or Simple Network Management Protocol (SNMP). Consistency checks are not performed when new information is obtained from a VTP message or when information is read from NVRAM. If the digest on a received VTP message is correct, its information is accepted without consistency checks.

Verifying VTP Operation

After configuring VTP, use the following command to verify the VLAN port assignments:

```
(privileged) show vtp status
```

Feature Example

In this example, Access_1, Distribution_1, and Distribution_2 will be assigned to a VTP domain named GO-CATS. Figure 6-2 shows that Access_1 will be in VTP client mode with an 802.1Q trunk connecting to Distribution_1. Distribution_1 will be configured in VTP server mode with an ISL trunk connecting it to Core_1, which is in VTP transparent mode. Core_1 has an ISL trunk to Distribution_2, which is also in VTP server mode. VTP pruning has also been enabled for the domain, and all switches are configured so that VLAN 10 is not prune-eligible on the trunk links. Because VTP runs across trunk links, it is not necessary to configure the VTP domain name on the Distribution_2 switch or the Access_1 switch. It is also not necessary to configure the pruning on each switch; this is also propagated by VTP.

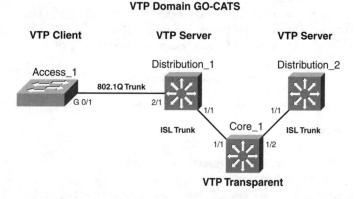

Figure 6-2 *Network Diagram for VTP Configuration on Access_1, Distribution_1, Distribution_2, and Core_1.*

An example of the configuration for Core_1 follows:

```
Core_1# conf t
Core_1 (config)# vtp mode transparent
Core_1 (config)# interface gigabitethernet 1/1
Core_1 (config-if)# switchport mode trunk
Core_1 (config-if)# switchport trunk encapsulation isl
Core_1 (config-if)# end
Core_1# conf t
Core_1 (config)# interface gigabitethernet 1/2
Core_1 (config-if)# switchport mode trunk
Core_1 (config-if)# switchport trunk encapsulation isl
Core_1 (config-if)# end
Core 1# copy running-config startup-config
```

An example of the configuration for Distribution_1 follows:

```
Distribution_1# conf t
```

```
Distribution_1 (config)# vtp domain GO-CATS
Distribution_1 (config)# interface gigabitethernet 1/1
Distribution_1 (config-if)# switchport mode trunk
Distribution_1 (config-if)# switchport trunk encapsulation isl
Distribution_1 (config-if)# end
Distribution_1 (config)# interface gigabitethernet 2/1
Distribution_1 (config-if)# switchport mode trunk
Distribution_1 (config-if)# switchport trunk encapsulation dot1q
Distribution_1 (config-if)# end
Distribution_1# copy running-config startup-config
```

An example of the configuration for Distribution_2 follows:

```
Router(config)# vtp pruning
Router(config)# interface gigabitethernet 1/1
Router (config-if)# switchport mode trunk
Router (config-if)# switchport trunk encapsulation isl
Router (config-if)# end
Router (config-if)# copy running-config startup-config
```

An example of the Layer 2 IOS configuration for Access_1 follows

```
Access_1 #config t
Access_1 (config)# vtp mode client
Access_1 (config)# interface gigabitethernet 0/1
Access_1 (config-if)# switchport mode trunk
Access_1 (config-if)# switchport trunk encapsulation dot1Q
Access_1 (config-if)# switchport trunk pruning vlan remove 10
Access_1 (config-if)# end
Access_1# copy running-config startup-config
```

6-5: Private VLANs

■ Private VLANs allow for additional security between devices in a common subnet.

■ Private edge VLANs can be configured to prevent connectivity between devices on access switches.

■ Private VLANs can be configured on the Catalyst 6000 and Catalyst 4000 series products.

■ Within a private VLAN, you can isolate devices to prevent connectivity between devices within the isolated VLAN.

■ Within a private VLAN, communities can be created to allow connection between some devices and to prevent them from communicating with others.

■ Promiscuous ports are mapped to private VLANs to allow for connectivity to VLANs outside of this network.

Configuring Private VLANs

Private VLANs provide a mechanism to control which devices can communicate within a single subnet. The private VLAN uses **isolated** and **community** secondary VLANs to control how devices communicate. The secondary VLANs are assigned to the primary VLAN, and ports are assigned to the secondary VLANs. Ports in an isolated VLAN cannot communicate with any device in the VLAN other than the promiscuous port. Ports configured in a community VLAN can communicate with other ports in the same community and the promiscuous port. Ports in different communities cannot communicate with one another. To configure private VLANs, use the following steps.

1. Set VTP transparent mode:

   (privileged) **vlan database**

   (vlan_database) **vtp transparent**

   You must configure VTP to transparent mode before you can create a private VLAN. Private VLANs are configured in the context of a single switch and cannot have members on other switches. Private VLANs also carry TLVs that are not known to all types of Cisco switches.

2. Create the primary private VLAN:

   (global) **vlan** *primary_number*

   (vlan-config) **private-vlan primary**

   You must first create a primary private VLAN. The number of the primary VLAN is used in later steps for binding secondary VLANs and mapping promiscuous ports.

3. Create isolated and community VLANs:

   (global) **vlan** *secondary_number*

   (vlan-config) **private-vlan [isolated | community]**

   Configure isolated or community secondary VLANs for assignment of ports and control of the traffic. The secondary number for each of these VLANs must be unique from one another and the primary number. Members of an isolated VLAN can only communicate with the promiscuous ports mapped in Step 6, whereas members of a community VLAN can communicate with members of the same community and the promiscuous ports. A two-way community acts like a regular community but has the additional aspect of allowing access control lists to check traffic going to and from (two ways) the VLAN and provides enhanced security within a private VLAN.

4. Bind isolated and community VLANs to the primary VLAN:

   (global) **vlan** *primary_number*

   (vlan-config) **private-vlan association** *secondary_number_list* [**add** *secondary_number_list*]

This command associates or binds the secondary VLANs to the primary VLAN. The **add** option enables other VLANs to be associated in the future.

5. Place ports into the isolated and community VLANs:

   (global) **interface** *type mod/port*

   (interface) **switchport**

   (interface) **switchport mode private-vlan host**

   (interface) **switchport mode private-vlan host-association** *primary_number secondary_number*

   After you create and associate the primary and secondary VLANs, you must assign ports to that VLAN.

6. Map the isolated and community VLANs to promiscuous ports:

   (global) **interface** *type mod/port*

   (interface) **switchport**

   (interface) **switchport mode private-vlan promiscuous**

   (interface) **switchport mode private-vlan mapping** *primary_number secondary_number*

   After you assign ports to the secondary VLANs, you must map the VLANs to a promiscuous port for access outside the isolated or community VLAN.

7. *(Optional)* Map the isolated and community VLANs to a *Multilayer Switch Feature Card* (MSFC) interface:

   (global) **interface** *primary_number*

   (interface) **ip address** *address mask*

   (interface) **private-vlan mapping** *primary_number secondary_number*

   If your switch has an MSFC, you can map the private VLANs to the MSFC. For an IOS switch, you go to the VLAN interface with the primary number and then map the primary and secondary VLANs to that port.

Configuring Private Edge VLANs

The 3500XL switch uses the concept of a protected port to allow for control of traffic on the switch. A protected port on a 3500XL will not forward traffic to another protected port on the same switch. This behavior is similar to an isolated VLAN in that protected ports cannot communicate with one another. Use the following optional command to configure a protected port:

(global) **interface** *type mod/port*
(interface) **port protected**

To configure a private edge VLAN, select the interface and type the command **port protected**. To verify that a port is in protected mode, use the command **show port protected**.

Verifying Private VLAN Operation

After configuring private VLANs, use the following commands to verify the operation:

```
show vlan private-vlan type
show interface private-vlan mapping
show interface type mod/port switchport
```

> **Note** A number of guidelines and restrictions apply to private VLANs. For a complete list of these items, go to http://www.tinyurl.com/cka68e.

Feature Example

Figure 6-3 shows the network diagram for a working private VLAN configuration example. In this example, the switch Access_1 is configured with ports 1 and 2 as protected ports both in VLAN 10. The VLAN 10 server on Distribution_1 is also in VLAN 10. This enables the PCs to connect to the server but not one another. Also on the distribution switch, private VLAN 90 has been created with a community VLAN 901 and an isolated VLAN 900. Server 2 in port 3/46 and Server 3 in port 3/48 are placed in the community VLAN, and servers connected to ports 3/1 and 3/2 are to be placed in the isolated VLAN. All these devices are mapped to the router connected to port 1/2 and the MSFC port 15/1 for interface VLAN 90.

Section 6-5

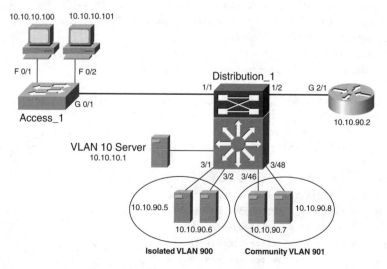

Figure 6-3 *Network Diagram for Private VLAN Configuration*

An example of the configuration for Distribution_1 follows:

```
Distribution_1# conf t
Distribution_1 (config)# vtp mode transparent
Distribution_1(config)# vlan 90
Distribution_1(config-vlan)# private-vlan primary
Distribution_1(config-vlan)# vlan 900
Distribution_1(config-vlan)# private-vlan isolated
Distribution_1(config-vlan)# vlan 901
Distribution_1(config-vlan)# private-vlan community
Distribution_1(config-vlan)# vlan 90
Distribution_1(config-vlan)# private-vlan association 900,901
Distribution_1(config-vlan)# interface range fastethernet 3/1 - 2
Distribution_1(config-if)# switchport
Distribution_1(config-if)# switchport mode private-vlan host
Distribution_1(config-if)# switchport mode private-vlan host-association 90 900
Distribution_1(config-if)# no shut
Distribution_1(config-if)# interface range fastethernet 3/46, 3/48
Distribution_1(config-if)# switchport
Distribution_1(config-if)# switchport mode private-vlan host
Distribution_1(config-if)# switchport mode private-vlan host-association 90 901
Distribution_1(config-if)# no shut
Distribution_1(config-if)# interface gigabitethernet 1/2
Distribution_1(config-if)# switchport
Distribution_1(config-if)# switchport mode private-vlan promiscuous
Distribution_1(config-if)# switchport mode private-vlan mapping 90 900,901
Distribution_1(config-if)# no shut
Distribution_1(config-vif)# interface vlan 90
Distribution_1(config-if)# ip address 10.10.90.1 255.255.255.0
Distribution_1(config-if)# private-vlan mapping 90 900,901
Distribution_1(config-if)# no shut
Distribution_1(config-if)# end
Distribution_1 # copy running-config startup-config
```

An example of the Layer 2 configuration for Access_1 follows:

```
Access_1 # config t
Access_1 (config)# interface fastethernet 0/1
Access_1 (config-if)# switchport access vlan 10
Access_1 (config-if)# port protected
Access_1 (config)# interface fastethernet 0/2
Access_1 (config-if)# switchport access vlan 10
Access_1 (config-if)# port protected
Access_1 (config)# interface gigabitethernet 0/1
Access_1 (config-if)# switchport mode trunk
Access_1 (config-if)# switchport trunk encapsulation dot1Q
```

```
Access_1 (config-if)# end
Access_1# copy running-config startup-config
```

Further Reading

Refer to the following recommended sources for further information about the topics covered in this chapter.

Clark, Kennedy and Kevin Hamilton. *Cisco LAN Switching*. Cisco Press, ISBN 157870-094-9.

Froom, Richard, Balaji Sivasubramanian, and Erum Frahim. *Building Cisco Multilayer Switched Networks (BCMSN) (Authorized Self-Study Guide)*, Fourth Edition. Cisco Press, ISBN 158705-273-3.

Hucaby, Dave. *CCNP BCMSN Official Exam Certification Guide*, Fourth Edition. Cisco Press, ISBN 1-58720-171-2.

Securing Networks with Private VLANs and VLAN Access Control Lists: http://www.tinyurl.com/hao6.

Configuring Isolated Private VLANs on Catalyst Switches: http://www.tinyurl.com/cq8zt9.

Chapter 7

Spanning Tree Protocol (STP)

See the following sections for configuration information about these topics:

- **7-1: STP Operation:** Explains the spanning-tree algorithm in relation to the processes and decisions made by a switch

- **7-2: STP Configuration:** Presents the basic steps needed to configure the *Spanning Tree Protocol (STP)*

- **7-3: STP Convergence Tuning:** Covers the more advanced steps needed to configure and tune STP convergence

- **7-4: Navigating the Spanning-Tree Topology:** Offers suggestions on how to find the root of a spanning-tree topology and how to map out an active topology by hand

7-1: STP Operation

- STP detects and prevents Layer 2 bridging loops from forming. Parallel paths can exist, but only one is allowed to forward frames.

- TP is based on the IEEE 802.1D bridge protocol standard.

- 802.1w is an enhancement to Spanning Tree that provides more rapid convergence during topology changes than with traditional Spanning Tree.

- Cisco Switches run one instance of STP per VLAN with PVST+ (per VLAN spanning tree) or Rapid-PVST+ (Rapid Per VLAN Spanning Tree). Trunking is required between switches to run RPVST.

- For industry standard IEEE 802.1Q trunks, only a single instance of STP is required for *all* VLANs. The *Common Spanning Tree (CST)* is communicated over VLAN 1.

- *PVST+* is a Cisco proprietary extension that allows switches to interoperate between

CST and PVST. PVST *bridge protocol data units (BPDU)* are tunneled over an 802.1Q trunk. Catalyst switches run PVST+ by default.

- *Rapid-PVST+* is a hybrid STP mode that uses IEEE 802.1w (Rapid Spanning Tree) combined with a per VLAN basis. This mode is compatible with IEEE 802.1w but uses a Cisco extension to allow per-vlan spanning tree.

- *Multiple Spanning Tree (MST)*, based on the IEEE 802.1s standard, extends the 802.1w *Rapid Spanning Tree Protocol (RSTP)* to have multiple STP instances.

    - MST is backward compatible with 802.1D, 802.1w, and PVST+ STP modes.

    - Switches configured with common VLAN and STP instance assignments form a single MST region.

    - MST can generate PVST+ BPDUs for interoperability.

    - MST supports up to 16 instances of STP.

- Switches send BPDUs out all ports every Hello Time interval (default 2 seconds).

- BPDUs are not forwarded by a switch; they are used only for further calculation and BPDU generation.

- Switches send two types of BPDUs:

    - Configuration BPDU

    - Topology change notification (TCN) BPDU

Note Standard BPDUs are sent to the well-known STP multicast address 01-80-c2-00-00-00, using each switch port's unique MAC address as a source address.

STP Process

1. **Root bridge election:** The switch with the lowest bridge ID becomes the root of the spanning tree. A *bridge ID* (BID) consists of a 2-byte priority and a 6-byte MAC address. The priority can range from 0 to 65535 and defaults to 32768.

2. **Root port election:** Each nonroot switch elects a root port, or the port "closest" to the root bridge, by determining the port with the lowest root path cost. This cost is carried along in the BPDU. Each nonroot switch along the path adds its local port cost of the port that *receives* the BPDU. The root path cost becomes cumulative as new BPDUs are generated.

3. **Designated port election:** One switch port on each network segment is chosen to handle traffic for that segment. The port that announces the lowest root path cost in the segment becomes the designated port.

4. **Bridging loops are removed:** Switch ports that are neither root ports nor designated ports are placed in the blocking state. This step breaks any bridging loops that would form otherwise.

STP Tiebreakers

When any STP decision has identical conditions or a tie, the final decision is based on this sequence of conditions:

1. The lowest BID
2. The lowest root path cost
3. The lowest sender BID
4. The lowest port ID

Path Costs

By default, switch ports have the path costs defined in Table 7-1.

Table 7-1 *Switch Port Path Costs*

Port Speed	Default Port Cost "Short Mode"	Default Port Cost "Long Mode"
4 mbps	250	—
10 mbps	100	2,000,000
16 mbps	62	—
45 mbps	39	—
100 mbps	19	200,000
155 mbps	14	—
622 mbps	6	—
1 gbps	4	20,000
10 gbps	2	2000
100 gbps	—	200
1000 gbps (1 tbps)	—	20
10 tbps	—	2

By default, Catalyst switches in RPVST+ mode use the "short mode" or 16-bit path or port cost values. When the port speeds in a network are less than 1 gbps, the short mode scale is sufficient. If you have any ports that are 10 gbps or greater, however, set *all* switches in the network to use the "long mode" or 32-bit path cost scale. This ensures that root path cost calculations are consistent on all switches.

Note   The IEEE uses a nonlinear scale to relate the port bandwidth of a single link to its port cost value. STP treats bundled links, such as Fast EtherChannel and Gigabit EtherChannel, as a single link with an aggregate bandwidth of the individual links. As a result, remember that the port or path cost used for a bundled EtherChannel will be based on the bundled bandwidth. For example, a two-link Fast EtherChannel has 200 mbps bandwidth and a path cost of 12. A four-link Gigabit EtherChannel has 4 gbps bandwidth and a path cost of 2. Use Table 7-1 to see how these EtherChannel aggregate bandwidth and port costs relate to the values of single or individual links.

STP Port States

Each switch port progresses through a sequence of states:

1.   **Disabled:** Ports that are administratively shut down or shut down due to a fault condition. (MST calls this state *discarding*.)

2.   **Blocking:** The state used after a port initializes. The port cannot receive or transmit data, cannot add MAC addresses to its address table, and can receive only BPDUs. If a bridging loop is detected, or if the port loses its root or designated port status, it will be returned to the blocking state. (MST calls this state discarding.)

3.   **Listening:** If a port can become a root or designated port, it is moved into the listening state. The port cannot receive or transmit data and cannot add MAC addresses to its address table. BPDUs can be received and sent. (MST calls this state discarding.)

4.   **Learning:** After the Forward Delay timer expires (default 15 seconds), the port enters the learning state. The port cannot transmit data but can send and receive BPDUs. MAC addresses can now be learned and added into the address table.

5.   **Forwarding:** After another Forward Delay timer expires (default 15 seconds), the port enters the forwarding state. The port can now send and receive data, learn MAC addresses, and send and receive BPDUs.

STP Topology Changes

■   If a switch port is moved into the forwarding state (except when PortFast is enabled), a topology change is signaled.

■   If a switch port is moved from the forwarding or learning state into the blocking state, a topology change is signaled.

■   To signal a topology change, a switch sends TCN BPDUs on its root port every Hello Time interval. This occurs until the TCN is acknowledged by the upstream designated bridge neighbor. Neighbors continue to relay the TCN BPDU on their root ports until it is received by the root bridge.

■   The root bridge informs the entire spanning tree of the topology change by sending a configuration BPDU with the *topology change* (TC) bit set. This causes all downstream switches to reduce their Address Table Aging timers from the default value (300 seconds) down to the Forward Delay (default 15 seconds). This flushes inactive MAC addresses out of the table faster than normal.

Improving STP Stability

- STP Root Guard helps enforce the root bridge placement and identity in a switched network. When enabled on a port, Root Guard disables the port if a better BPDU is received. This prevents other unplanned switches from becoming the root.

- STP Root Guard should be enabled on all ports where the root bridge should not appear. This preserves the current choice of the primary and secondary root bridges.

- *Unidirectional Link Detection (UDLD)* provides a means to detect a link that is transmitting in only one direction, enabling you to prevent bridging loops and traffic black holes that are not normally detected or prevented by STP.

- UDLD operates at Layer 2 by sending packets containing the device and port ID to connected neighbors on switch ports. As well, any UDLD packets received from a neighbor are reflected back so that the neighbor can see it has been recognized. UDLD messages are sent at the *message interval* times, usually defaulting to 15 seconds.

- UDLD operates in two modes:

  - **Normal mode:** Unidirectional links are detected and reported as an error, but no other action is taken.

  - **Aggressive mode:** Unidirectional links are detected, reported as an error, and disabled after eight attempts (once a second for eight seconds) to reestablish the link. Disabled ports must be manually reenabled.

- STP Loop Guard detects the absence of BPDUs on the root and alternate root ports. Nondesignated ports are temporarily disabled, preventing them from becoming designated ports and moving into the forwarding state.

- STP Loop Guard should be enabled on the root and alternate root ports (both nondesignated) for all possible active STP topologies.

STP Operation Example

As an example of STP operation, consider a network of three Catalyst switches connected in a triangle fashion as illustrated in Figure 7-1. RP labels the root ports, DP labels designated ports, F labels ports in the forwarding state, and X labels ports that are in the blocking state.

The spanning-tree algorithm proceeds as follows:

1. **The root bridge is elected:** All three switches have equal bridge priorities (32768, the default). However, Catalyst A has the lowest MAC address (00-00-00-00-00-0a), so it becomes the root bridge.

2. **The root ports are chosen:** The lowest root path costs are computed on each switch. These are Catalyst B port 1/1, which has a root path cost of 0+19, and Catalyst C port 1/1, which also has a root path cost of 0+19.

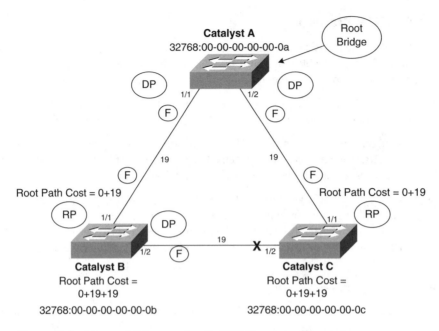

Figure 7-1 *Network Diagram for the STP Operation Example*

3. **The designated ports are chosen:** By definition, all ports on the root bridge become designated ports for their segments. Therefore, ports 1/1 and 1/2 on Catalyst A are designated. Catalyst B port 1/2 and Catalyst C port 1/2 share a segment, requiring that one of them become designated. The root path cost for each of these ports is 0+19+19 or 38, resulting in a tie. The lowest-sending BID breaks the tie, so Catalyst B (having the lowest MAC address of the two) port 1/2 becomes the designated port.

4. **All ports that are neither root nor designated ports are put in the blocking state:** The only remaining port that is neither root nor designated is Catalyst C port 1/2. This port is moved to the blocking state (as shown by the X in the figure).

7-2: STP Configuration

1. *(Optional)* Enable or disable STP:

    ```
    (global) [no] spanning-tree [vlan vlan]
    ```

    STP is enabled by default on VLAN 1 and any newly created VLANs. Without a specified VLAN, STP is enabled or disabled on all VLANs. Be aware that if STP is disabled, bridging loops are not detected and prevented. You should always enable STP.

2. *(Optional)* Set the STP mode for the switch:

    ```
    spanning-tree mode {pvst | mst | rapid-pvst}
    ```

By default, all Catalyst switches run PVST+ STP for one instance of STP on each VLAN. To configure other STP modes, **rapid-pvst** (802.1w per vlan with IEEE compatibility) or **mst** must be explicitly enabled.

3. *(MST only)* Activate an MST instance:

   a. Enter MST Configuration mode:

   spanning-tree mst configuration

   b. Identify the MST region:

   name *name*

   revision *revision-number*

   The MST region is identified by *name* (a text string up to 32 characters). If no name is given, no region name is used. You can use a region revision number to indicate the number of times the region configuration has changed. The *revision-number* (0 to 65535, default 1) must be explicitly set and is not automatically incremented with region changes.

   c. Map one or more VLANs to the instance:

   instance *instance-id* **vlan** *vlan-range*

   A *vlan* number (1 to 1005, 1025 to 4094) is mapped to the MST *instance* (0 to 15). This mapping is held in the MST region buffer until the changes are committed.

   d. Exit MST configuration mode:

   end

   When you end this mode, you will be returned to privileged EXEC mode. The changes to the configuration will be immediate, but you must save the configuration to NVRAM to make them permanent.

4. *(Optional)* Placement of the root bridge switch.

Note The root bridge (and secondary root bridges) should be placed near the "center" of the network so that an optimum spanning-tree topology is computed. Typically, the root is located in the core or distribution layers of the network. If you choose not to manually configure the root placement, the switch with the lowest BID wins the root election. This almost always produces a spanning-tree topology that is inefficient.

(global) **spanning-tree vlan** *vlan* **root** {**primary** | **secondary**} [**diameter** *net-diameter* [**hello-time** *hello-time*]]

The switch becomes the primary root bridge for the VLANs (a list of VLAN numbers 1 to 1005 and 1025 to 4094) or STP instances (1 to 16) specified (VLAN 1 if unspecified). The bridge priority value is modified as follows: If it is more than 8192, it is set to 8192; if it is already less than 8192, it is set to a value less than the current root bridge's priority. You can use the **secondary** keyword to place a secondary or backup root bridge, in case of a primary root failure. Here, the bridge priority is set to 16384. (For MST, the root priority is set to 24576, and the secondary priority to 28672.)

The **diameter** keyword specifies the diameter or the maximum number of bridges or switches between two endpoints across the network (1 to 7, default 7). The BPDU Hello Time interval can also be set (default 2 seconds). Setting the network diameter causes other STP timer values to be automatically calculated and changed. You can adjust the timers explicitly with other commands, but adjusting the diameter hides the complexity of the timer calculations.

5. *(Optional)* Adjust the bridge priority:

    `(global)` **spanning-tree vlan** *vlan* **priority** *priority*

    You can also directly modify the bridge priority to achieve other values than the automatic root or secondary priorities. The priority can be set on a per-VLAN or instance basis. Instances can be given as an *instance-list*, as one or more instance numbers separated by commas, or a hyphenated range of numbers.

    To force a switch to become the root, the priority should be chosen so that the root bridge has a *lower* priority than all other switches on that VLAN or STP instance. The bridge priority ranges from 0 to 65535 (default 32768) for PVST+, or one of the values 0 (highest), 4096, 8192, 12288, 16384, 20480, 24576, 28672, 32768, 36864, 40960, 45056, 49152, 53248, 57344, and 61440 (lowest) when enabling extended VLAN support.

6. *(Optional)* Prevent a port from becoming a STP root port:

    `(interface)` **spanning-tree rootguard**

    STP Root Guard will be enabled on the port or interface. If another bridge connected to that port reports a lower bridge ID, becoming the root, the port will be moved to *root-inconsistent* (listening) STP state. When the BPDUs of a root bridge are no longer detected on the port, it will be moved back into normal operation.

7. *(Optional)* Tune the root path cost.

    a. *(Optional)* Set the port cost scale

        `(global)` **spanning-tree pathcost defaultcost-method {long | short}**

        By default, PVST+ switches use the **short** (16-bit) port cost values. If you have any ports that are 10 gbps or greater, you should set the port cost scale to **long** (32-bit) values on *every* switch in your network. MISTP, MISTP-PVST+, and MST modes use long mode by default.

    b. Set the port cost for all VLANs or instances:

        `(interface)` **spanning-tree cost** *cost*

The port cost can be set to *cost* (1 to 65535 short or MISTP mode, 1 to 2000000 long mode) for all VLANs or STP instances. The **mst** keyword signifies a port used in MST.

c. Set the port cost per VLAN or per instance:

```
(interface) spanning-tree vlan vlan-id cost cost
```

The port cost can be set to *cost* (1 to 65535 short mode, 1 to 2000000 long mode) for the VLAN *vlan-id* or the list of VLANs, *vlan-list,* or STP instance (0 to 15).

8. *(Optional)* Tune the port priority.

a. Set the port priority for all VLANs or instances:

```
(interface) spanning-tree port-priority port-priority
```

The port priority can be set to *priority* (2 to 255).

b. Set the port priority per VLAN or per instance:

```
(interface) spanning-tree vlan vlan-list port-priority priority
```

The port priority can be set to *priority* (0 to 255) for the VLAN *vlan-id* or the list of VLANs, *vlan-list,* or STP instance (0 to 15).

9. *(Optional)* Detect unidirectional connections with UDLD.

a. Enable UDLD on the switch:

```
(global) udld {enable | aggressive}
```

By default, UDLD is disabled. It must be enabled before it can be used on specific ports. The Supervisor IOS enables the keyword **aggressive** to be used to globally enable UDLD aggressive mode on all Ethernet fiber-optic interfaces.

b. *(Optional)* Adjust the UDLD message interval timer:

```
(global) udld message time interval
```

The UDLD message interval can be set to *interval* (7 to 90 seconds; COS default is 15 seconds, Supervisor IOS is 60 seconds).

c. Enable UDLD on specific ports:

```
(interface) udld {enable | disable}
```

After UDLD has been globally enabled on a switch, UDLD is also enabled by default on all Ethernet fiber-optic ports. UDLD is disabled by default on all Ethernet twisted-pair media ports.

d. *(Optional)* Enable UDLD aggressive mode on specific ports:

```
(interface) udld aggressive
```

After aggressive mode has been enabled on a port, the port is disabled when a unidirectional connection is detected. It must be manually reenabled after the problem has been corrected. On the Supervisor IOS, use the EXEC command **udld reset** to reenable all ports that are disabled by UDLD.

10. *(Optional)* Improve STP stability with Loop Guard:

```
(interface) spanning-tree loopguard
```

Loop Guard should be enabled only on the ports that you know are root or alternate root ports. For example, the uplink ports on an access layer switch would always be root or alternate root ports because they are closest to the root bridge. (This assumes that you have placed the root bridge toward the center of your network.)

Displaying Information About STP

Table 7-2 lists the switch commands that you can use to display helpful information about STP.

Table 7-2   *Switch Commands to Display STP Information*

Display Function	Command
STP for a specific VLAN	(exec) **show spanning-tree vlan** *vlan*
STP state for all VLANs on a trunk	(exec) **show spanning-tree interface** *mod/num*

STP Configuration Examples

As a good practice, you should always configure one switch in your network as a primary root bridge for a VLAN and another switch as a secondary root. Suppose you build a network and forget to do this. What might happen if the switches are left to sort out a spanning-tree topology on their own, based on the default STP parameters?

Poor STP Root Placement

The top half of Figure 7-2 shows an example network of three Catalyst switches connected in a triangle fashion. Catalysts C1 and C2 form the core layer of the network, whereas Catalyst A connects to the end users in the access layer. (C1 and C2 might also be considered distribution layer switches if the overall campus network doesn't have a distinct core layer. In any event, think of them as the highest layer or the backbone of the network.)

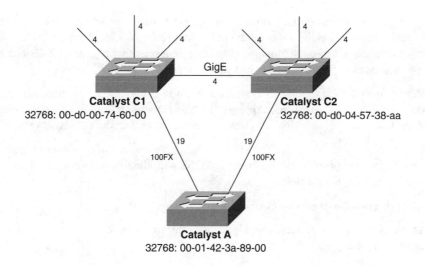

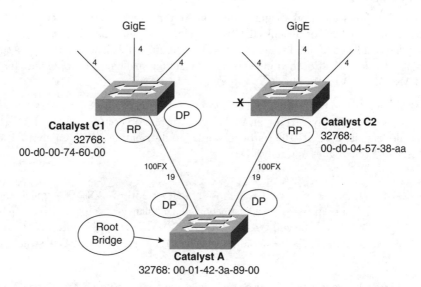

Figure 7-2 *Network Diagram Demonstrating Poor STP Root Placement*

As it might be expected, the links between the core and other switches are Gigabit Ethernet. The uplinks from Catalyst A into the core, however, are Fast Ethernet.

When the root bridge is elected, Catalyst A wins based on its lower MAC address. (All switches have their default bridge priorities of 32768.) Both of the uplink ports on switch A become designated ports because it is now the root. The downlinks from C1 and C2 to switch A become root ports. Switch C1 makes its Gigabit Ethernet link to C2 a designated port because it has the lower sending BID. And sadly, switch C2 must move its Gigabit Ethernet link to C1 into the blocking state because it is neither a root nor a designated port. You can see this in the lower half of the figure.

Clearly, an inefficient topology has surfaced because all the traffic passing across the network core must now pass across lower-speed links through switch A. Switch A, being an access layer switch, is also likely to have less horsepower than the core layer switches.

To remedy this situation, place the STP root bridge somewhere in the core or highest hierarchical layer of the network. You can do this with the following command for VLAN 10 on switch C1, for example:

```
(global) spanning-tree vlan 10 root primary
```

Alternatively, you can explicitly set the bridge priorities with these commands (available on all Catalyst models):

```
(global) spanning-tree vlan 10 priority 8192
```

STP Load Balancing

Figure 7-3 shows a network diagram consisting of three switches that are connected in a triangle fashion. Each of the links between switches is a trunk, carrying two VLANs. The switches will be configured so that the two VLANs are load balanced across the available trunks. The lower half of the figure shows the resulting spanning-tree topologies for VLAN 100 and VLAN 101.

Distribution switch Catalyst D1 will be chosen as the root bridge. Some users connected to access switch Catalyst A1 are on VLAN 100, whereas other users are on VLAN 101. The idea is to have VLAN 100 traffic forwarded to distribution switch Catalyst D1, while VLAN 101 traffic goes to Catalyst D2.

Note   Switch D1 has been selected as the root bridge for both VLANs for simplicity and to demonstrate the use of port cost adjustments in load balancing. You can also configure D1 as the root for VLAN 100 and D2 as the root for VLAN 101. The resulting STP topologies would be the same, but there would be no need to adjust the port costs in switch A1.

An additional benefit is that the two trunk links will failover to each other. Should one trunk link fail, the other moves from blocking into forwarding mode, forwarding both VLANs 100 and 101 across the same trunk. If the STP UplinkFast feature is also used on both switches, the link failover is almost instantaneous.

Switch Catalyst D1 will be configured as the primary root bridge for both VLANs, whereas Catalyst D2 will become the secondary root bridge. If D1 fails, D2 becomes the new root.

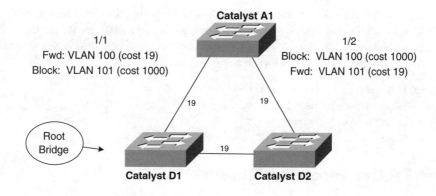

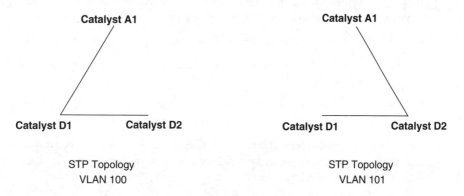

Figure 7-3 *Network Diagram for the STP Load-Balancing Example*

Catalyst D1 can be configured with these commands:

```
(global) spanning-tree vlan 100 root primary
(global) spanning-tree vlan 101 root primary
```

Alternatively, you can explicitly set the bridge priorities with these commands (available on all Catalyst models):

```
(global) spanning-tree vlan 100 priority 8192
(global) spanning-tree vlan 101 priority 8192
```

Catalyst D2 can be configured with these commands to become the secondary root:

```
(global) spanning-tree vlan 100 root secondary
(global) spanning-tree vlan 101 root secondary
```

Alternatively, you can explicitly set D2's bridge priorities:

```
(global) spanning-tree vlan 100 priority 8200
(global) spanning-tree vlan 101 priority 8200
```

Finally, Catalyst A1 will have the port cost adjusted for ports 1/1 and 1/2 for the two VLANs. Recall that the default port cost is shown as 19 in the diagram. We set the new costs to 1000 on the undesirable paths so that those ports will be blocking. For example, VLAN 101 on port 1/1 will be blocked because it has a higher port cost of 1000:

```
(global) interface fastethernet 1/1
(interface) spanning-tree vlan 101 cost 1000
(global) interface fastethernet 1/2
(interface) spanning-tree vlan 100 cost 1000
```

7-3: STP Convergence Tuning

- STP bases its operation on several timers. Usually, the default timer values are used for proper STP behavior. The defaults are based on a network diameter of seven switches but can be adjusted for faster convergence times.

  - The Hello Timer triggers periodic hello messages to neighboring switches.

  - The Forward Delay timer specifies the time a port stays in each of the listening and learning states.

  - The MaxAge timer specifies the lifetime of a stored BPDU received on a designated port. After the timer expires, other ports can become designated ports.

- BPDUs are expected at regular intervals. If they are delayed beyond the lapse of an STP timer, topology changes can be triggered in error. This condition can be detected with the *BPDU skewing* feature.

- *STP PortFast* allows ports that connect to hosts or nonbridging network devices to enter the forwarding mode immediately when the link is established. This bypasses the normal STP port states for faster startup but allows the potential for bridging loops to form.

- *STP UplinkFast* is used only on leaf-node switches (the ends of the ST branches), usually located in the access layer. The switch keeps track of all potential paths to the root, which are in the blocking state.

  - When the root port fails, an alternate port is brought into the forwarding state without the normal STP port state progression and delays.

  - When UplinkFast is enabled, the bridge priority is raised to 49152, making it unlikely to become the root bridge. All switch ports have their port costs increased by 3000 so that they won't be chosen as root ports.

  - When an alternate root port comes up, the switch updates upstream switches with the new location of downstream devices. Dummy multicasts are sent to destination 01-00-0C-CD-CD-CD that contains the MAC addresses of stations in the bridging table.

- *STP BackboneFast* causes switches in the network core to actively look for alternate paths to the root bridge in case of an indirect failure.

- When used, this feature should be enabled on all switches in the network. Switches use a request-and-reply mechanism to determine root path stability, so all switches must be able to participate.

- BackboneFast can only reduce the convergence delay from the default 50 seconds (20 seconds for the MaxAge timer to expire, and 15 seconds in both listening and learning states) to 30 seconds.

Configuring STP Convergence Tuning

1. *(Optional)* Tune the STP timers to adjust convergence.

> **Note** STP timer values should be modified only on the root bridge. The root propagates the values to all other switches through its configuration BPDUs.
>
> If you think that the STP timers must be adjusted, consider doing this by setting the network diameter on the STP root bridge. After the diameter has been set, all the other STP timer values are computed and adjusted automatically. Refer to Step 4 in section "7-2: STP Configuration" for more details.

a. *(Optional)* Adjust the STP Hello timer:

```
(global) spanning-tree [vlan vlan] hello-time interval
```

The Hello timer can be set to *interval* (1 to 10 seconds, default 2 seconds). It can be set for specific VLANs or STP instances, or globally for VLAN 1 (COS) or all VLANs (IOS) if the VLAN number is not given.

b. (Optional) Adjust the STP Forward Delay timer:

```
(global)spanning-tree vlan vlan forward-time delay
```

The Forward Delay interval can be set to *delay* (4 to 30 seconds, default 15 seconds) for specific VLANs, specific instances, or globally for VLAN 1 (COS) or all VLANs (IOS) if the VLAN number is not given.

c. (Optional) Adjust the STP MaxAge timer:

```
(global) spanning-tree [vlan vlan] max-age agingtime
```

The MaxAge timer can be set to *agingtime* (6 to 40 seconds, default 20 seconds) for specific VLANs, instances, or globally for VLAN 1 (COS) or all VLANs (IOS) if the VLAN number is not given.

2. *(Optional)* Use PortFast STP convergence for access layer nodes.

a. Use PortFast on specific ports:

```
(interface) spanning-tree portfast [trunk]
```

You can **enable** or **disable** PortFast on nontrunking ports. As well, you can use the keyword **trunk** to force PortFast to be used on a trunking link.

> **Note** Enabling PortFast on a port also prevents TCN BPDUs from being generated due to a state change on the port. Although STP is still operating on the port to prevent bridging loops, topology changes are not triggered when the attached host goes up or down.
>
> You should use the PortFast feature only on switch ports where single hosts connect. In other words, don't enable PortFast on switch ports that connect to other switches or hubs, whether the ports or trunking.

     b. *(Optional)* Enable PortFast BPDU Guard to improve STP stability:

        `(global)` **`spanning-tree portfast bpduguard`**

        On a nontrunked port with PortFast enabled, BPDU Guard moves the port into the *Errdisable* state if a BPDU is detected. You can use **enable** or **disable** to control the BPDU filtering state on the port. Use the **default** keyword to return the port to the global default set by the optional command **set spantree global-default bpdu-guard** {enable | disable}.

        On the Supervisor IOS, BPDU Guard is enabled globally on all ports that have PortFast enabled.

     c. *(Optional)* Enable PortFast BPDU Filtering to stop BPDU processing on a port:

        `(interface)` **`spanning-tree bpdu-filter`**

        BPDU Filtering causes the switch to stop sending BPDUs on the specified port. As well, incoming BPDUs on that port will not be processed. You can use **enable** or **disable** to control the BPDU Filtering state on the port.

3. *(Optional)* Use UplinkFast STP convergence for access layer uplinks:

    `(global)` **`spanning-tree uplinkfast`** [**`max-update-rate`** *packets-per-second*]

    The switch can generate dummy multicasts at a rate up to *station-update-rate* per 100 milliseconds (Catalyst OS, default 15 per 100 ms) or *packets-per-second* (Supervisor IOS, default 150 packets per second). The **all-protocols** keyword generates multicasts for each protocol filtering group.

4. *(Optional)* Use BackboneFast STP convergence for redundant backbone links:

    `(global)` **`spanning-tree backbonefast`**

    When used, you should enable on all switches in the network. BackboneFast is enabled or disabled for all VLANs on the switch.

7-4: Navigating the Spanning-Tree Topology

Although navigating a spanning-tree topology is a rather tedious process, it is usually the only way to verify that the STP is operating as it was intended. Many times, you will have a diagram of the switches in the network showing the physical or logical interconnections. The spanning-tree topology, however, usually goes undocumented until there is a problem.

You might have to troubleshoot a network that is foreign to you, or one that is not completely documented. In this case, you need to get an idea of the current active STP topology, especially the root bridge location.

1. Find the root bridge.

   a. Choose a switch to use as a starting point.

      Ideally, you want to start out on the root bridge at the "top" of the STP hierarchy. If you don't know which switch is the root for a given VLAN, any switch will do as a starting point.

   b. Display the root ID, local BID, and root port:

      ```
      (exec) show spanning-tree vlan vlan
      ```

      An example of the Supervisor IOS command follows:

      ```
      switch# show spanning-tree vlan 534


      Spanning tree 534 is executing the IEEE compatible Spanning Tree protocol
        Bridge Identifier has priority 49152, address 0005.32f5.45ef
      Configured hello time 2, max age 20, forward delay 15
        Current root has priority 8000, address 00d0.0457.3a15
        Root port is 67, cost of root path is 3006
      Topology change flag not set, detected flag not set, changes 132
        Times:  hold 1, topology change 35, notification 2
                hello 2, max age 20, forward delay 15
        Timers: hello 0, topology change 0, notification 0
        Fast uplink switchover is enabled
        Stack port is GigabitEthernet0/2


      Interface Fa0/1 (port 13) in Spanning tree 534 is FORWARDING
        Port path cost 3019, Port priority 128
        Designated root has priority 8000, address 00d0.0457.3a15
        Designated bridge has priority 49152, address 0005.32f5.45ef
        Designated port is 14, path cost 3006
        Timers: message age 0, forward delay 0, hold 0
        BPDU: sent 2967446, received 0
      ```

```
      The port is in the portfast mode
...(output removed)...
Interface Gi0/1 (port 67) in Spanning tree 534 is FORWARDING
      Port path cost 3004, Port priority 128
      Designated root has priority 8000, address 00d0.0457.3a15
      Designated bridge has priority 32768, address 00d0.ff8a.2a15
      Designated port is 7, path cost 2
      Timers: message age 3, forward delay 0, hold 0
      BPDU: sent 3, received 2967537


Interface Gi0/2 (port 75) in Spanning tree 534 is FORWARDING
      Port path cost 4, Port priority 128
      Designated root has priority 8000, address 00d0.0457.3a15
      Designated bridge has priority 49152, address 0005.32f5.45ef
      Designated port is 75, path cost 3006
      Timers: message age 0, forward delay 0, hold 0
      BPDU: sent 2967519, received 1
switch#
```

   c. Follow the root port toward the root bridge.

Remember that a switch has only one root port, and that port leads toward the root bridge. A switch can have many designated ports, and those lead away from the root bridge. Our goal is to find the neighboring switch that connects to the root port.

IOS shows the root port as a logical port number (port 67). The port number is an index into the interfaces according to the STP. You can either page through the output until you find the interface with the port number, or you can use the EXEC command **show spanning-tree brief | begin VLAN***vlan* to see only the port number associated with the specific VLAN number. An example of this follows:

```
switch# show spanning-tree brief | begin VLAN534

VLAN534

   Spanning tree enabled protocol IEEE

   ROOT ID    Priority 8000

                   Address 00d0.0457.3a15

                   Hello Time   2 sec  Max Age 20 sec  Forward Delay 15 sec
```

```
Bridge ID   Priority    49152

            Address     0005.32f5.45ef

            Hello Time  2 sec  Max Age 20 sec  Forward Delay 15 sec


Port                                Designated

Name    Port ID Prio Cost Sts  Cost  Bridge ID      Port ID

___. ___. __ __ __.  __  _____ ___.

Fa0/1   128.13   128  3100 BLK  3006  0005.32f5.45ef 128.13

Fa0/2   128.14   128  3019 FWD  3006  0005.32f5.45ef 128.14

...(output removed)...


Gi0/1   128. 67  128  3004 FWD  2     00d0.ff8a.2a15 129.7

Gi0/2   128.75   128  4    FWD  3006  0005.32f5.45ef 128.75
```

Here, STP port 67 corresponds to the physical interface Gigabit0/1. The output
also shows a bonus piece of information: the MAC address of the designated
bridge on the root port.

d. Identify the designated bridge on the root port:

(exec) **show cdp neighbor** *type mod/num* **detail**

The neighboring switch can be found as a *Cisco Discovery Protocol (CDP)*
neighbor if CDP is in use. Look for the neighbor's IP address in the output. An
example follows:

switch# **show cdp neighbor gigabitEthernet 0/1 detail**

_____

Device ID: SCA03320048(Switch-B)

Entry address(es):

 IP address: 192.168.254.17

Platform: WS-C6509, Capabilities: Trans-Bridge Switch

Interface: GigabitEthernet0/1, Port ID (outgoing port): 5/7

Holdtime : 120 sec

After the IP address has been found, you can open a Telnet session to the neighboring switch.

e.   Repeat Steps 1b, 1c, and 1d until you are at the root.

How will you know when you have reached the root bridge? The local BID will
be identical to the root bridge ID, and the root cost will be 0.

2.   Draw out the active topology from the top down.

Beginning at the root bridge, look for other switches that are participating in the
spanning tree for a specific VLAN.

a.   Identify other neighboring switches:

(exec) **show cdp neighbor detail**

Every neighbor can be identified by name, IP address, and connecting port.
There will usually be more neighbors listed on switches that are toward the core
layer and fewer neighbors on the access layer.

b.   Identify the BID, the root and designated ports, and their costs:

(exec) **show spanning-tree brief | begin VLAN**_vlan_

The BID and the root port will be listed first. The switch ports on VLAN number
vlan will be listed, along with their STP states and port costs. The designated
ports are the ones marked in the _forwarding_ state.

c.   Identify the blocking ports:

(exec) **show spanning-tree vlan** _vlan_ **| include BLOCKING**

d.   Move to a neighboring switch and repeat Steps 2a through 2c.

Further Reading

Refer to the following recommended sources for further information about the topics
covered in this chapter.

802.1D MAC bridges, IEEE, at http://www.ieee802.org/1/pages/802.1D.html.

802.1s Multiple Spanning Trees, IEEE, at http://www.ieee802.org/1/pages/802.1s.html.

Boyles, Tim and David Hucaby. _CCNP Switching Exam Certification Guide._ Cisco
Press, ISBN 1-58720-000-7.

Clark, Kennedy and Kevin Hamilton. _Cisco LAN Switching._ Cisco Press, ISBN 157870-
094-9.

Perlman, Radia. _Interconnections: Bridges, Routers, Switches, and Internetworking
Protocols._ Addison-Wesley, ISBN 0-20163-448-1.

Understanding and Configuring the Cisco Uplink Fast Feature at
http://www.cisco.com/warp/customer/473/51.html.

Understanding Spanning Tree Protocol's Backbone Fast Feature at
http://www.cisco.com/warp/customer/473/18.html.

Chapter 8

Configuring High Availability Features

See the following sections to configure and use these features:

- **8-1: Route Processor Redundancy (RPR/RPR+): Supervisor Redundancy:** Discusses the steps needed to configure configuration redundancy and failover for a Catalyst 6500 with redundant supervisor modules

- **8-2: Non-Stop Forwarding/Supervisor Switchover (NSF/SSO) with Supervisor Redundancy:** Covers the steps to configure and tune non-stop forwarding and supervisor switchover on a Catalyst 6500 with redundant supervisor modules

- **8-3: Router Redundancy with HSRP:** Discusses the configuration steps required for Layer 3 switches to share a common IP address for gateway redundancy

- **8-4: Fast Software Upgrade (FSU) and Enhanced Fast Software Upgrade (eFSU):** Discusses upgrading the software of supervisors when in redundancy mode

8-1: Route Processor Redundancy (RPR/RPR+)

- Catalyst 6500 series switches support fault resistance by allowing a redundant Supervisor engine to take over if the primary Supervisor engine fails.

- RPR supports a switchover time of two or more minutes.

- RPR+ decreases the switchover time by initializing the second processor and synchronizing the configurations.

- When the switch is powered on, RPR runs between the two Supervisor engines. The Supervisor engine that boots first becomes the RPR active Supervisor engine. The Multilayer Switch Feature Card and Policy Feature Card become fully operational. The route processor (RP) and PFC on the redundant Supervisor engine come out of reset but are not operational.

- The following events cause a switchover:

  - A hardware failure on the active Supervisor engine

  - Clock synchronization failure between Supervisor engines

  - A manual switchover

Configuration

1. Enter router redundancy configuration mode.

   (global) **redundancy**

   This places the switch into redundancy configuration mode so that redundancy can be enabled.

2. Select route processor redundancy.

   (redundancy) **mode rpr | rpr-plus**

   This enables route processor redundancy mode. During normal operation, the start-up-config and config-registers configuration are synchronized by default between the two Supervisor engines. In a switchover, the new active Supervisor engine uses the current configuration.

3. Save configuration.

   (exec) **copy running-configuration startup-configuration**

Displaying Information About RPR

To show the status of RPR, enter the following command:

(exec) **show redundancy states**

8-2: Non-Stop Forwarding/Supervisor Switchover (NSF/SSO) with Supervisor Redundancy

Cisco NSF works with SSO to minimize the amount of time a network is unavailable to its users following a switchover while continuing to forward IP packets.

SSO establishes one of the Supervisor engines as active while the other Supervisor engine is designated as standby, and then SSO synchronizes information between them. A switchover from the active to the redundant Supervisor engine occurs when the active Supervisor engine fails, is removed from the switch, or is manually shut down for maintenance. This type of switchover ensures that Layer 2 traffic is not interrupted. In networking devices running SSO, both Supervisor engines must be running the same configuration so that the redundant Supervisor engine is always ready to assume control following a fault on the active Supervisor engine.

SSO switchover also preserves FIB and adjacency entries and can forward Layer 3 traffic after a switchover. Configuration information and data structures are synchronized from the active to the redundant Supervisor engine at startup and whenever changes to the active Supervisor engine configuration occur. Following an initial synchronization between the two Supervisor engines, SSO maintains state information between them, including forwarding information.

During switchover, system control and routing protocol execution is transferred from the active Supervisor engine to the redundant Supervisor engine. The switch requires between 0 and 3 seconds to switchover from the active to the redundant Supervisor engine.

Cisco NSF always runs with SSO and provides redundancy for Layer 3 traffic. NSF works with SSO to minimize the amount of time that a network is unavailable to its users following a switchover. The main purpose of NSF is to continue forwarding IP packets following a Supervisor engine switchover

The following events cause a switchover:

- A hardware failure on the active Supervisor engine

- Clock synchronization failure between Supervisor engines

- A manual switchover

SSO/NSF Configuration

1. Enter redundancy configuration mode:

   `(global) redundancy`

   From Global configuration mode, enter the command **redundancy** to move into redundancy configuration mode.

2. Select SSO redundancy mode.

   `(redundancy) mode sso`

   This enables redundant supervisor modules to run in SSO mode. This mode enables the support of NSF for applicable protocols.

3. Save configuration:

   `(exec) copy running-config startup-config`

   After you configure SSO, you need to save the configuration.

4. *(Optional)* Configuring Multicast MLS NSF with SSO.

   Multicast MLS NSF with SSO is on by default when you select SSO as the redundancy mode:

   a. *(Optional)* Configure MLS wait time:

      `(global) mls ip multicast sso convergence-time time`

Specifies the maximum time to wait for protocol convergence; valid values are from 0 to 3600 seconds.

    b. *(Optional)* Configure Packet Leak interval:

       (global) **mls ip multicast sso leak** *interval*

Specifies the packet leak interval; valid values are from 0 to 3600 seconds. For PIM sparse mode and PIM dense mode, this is the period of time after which packet leaking for existing PIM sparse mode and PIM dense mode multicast forwarding entries should be completed.

    c. *(Optional)* Configure multicast flow value:

       (global) **mls ip multicast sso leak** *percentage*

Specifies the percentage of multicast flows; valid values are from 1 to 100 percent. The value represents the percentage of the total number of existing PIM sparse mode and PIM dense mode multicast flows that should be flagged for packet leaking.

5.   Configuring L3 NSF with SSO.

If you want to have NSF for your routing protocols so that L3 forwarding is not interrupted, you will be required to configure NSF for each routing protocol.

    a. To configure BGP for NSF, perform this task:

       (global) **router bgp as-number** *number*

       (router) **bgp graceful-restart**

This command enables NSF awareness on the BGP router. This must be configured on BGP peer device for this switch regardless of whether it has dual supervisors.

    b. To configure OSPF for NSF, perform this task:

       (global) **router ospf** *process-id*

       (router) **nsf**

This command enables NSF awareness on the BGP router. This must be configured on OSPF peer device for this switch regardless of whether it has dual supervisors.

    c. To configure BGP for NSF, perform this task:

       (global) **router EIGRP** *as-number*

       (router) **nsf**

This command enables NSF awareness on the BGP router. This must be configured on EIGRO peer device for this switch regardless of whether it has dual supervisors.

Displaying Information About SSO and NSF

You can use the switch commands in Table 8-1 to display helpful information about SSO and NSF.

Table 8-1 *Commands to Display SSO and NSF Information*

Display Function	Command
Displays redundancy states	**(exec)** show redundancy states
Verifies Multicast NSF with SSO	**(exec)** show mls ip sip multicast sso

8-3: Router Redundancy with HSRP

- Route processors in the same or another chassis can share redundant gateway addresses on a VLAN by using the *Hot Standby Router Protocol (HSRP)*.

- Route processors sharing a common HSRP IP address must belong to the same HSRP group number.

- The HSRP address appears on the network with a special virtual MAC address—0000-0C-07-AC-*XX*, where *XX* is the HSRP group number (0 to 255). The hosts on the HSRP VLAN use this MAC address as the default gateway.

- Although HSRP is enabled on an interface, each route processor still maintains its own unique IP and MAC addresses on the VLAN interface. These addresses are used by other routers for routing protocol traffic.

- When an HSRP group is enabled, the highest-priority HSRP device at that time becomes the active router, whereas the second-highest-priority stays in the standby state. All other HSRP devices in the group maintain a "listening" state, waiting for the active device to fail. A new active router election occurs only when the active device fails. The previous active router (having the highest priority) might reclaim its active role by preempting the other HSRP routers in the group.

- HSRP devices communicate by sending a hello message over UDP at multicast address 224.0.0.2. These messages are sent every three seconds by default.

- Devices on a VLAN use the HSRP address as their default gateway. If one of the HSRP devices fails, there will always be another one to take its place as the default gateway address.

Configuration

1. Specify the HSRP group number and IP address:

   (interface) **standby** [*group-number*] **ip** [*ip-address* [**secondary**]]

   The VLAN interface participates in HSRP group *group-number* (0 to 255, default 0) as HSRP IP address *ip-address*. Use the **secondary** keyword if this address corresponds to a secondary address on the actual VLAN interface. This enables HSRP addresses to be activated for both primary and secondary interface addresses.

   The group number and the IP address should be the same across all Layer 3 devices participating in HSRP on the VLAN. This also makes the HSRP virtual MAC address identical on all the HSRP devices.

   Tip   It is common practice to use the VLAN number as the HSRP group number for convenient reference. However, the Catalyst 6500 2 with PFC2/MSFC2 combination supports only up to 16 different HSRP groups (each numbered 1 to 255). You can, however, reuse a group number on several VLAN interfaces if no bridging exists between the VLANs.

2. *(Optional)* Set the HSRP priority:

   (interface) **standby** [*group-number*] **priority** *priority* [**preempt** [**delay minimum** *delay*]]

   The interface negotiates with other HSRP devices in the group to become the active device. Assign a *priority* (1 to 255, default 100) value to each HSRP device so that the one with the highest priority (255 is the highest) becomes active. Adjust the priorities of all other devices to achieve expected elections if the active device fails.

   If the active device (highest priority) fails, it waits until the new active device (lower priority) fails before becoming active again. Use the **preempt** keyword to enable the device to immediately take over the active role again. You can add the **delay minimum** keywords to cause preemption to wait until *delay* (0 to 3600 seconds, default 0 or no delay) time after the Layer 3 switch has been restarted. This allows a period of time for the routing protocols to converge.

3. *(Optional)* Use HSRP authentication:

   (interface) **standby** [*group-number*] **authentication** *string*

   By default, any device can participate in HSRP communications. You can use the **authentication** keyword to force HSRP devices to authenticate with one another by using *string* (text string, up to eight characters) as a clear-text key.

4. *(Optional)* Tune the HSRP timers:

   (interface) **standby** [*group-number*] **timers** [**msec**] *hellotime* [**msec**] *holdtime*

   You can adjust the time between HSRP hello messages to *hellotime* (1 to 254 seconds, default 3 seconds, or 50 to 999 milliseconds, by using **msec**.

HSRP devices listen for hellos from the active device until a holdtime period expires. After this, the active device is declared dead, and the next-highest-priority device becomes active. You can adjust this to *holdtime* (up to 255 seconds, default 10 seconds, or up to 3000 milliseconds) by using **msec**. Make sure the holdtime is set consistently across all HSRP devices in the group.

> **Tip**   To be notified of HSRP active device changeovers, you can enable SNMP traps from the HSRP MIB. Use the **snmp-server enable traps hsrp** command. See Section "12-2: Simple Network Management Protocol" in Chapter 12, Switch Management," for more information about SNMP configuration.

HSRP Example

Two Layer 3 switches have interfaces on VLAN 199. These devices can be two MSFC modules in a single Catalyst 6000 chassis or in two separate chassis, or two Catalyst 3550 switches, and so on.

Here, HSRP group 1 is used. In fact, HSRP group 1 can be used on every VLAN interface, provided that no Layer 2 bridging is configured. The HSRP devices share the 192.168.104.1 IP address so that the hosts on VLAN 199 always have a default gateway available. Note that IP address 192.168.104.1 appears as the virtual MAC address 00-00-0C-07-AC-01 (01 signifying HSRP group 1).

The devices are set with an HSRP hello time of 3 seconds and a holdtime of 40 seconds. Device A is configured with priority 210, making it the active device over device B's priority of 200. Device A is configured to preempt all other lower-priority HSRP devices that might become active but only if this is at least 60 seconds after it has been restarted. This allows it to immediately take over its active role if needed. (This is not necessary in a two-router HSRP scenario because the two devices always trade off the active role. Preemption can be useful when more than two HSRP devices participate in a group.)

Finally, the HSRP devices use the string *myhsrpkey* in all HSRP communication as a simple form of authentication. If a host attempts to use HSRP messages without the authentication key, none of the other devices listen to it.

Layer 3 Device A configuration:

```
(global) interface vlan 199
(interface) standby 1 ip 192.168.104.1
(interface) standby 1 priority 210 preempt delay 60
(interface) standby 1 authentication myhsrpkey
(interface) standby 1 timers 3 40
```

Layer 3 Device B configuration:

```
(global) interface vlan 199
(interface) standby 1 ip 192.168.104.1
```

Section 8-3

```
(interface) standby 1 priority 200 preempt
(interface) standby 1 authentication myhsrpkey
(interface) standby 1 timers 3 40
```

Displaying Information About HSRP

You can use the switch commands in Table 8-2 to display helpful information about HSRP on interfaces.

Table 8-2   *Commands to Display HSRP Information*

Display Function	Command
Concise HSRP status	**(exec)** show standby brief
HSRP on a specific VLAN interface	**(exec)** show standby Vlan **vlan-number** **[hsrp-group]** [brief]

8-4: Fast Software Upgrade (FSU) and Enhanced Fast Software Upgrade (eFSU)

The Fast Software Upgrade (FSU) procedure supported by RPR enables you to upgrade the Cisco IOS image on the Supervisor engines without reloading the system. To perform an FSU complete the following steps:

1. Copy the IOS image to the active supervisor:

    ```
    (exec) copy source_device:source_filename {disk0 | disk1 | sup-
    bootflash}:target_filename
    ```

    Copies the new Cisco IOS image to the disk0: device or the disk1: or the bootflash: device on the active Supervisor engine.

    OR

    Copy the IOS image to the redundant supervisor:

    ```
    (exec) copy source_device:source_filename {slave-disk0 | slave-disk1 |
    slavesup-bootflash}:target_filename
    ```

    Copies the new Cisco IOS image to the disk0: device or the disk1: or the bootflash: device on the redundant Supervisor engine.

    After you copy the file to the appropriate location, make sure that it has synchronized to both supervisors before moving to the next step by showing the appropriate device or slave device.

2. Configure the system to boot from the new image:

    ```
    (global) boot system flash device:file_name
    ```

This should be the name of the new file copied in Step 1. Also verify that the configuration register is set to 0x2102. If not, set using the command:

```
(global)configuration-register 0x2101
```

3. Save the configuration.

```
(exec) copy running-configuration startup-configuration
```

This saves the boot parameter set in Step 2.

4. Save the configuration.

```
(exec) hw-module {module num} reset
```

Use the module number of the redundant supervisor. For example, if the supervisor in slot 5 is active and the one in slot 6 is standby, you would use 6 as the module number in this command.

Reloads the redundant Supervisor engine and brings it back online (running the new version of the Cisco IOS Software).

> **Note** Before reloading the redundant Supervisor engine, make sure you wait long enough to ensure that all configuration synchronization changes have completed.

5. Force the switch to switch to the backup supervisor running the new code.

```
(exec) redundancy force-switchover
```

Conducts a manual switchover to the redundant Supervisor engine. The redundant Supervisor engine becomes the new active Supervisor engine running the new Cisco IOS image. The modules are reloaded, and the module software is downloaded from the new active Supervisor engine.

Further Reading

Refer to the following recommended sources for further information about the topics covered in this chapter.

Campus Network for High Availability Design Guide at http://www.tinyurl.com/d3e6dj.

Understanding and Troubleshooting HSRP Problems in Catalyst Switch Networks at http://www.tinyurl.com/2c6xtv.

Using HSRP for Fault-Tolerant IP Routing at http://www.tinyurl.com/68axpm.

Section 8-4

Chapter 9

Multicast

Refer to the following sections to configure and use these features:

- **9-1: Multicast Addressing:** Describes multicast flows and multicast addressing in relation to networking devices

- **9-2: IGMP Snooping:** Explains how to configure a switch to constrain multicast traffic by listening to *Internet Group Management Protocol* (IGMP) messages

9-1: Multicast Addressing

Multicasts are directed flows in the network. Application servers send packets and messages to addresses that must be forwarded by network devices and then picked up by the appropriate end devices. The network devices choose which links to forward based on these addresses. The devices track flows from the servers. The list that follows summarizes the characteristics of multicast:

- IP multicast flows can be designated by these notations:

  - **(S,G):** A unique shortest path tree structure between the source and the multicast destinations, pronounced "S comma G." S is an IP unicast source address, and G is the IP multicast destination address or group.

  - **(*,G):** A common shared tree structure, where a multicast rendezvous point (RP) accepts multicast traffic from the source and then forwards it on to the destinations, pronounced "Star comma G." The star or asterisk (*) represents the RP because it is a wildcard source that accepts input from any real multicast source. The G represents the IP multicast destination address or group.

- IP multicast or Class D addresses begin with 1110 in the most significant address bits—Addresses within the range 224.0.0.0 to 239.255.255.255.

- Hosts anywhere in the network can register to join a multicast group defined by a specific multicast IP address. Registration is handled through the IGMP.

- IP multicast addresses 224.0.0.1 (all hosts on a subnet) and 224.0.0.2 (all routers on a subnet) are well known and don't require registration. You can find other well-known multicast addresses listed in Appendix B, "Well-Known Protocol, Port, and other Numbers."

■   Multicast also uses Ethernet or MAC addresses beginning with 01-00-5e. (The least-significant bit of the high-order byte is always 1.) The multicast IP addresses must be translated into multicast MAC addresses in this fashion, following the structure shown in Figure 9-1:

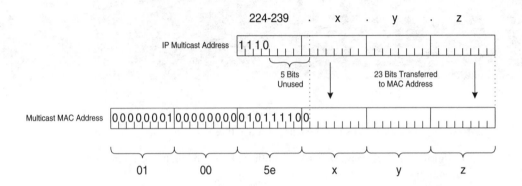

Figure 9-1   *Multicast Address Translation*

■   The 25 most-significant bits in the MAC address are always 01-00-5e.

■   The 23 lowest-significant bits are copied from the 23 lowest-significant bits of the IP address.

■   The address translation is not unique; 5 bits of the IP address are not used, therefore, 32 different IP addresses can all correspond to a single multicast MAC address.

9-2: IGMP Snooping

■   Some Catalyst switches can be configured to intercept IGMP join requests as hosts ask to join IP multicast groups.

■   IGMP join requests can occur as the following happens:

■   Hosts send unsolicited membership reports to join specific multicast groups.

■   Multicast routers acting as IGMP queriers send IGMP membership query messages to the all-hosts multicast group 224.0.0.1 every 60 seconds. Interested hosts respond with membership reports to join specific multicast groups.

■   The switch keeps a record of the IP multicast group, its Layer 2 MAC address, and the switch ports that connect to the requesting host and the multicast router.

- Multicast routers cannot keep a detailed list of all hosts belonging to a multicast group. Rather, a router knows only which multicast groups are active on specific subnets.

- The switch also relays the initial join request for a multicast group to all its known multicast routers.

- If no multicast routers are present in the network, the switch can be configured to act as an IGMP querier.

- When a host wants to leave a multicast group, IGMPv1 detects only the absence of its membership reports. IGMPv2, however, allows the host to send an IGMP leave group message to the "all-routers" multicast group 224.0.0.2 at any time.

- When the switch intercepts an IGMP leave group message on a switch port, it normally sends a query to that multicast group back out the same switch port. If no hosts respond to the query and no multicast routers have been discovered on the switch port, that port is removed from the multicast group. *IGMP Fast-Leave Processing* can be used to allow the switch to immediately remove a port from a multicast group after a Leave Group message is received.

- Spanning tree topology changes that occur in a VLAN also cause the switch to purge any multicast group information learned through IGMP snooping. That information must be relearned.

Configuration

1. *(Optional)* Enable IGMP snooping:

   `(interface)` **`ip igmp snooping`**

   IGMP snooping is enabled by default. Use the **no** form of this command to disable IGMP.

2. (Optional) Enable IGMP on a per VLAN basis:

   `(interface)` **`ip igmp snooping vlan`** *`vlan-id`*

   IGMP snooping is enabled on every VLAN. By disabling IGMP globally with the **no igmp snooping** command, you can enable IGMP on a per VLAN basis with this command.

3. *(Optional)* Allow snooping to learn from another source:

   `(interface)` **`ip igmp snooping mrouter learn {cgmp | pim-dvmrp}`**

   In addition to normal IGMP snooping, the switch can also learn by listening to CGMP messages (**cgmp**) or PIM-DVMRP messages (**pim-dvmrp**).

4. *(Optional)* Use IGMP Fast-Leave Processing:

   `(interface)` **`ip igmp snooping fast-leave`**

   By default, Fast-Leave Processing is disabled. Fast-Leave improves the latency of multicast group removal but should be used only on VLANs where single hosts connect to each switch port.

5. *(Optional)* Statically identify a multicast router port:

```
(interface) ip igmp snooping mrouter {interface {interface interface-number}
 | {Port-channel number}}
```

IGMP snooping automatically detects ports where multicast routers connect. You can also give a static definition of a multicast router port.

6. (Optional) Define a static multicast host entry:

```
(interface) ip igmp snooping static {mac-address} {interface {interface
    interface-number}} | {port-channel number}}
```

The host connected to the specified interface is statically joined to multicast group *mac-address* (dotted-triplet format) on the current VLAN interface. On the COS switch, the static entry can be used until the next reboot (**static**) or even across the next reboot (**permanent**).

7. *(Optional)* Act as an IGMP querier.

   a. Enable the querier:

```
(interface) ip igmp snooping querier
```

     By default, the IGMP querier function is disabled. If no other multicast routers are available and there is no need to route multicast packets on the local network, the switch can provide the IGMP querier function. Use the **enable** keyword and specify the *vlan* number where the querier will be used.

   b. *(Optional)* Adjust the query interval:

```
(global) ip igmp query-interval seconds
```

     The time between general IGMP queries or the query interval on the *vlan* number can be set to *seconds*. (The default is 125 seconds.)

   c. *(Optional)* Adjust the self-election interval:

```
(global) ip igmp query-timeout seconds
```

If more than one querier is present on a VLAN, only one of them is elected to remain the querier. If no other general IGMP queries are overheard on the *vlan* number for *seconds* (default 300 seconds), the switch elects itself as the querier.

Tip   Querier election takes place by using the source IP address in the general query messages. For a specific VLAN, switches use the IP address from their VLAN interface as the IGMP source address. The lowest IP address wins the querier election.

IGMP Snooping Example

IGMP snooping is enabled globally on the COS switch and on specific interfaces on the IOS switch. IGMP Fast-Leave Processing is enabled. A static entry for IP multicast group address 224.100.1.35 (MAC address 01-00-5e-64-01-23) is configured that lists switch ports 2/1 and 2/3 as permanent members. These switch ports are assigned to a common VLAN 199.

```
(global) interface fastethernet 2/1
(interface) ip igmp snooping
(interface) ip igmp snooping fast-leave
(interface) switchport access vlan 199
(global) interface fastethernet 2/3
(interface) ip igmp snooping
(interface) ip igmp snooping fast-leave
(interface) switchport access vlan 199

(global) interface vlan 199
(interface) ip igmp snooping static 0100.5364.0123 interface fastethernet 2/1
(interface) ip igmp snooping static 0100.5364.0123 interface fastethernet 2/3
```

Displaying Information About IGMP Snooping

Table 9-1 lists some switch commands that you can use to display helpful information about IGMP snooping.

Table 9-1   *Commands to Display IGMP Snooping Information*

Display Function	Command
IGMP statistics	(exec) **show ip igmp interface** *interface interface-number*
Multicast routers discovered	(exec) **show ip igmp snooping mrouter interface** vlan *vlan-id*
Number of multicast groups in a VLAN	(exec) **show mac-address-table multicast** *vlan-id* **count**
Multicast group information	(exec) **show mac-address-table multicast** {*mac-group-address* [*vlan-id*]}
IGMP snooping on an interface	(exec) **show ip igmp interface** *vlan-id*

Further Reading

Refer to the following recommended sources for further information about the topics covered in this chapter.

Internet Protocol (IP) Multicast Technology Overview at www.cisco.com/warp/public/cc/pd/iosw/prodlit/ipimt_ov.htm.

Williamson, Beau. *Developing IP Multicast Networks*, Volume 1 by Cisco Press, ISBN 157870-077-9.

Barnes, David and Basir Sakandar. *Cisco LAN Switching Fundamentals*. Cisco Press, ISBN 1-58705-849-9.

Chapter 10

Server Load Balancing (SLB)

See the following sections to configure and use these features:

- **10-1: SLB:** Covers the configuration steps needed to provide load balancing of traffic to one or more server farms

- **10-2: SLB Firewall Load Balancing:** Discusses the configuration steps necessary to load balance traffic to one or more firewall farms

- **10-3: SLB Probes:** Explains the configuration steps needed to define probes that test server and firewall farm functionality

10-1: SLB

- SLB provides a virtual server IP address to which clients can connect, representing a group of real physical servers in a server farm. Figure 10-1 shows the basic SLB concept. A client accesses a logical "virtual" server (IP address v.v.v.v), which exists only within the Catalyst 6500 SLB configuration. A group of physical "real" servers (IP addresses x.x.x.x, y.y.y.y, and z.z.z.z) is configured as a server farm. Traffic flows between clients and the virtual server are load balanced across the set of real servers, transparent to the clients.

- As clients open new connections to the virtual server, SLB decides which real server to use based on a load-balancing algorithm.

- Server load balancing is performed by one of these methods:

    - **Weighted round-robin:** Each real server is assigned a weight that gives it the capability to handle connections, relative to the other servers. For a weight n, a server is assigned n new connections before SLB moves on to the next server.

    - **Weighted least connections:** SLB assigns new connections to the real server with the least number of active connections. Each real server is assigned a weight *m*, where its capacity for active connections is *m* divided by the sum of all server weights. SLB assigns new connections to the real server with the number of active connections farthest below its capacity.

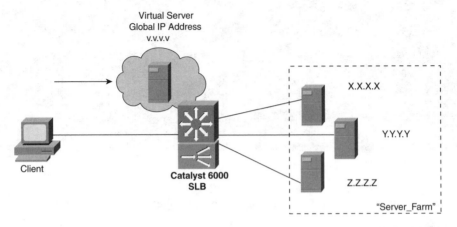

Figure 10-1   *SLB Concept*

- With weighted least connections, SLB controls the access to a new real server, providing a slow start function. New connections are rate limited and allowed to increase gradually to keep the server from becoming overloaded.

- The virtual server can masquerade as the IP address for all TCP and UDP ports of the real server farm. As well, the virtual server can appear as the IP address of a single port or service of a server farm.

- *Sticky* connections enable SLB to assign new connections from a client to the last real server the client used.

- SLB can detect a real server failure by monitoring failed TCP connections. SLB can take the failed server out of service and return it to service when it is working again.

- SLB can use *server Network Address Translation (NAT)* to translate between the real and virtual server addresses if they reside on different Layer 3 subnets.

- SLB can use *client NAT* to translate the source addresses of client requests into addresses on the server side of the SLB device. This is used when several SLB devices are operating so that return traffic can be sent to the correct SLB device.

- SLB provides a control mechanism over incoming TCP SYN floods to the real servers. This can prevent certain types of denial-of-service attacks.

- SLB can coexist with *Hot Standby Router Protocol (HSRP)* to provide a "stateless backup." If one SLB router fails, a redundant router can take over the SLB function. However, existing SLB connections will be lost and will have to be reestablished from the client side.

■ IOS SLB can also operate as a *Dynamic Feedback Protocol (DFP)* load-balancing manager. The DFP manager collects capacity information from DFP agents running on the real servers.

Configuration

1. Define a server farm.

    a. Assign a name to the server farm:

```
(global) ip slb serverfarm serverfarm-name
```

The server farm is identified by *serverfarm-name* (text string up to 15 characters).

    b. *(Optional)* Select a load-balancing algorithm for the server farm:

```
(server-farm) predictor {roundrobin | leastconns}
```

SLB selects a real server using **roundrobin** (weighted round-robin the default) or **leastconns** (weighted least connections).

    c. *(Optional)* Use server NAT:

```
(server-farm) nat server
```

By default, the virtual server and real server addresses must be Layer 2-adjacent. In other words, SLB forwards packets between the virtual server and a real server by substituting the correct MAC addresses. Server NAT can be used instead, allowing the virtual and real servers to have addresses from separate IP subnets. SLB then substitutes the Layer 3 IP addresses to forward packets between the virtual and real servers, allowing the servers to be separated by multiple routing hops.

    d. *(Optional)* Use client NAT.

      ■ Define a NAT pool of addresses:

```
(global) ip slb natpool pool-name start-ip end-ip {netmask netmask |
prefix-length leading-1-bits} [entries init-addr [max-addr]]
```

A pool of IP addresses is given the name *pool-name* (text string up to 15 characters), consisting of addresses bounded by *start-ip* and *end-ip*. The subnet mask associated with the pool can be given as a regular subnet mask, *netmask* (x.x.x.x format), or as the number of leading 1 bits in the mask, *leading-1-bits* (1 to 32).

For IOS SLB, client NAT allocates a number of entries as IP addresses and port numbers, *init-addr* (1 to 1,000,000; default 8000) as an initial set to use. When the number of dynamically allocated entries reaches half of the initial number, more entries are allocated. The maximum number of NAT entries can be defined as *max-addr* (1 to 8,000,000; default is the pool size times the number of ports available, or 65,535 to 11,000, or 54,535). Port numbers for translation begin at 11,000.

■ Enable client NAT with a pool:

```
(server-farm) nat client pool-name
```

The SLB NAT pool is identified by *pool-name* (up to 15 characters).

e. *(Optional)* Assign a unique identifier for DFP:

```
(server-farm) bindid [bind-id]
```

Sometimes, a real server is assigned to multiple server farms. The *bind-id* (0 to 65533; default 0) is an arbitrary identification value given to a server farm. Each instance of a real server references this value, allowing DFP to assign a unique weight to it.

f. *(Optional)* Test the server with a probe:

```
(server-farm) probe name
```

The probe defined as *name* (text string, up to 15 characters) periodically tests for server connectivity and operation. IOS SLB offers ping, HTTP, and *Wireless Session Protocol (WSP)* probes. The CSM also offers TCP, FTP, SMTP, Telnet, and DNS probes. See section "10-3: SLB Probes" for more information about configuring probes.

2. Specify one or more real servers in the server farm.

a. Identify the real server:

```
(server-farm) real ip-address
```

The real server has the IP address given by *ip-address*.

b. *(Optional)* Specify a connection threshold.

■ Set the maximum number of connections:

```
(real-server) maxconns number
```

At any given time, the real server will be limited to *number* (1 to 4,294,967,295 connections; default 4,294,967,295) active connections.

c. *(Optional)* Assign a relative capacity weight:

```
(real-server) weight weighting-value
```

The real server is assigned a *weighting-value* (1 to 255; default 8) that indicates its capacity relative to other real servers in the server farm. For weighted round-robin, *weighting-value* defines the number of consecutive connections the server receives before SLB moves to the next server. For weighted least connections, the next connection is given to the server whose number of active connections is furthest below its capacity. The capacity is computed as the *weighting-value* divided by the sum of all real server weighting values in the server farm.

d. *(Optional; IOS SLB only)* Reassign connections when a server doesn't answer:

```
(real-server) reassign threshold
```

SLB attempts to assign a new connection to a real server by forwarding the client's initial SYN. If the server doesn't answer with a SYN handshake before the client retransmits its SYN, an unanswered SYN is recorded. After *threshold* (1 to 4, default 3) unanswered SYNs occur, SLB reassigns the connection to the next server.

e. *(Optional; IOS SLB only)* Define a failed server threshold:

```
(real-server) faildetect numconns number-conns [numclients number-clients]
```

A server is determined to have failed if *number-conns* (1 to 255, default 8 connections) TCP connections have been reassigned to another server. You can also use the **numclients** keyword to specify the *number-clients* (1 to 8, default 2) of unique clients that have had connection failures.

f. *(Optional; IOS SLB only)* Specify the amount of time before retrying a failed server:

```
(real-server) retry retry-value
```

After a real server has been declared "failed," SLB attempts to assign a new connection to it after *retry-value* (1 to 3600 seconds, default 60 seconds) time has elapsed. You can also use a value of 0 to indicate that new connections should not be attempted.

g. Allow SLB to begin using the real server:

```
(real-server) inservice
```

By default, the real server is not used by SLB unless it is placed in service. To remove a server from service, use **no inservice**.

3. Define a virtual server for the server farm.

a. Name the virtual server:

```
(global) ip slb vserver virtual-server-name
```

The virtual server is given the name *virtual-server-name* (text string up to 15 characters).

b. Assign the virtual server to a server farm:

```
(virtual-server) serverfarm serverfarm-name
```

SLB uses the virtual server as the front end for the server farm named *serverfarm-name* (text string up to 15 characters).

c. Define the virtual server capabilities:

```
(virtual-server) virtual ip-address [network-mask] {tcp | udp} [port | wsp
| wsp-wtp | wsp-wtls | wsp-wtp-wtls] [service service-name]
```

The virtual server appears as IP address *ip-address* (default 0.0.0.0 or "all networks") with *network-mask* (default 255.255.255.255).

With IOS SLB, it provides load balancing for the specified **tcp** or **udp** *port*: **dns** or **53** (Domain Name System), **ftp** or **21** (File Transfer Protocol), **https** or **443** (HTTP over Secure Socket Layer), **www** or **80** (HTTP), **telnet** or **23** (Telnet), **smtp** or **25** (SMTP), **pop3** or **110** (POPv3), **pop2** or **109** (POPv2), **nntp** or **119** (Network News Transport Protocol), or **matip-a** or **350** (Mapping of Airline Traffic over IP, type A). A port number of 0 can be given to indicate that the virtual server accepts connections on all ports.

Other alternatives to a port number are **wsp** (connectionless WSP, port 9200), **wsp-wtp** (connection-oriented WSP, port 9201 with WAP FSM), **wsp-wtls** (connectionless secure WSP, port 9202), and **wsp-wtp-wtls** (connection-oriented secure WSP, port 9203).

The **service** keyword can be given to force SLB to assign all connections associated with a given *service-name* (**ftp** or **wsp-wtp**) to the same real server. On a CSM, only **ftp** connections are allowed to be coupled to the originating control session.

d. *(Optional)* Control access to the virtual server. To allow only specific clients to use the virtual server, enter

```
(virtual-server) client ip-address network-mask
```

Clients having IP addresses within the range given by *ip-address* (default 0.0.0.0, or all addresses) and *network-mask* (default 255.255.255.255, or all networks) are allowed to connect to the virtual server. The *network-mask* in this case resembles the mask of an access list, where a 1 bit ignores and a 0 bit matches. On a CSM, you can use the **exclude** keyword to disallow the IP addresses specified.

e. *(Optional)* Assign connections from the same client to the same real server:

```
(virtual-server) sticky duration [group group-id] [netmask netmask]
```

For a given client, connections are assigned to the last-used real server for *duration* in seconds (0 to 65,535). Virtual servers can be assigned to a *group-id* (0 to 55; default 0), associating them as a single group. A *netmask* (default 255.255.255.255) can be given such that all client source addresses within the mask are assigned to the same real server.

f. *(Optional)* Hold connections open after they are terminated:

```
(virtual-server) delay duration
```

After a TCP connection is terminated, SLB can maintain the connection context for *duration* (1 to 600 seconds, default 10 seconds). This can be useful when packets arrive out of sequence, and the connection is reset before the last data packet arrives.

g. *(Optional)* Hold connections open after no activity:

```
(virtual-server) idle duration
```

When SLB detects an absence of packets for a connection, it keeps the connection open for *duration* in seconds (IOS: 10 to 65,535; default 3600 seconds or 1 hour) before sending an RST.

h. *(Optional)* Prevent a SYN flood to the real servers:

```
(virtual-server) synguard syn-count [interval]
```

SLB monitors the number of SYNs that are received for the virtual server. If more than *syn-count* (0 to 4294967295; default 0 or no SYN monitoring) SYNs are received within the *interval* (50 to 5000 milliseconds; default 100 ms), any subsequent SYNs are dropped.

i. *(Optional)* Control the advertisement of the virtual server:

```
(virtual-server) advertise [active]
```

By default, SLB creates a static route for the virtual server address to the Null0 logical interface. This static route can then be redistributed and advertised by a routing protocol. The **active** keyword causes the route to be advertised only when at least one real server is available. You can disable the advertisement with **no advertise**, preventing the static route from being created.

j. Enable SLB to begin using the virtual server:

```
(virtual-server) inservice [standby group-name]
```

By default, the virtual server is not used by SLB unless it is placed in service. To remove a virtual server from service, use **no inservice**.

Tip   You can use multiple IOS SLB devices to provide redundancy for virtual servers. *IOS SLB stateless backup* enables each SLB device to listen to HSRP messages from Layer 3 interfaces on redundant switches. When one switch (and its IOS SLB) fails, another HSRP interface becomes the primary gateway. When the other IOS SLB also detects the failure, the virtual servers that are associated with the HSRP *group-name* (defined previously) become active. No SLB state information is kept, however, so existing connections are dropped and must be reestablished.

Stateless backup requires that HSRP be configured on all the redundant Layer 3 devices on the *server-side* VLAN. Be sure that the *group-name* matches between the HSRP and virtual server configurations. See section "8-6: Router Redundancy with HSRP" in Chapter 8, "Configuring High Availability Features," for further HSRP configuration information.

k. *(Optional)* Use SLB stateful backup:

```
(virtual-server) replicate casa listening-ip remote-ip port-number
[interval] [password [0|7] password [timeout]]
```

IOS SLB replicates and exchanges its load-sharing decision tables with other stateful backup devices using the *Cisco Appliance Services Architecture*

(CASA) mechanism. When a failure occurs, the backup SLB device already has the current state information and can immediately take over.

This information is sent from the *listening-ip* address (an interface on the local device) to the *remote-ip* address (an interface on the backup device), using TCP port *port-number* (1 to 65,535). Replication messages are sent at *interval* seconds (1 to 300, default 10).

A *password* (text string; use **0** if unencrypted, the default, or **7** if encrypted) can be used for MD5 authentication with the backup device. The optional *timeout* (0 to 65,535 seconds; default 180 seconds) defines a time period when the password can be migrated from an old value to a new one. During this time, both old and new passwords are accepted.

CSM replicates its connection information using the *Content Switching Replication Protocol (CSRP)*. The **sticky** connection database or the regular **connection** database can be replicated. To replicate both, choose each one in a separate **replicate csrp** command.

4. (Optional) Use SLB Dynamic Feedback Protocol (DFP).

   a. *(Optional)* Use the DFP manager to communicate with DFP agents on servers.

      ■ Enable the DFP manager:

      ```
      (global) ip slb dfp [password [0|7] password [timeout]]
      ```

      The router can become a DFP load-balancing manager. DFP can be configured with a *password* (text string; use **0** if unencrypted, the default, or **7** if encrypted) for MD5 authentication with a host agent. The optional *timeout* (0 to 65,535 seconds; default 180 seconds) defines a time period when the password can be migrated from an old value to a new one. During this time, both old and new passwords are accepted.

      ■ Specify a DFP agent:

      (slb-dfp) **agent** *ip-address port-number* [*timeout* [*retry-count* [*retry-interval*]]]

      A DFP agent on a real server is identified by its *ip-address* and the *port-number* number used. The DFP agent (the server) must contact the DFP manager (the IOS SLB device) at *timeout* intervals (0 to 65,535 seconds; default 0 seconds or no timeout period). The DFP manager attempts to reconnect to the agent *retry-count* (0 to 65,535 retries; default 0 retries or an infinite number) times, at intervals of *retry-interval* (1 to 65,535 seconds; default 180 seconds).

   b. *(Optional)* Use a DFP agent to provide DFP reports.

      ■ Define the agent:

      ```
      (global) ip dfp agent subsystem-name
      ```

      The DFP agent sends periodic reports to its manager, a distributed director device. The *subsystem-name* (text string up to 15 characters) enables the manager to associate the server reports with a subsystem (controlled by the SLB device) for global load balancing. To see what *subsystem-name* values are available from the global manager, use the **ip dfp agent ?** command.

- *(Optional)* Set a DFP agent password:

  (dfp) **password** [**0|7**] *password* [*timeout*]

  A *password* (text string; use 0 if unencrypted, the default, or 7 if encrypted) can be used for MD5 authentication with a DFP manager. The optional *timeout* (0 to 65,535 seconds; default 180 seconds) defines a time period when the password can be migrated from an old value to a new one. During this time, both old and new passwords are accepted.

- Set the DFP port number:

  (dfp) **port** *port-number*

  The DFP manager and agents communicate over a common port number, *port-number* (1 to 65535, no default). DFP managers discover their agents dynamically, requiring the port number to be identical between the manager (distributed director) and the agents (IOS SLB).

- *(Optional)* Set the interval for recalculating weights:

  (dfp) **interval** *seconds*

  DFP server weights are recalculated at an interval of *seconds* (5 to 65,535 seconds; default 10 seconds) before they are supplied to the DFP manager.

- Enable the DFP agent:

  (dfp) **inservice**

  By default, the DFP agent is disabled.

SLB Example

See Figure 10-2 for a network diagram. SLB is configured to provide load balancing for two server farms: FARM1 and FARM2.

FARM1 is a server farm of three real web servers having IP addresses 192.168.250.10, 192.168.250.11, and 192.168.250.12. The real servers are considered in a "failed" state if four consecutive TCP connections cannot be established with the server. SLB waits 30 seconds before attempting another connection to a failed server. (The number of failed TCP connections and the retry interval are supported only in the IOS command set.) An HTTP probe is configured to try a connection to each real server in the server farm every 120 seconds.

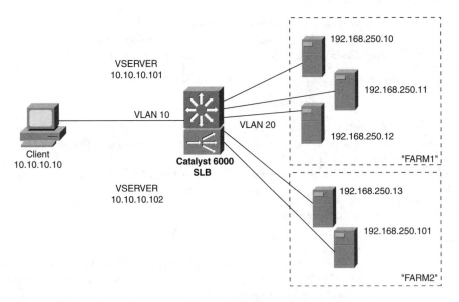

Figure 10-2 *Network Diagram for the SLB Example*

The virtual server VSERVER1 at 10.10.10.101 uses the weighted least connections algorithm for load balancing between the real servers. New connections are made sticky (passed to the real server last used by the same client) for 60 seconds.

The CSM version of this example also includes the client and server-side VLAN numbers (10 and 20) and IP addresses (10.10.10.2 and 192.168.250.1).

One server is given a weight of 32, one server has a weight of 16, and one server has a weight of 8. New connections are assigned to the server with the least number of active connections, as measured by the server capacities. For example, server 192.168.254.10 has a weight of 32 and a capacity of 32 /(32 + 16 + 8) or 32 / 56. Server 192.168.254.11 has a weight of 16 and a capacity of 16 /(32 + 16 + 8) or 16 / 56. Server 192.168.254.12 has a weight of 8 and a capacity of 8 /(32 + 16 + 8) or 8 / 56. At any given time, the server with the number of active connections furthest below its capacity is given a new connection.

The configuration that follows shows the commands that are necessary for server farm FARM1 and virtual server VSERVER1. The same configuration is shown for an IOS-based switch and a CSM module:

```
(global) ip slb serverfarm FARM1
(server-farm) predictor leastconns
(server-farm) nat server
(server-farm) probe HTTP1
(server-farm) real 192.168.250.10
(real-server) weight 32
```

```
(real-server) faildetect numconns 4
(real-server) retry 30
(real-server) inservice
(real-server) exit
(server-farm) real 192.168.250.11
(real-server) weight 16
(real-server) faildetect numconns 4
(real-server) retry 30
(real-server) inservice
(real-server) exit
(server-farm) real 192.168.250.12
(real-server) weight 8
(real-server) faildetect numconns 4
(real-server) retry 30
(real-server) inservice
(real-server) exit

(global) ip slb vserver VSERVER1
(virtual-server) serverfarm FARM1
(virtual-server) virtual 10.10.10.101 tcp www
(virtual-server) sticky 60 group 1
(virtual-server) advertise active
(virtual-server) inservice
(virtual-server) exit

(global) ip slb dfp password 0 test123
(slb-dfp) agent 192.168.250.10 2000
(slb-dfp) agent 192.168.250.11 2000
(slb-dfp) agent 192.168.250.12 2000
(slb-dfp) exit

(global) probe HTTP1 http
(probe) interval 120
(probe) port 80
(probe) request method get
(probe) exit
```

Displaying Information About SLB

Table 10-1 lists some switch commands that you can use to display helpful information about SLB configuration and status.

Table 10-1   *Commands to Display SLB Configuration and Status Information*

Display Function	Command
Server farms	(exec) **show ip slb serverfarms** [**name** *serverfarm-name*] [**detail**]
Real servers	(exec) **show ip slb reals** [**vserver** *virtual-server-name*] [**detail**]
Virtual servers	(exec) **show ip slb vserver** [**name** *virtual-server-name*] [**detail**]
SLB connections	(exec) **show ip slb conns** [**vserver** *virtual-server-name* |**client** *ip-address*] [**detail**]
DFP status	(exec) **show ip slb dfp** [**agent** *agent-ip-address* *port-number* | **manager** *manager-ip-address* |**detail**|**weights**]
SLB redundancy	(exec) **show ip slb replicate**
Probes	(exec) **show ip slb probe** [**name** *probe_name*] [**detail**]
SLB statistics	(exec) **show ip slb stats**

10-2: SLB Firewall Load Balancing

- Firewall load balancing balances traffic flows to one or more firewall farms.

- A firewall farm is a group of firewalls that are connected in parallel or that have their "inside" (protected) and "outside" (unprotected) interfaces connected to common network segments.

- Firewall load balancing requires a load-balancing device (IOS SLB) to be connected to each side of the firewall farm. A firewall farm with "inside" and "outside" interfaces would then require two load-balancing devices, each making sure that traffic flows are directed toward the same firewall for the duration of the connection. Figure 10-3 illustrates the basic firewall load-balancing concept.

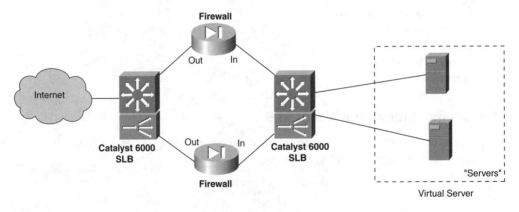

Figure 10-3   *Firewall Load-Balancing Concept*

- Firewall load balancing is performed by computing a hash value of each new traffic flow (source and destination IP addresses and ports). This is called a *route lookup*.

- The firewall load-balancing device then masquerades as the IP address for all firewalls in the firewall farm.

- Firewall load balancing can detect a firewall failure by monitoring probe activity.

- The HSRP can be used to provide a "stateless backup" redundancy for multiple firewall load-balancing devices. If one device fails, a redundant device can take over its function.

- Multiple firewall load-balancing devices can also use "stateful backup" for redundancy. Backup devices keep state information dynamically and can take over immediately if a failure occurs.

Section 10-2

Configuration

1. Define a firewall farm.

   a. Assign a name to the firewall farm:

   ```
   (global) ip slb firewallfarm firewallfarm-name
   ```

   In IOS SLB, the collection of firewalls is referenced by *firewallfarm-name* (text string up to 15 characters).

   b. Identify one or more firewalls in the farm.

   - Specify the firewall's IP address:

   ```
   (firewall-farm) real ip-address
   ```

   The firewall is directly connected (same logical subnet) to the load-balancing device with an interface at IP address *ip-address*.

   - *(Optional)* Assign a relative capacity weight:

   ```
   (real-firewall) weight weighting-value
   ```

   The real firewall is assigned a *weighting-value* (1 to 255; default 8) that indicates its capacity relative to other real firewalls in the firewall farm. These values are statically defined and are based on what you think the firewall can handle, relative to the others. The weight values are used only for round-robin or least-connections algorithms.

   - *(Optional)* Define one or more probes to detect a firewall failure:

   ```
   (real-firewall) probe probe-name
   ```

   The probe that is defined by *probe-name* (text string) is used periodically to determine whether the firewall has failed. Even if more than one probe is defined, the firewall is declared down if it fails just one probe. A firewall must pass all probes to be recovered again.

Tip   You must also define the probes separately, as described in section "10-3: SLB Probes." Ping probes are the most useful for firewall load balancing. For each firewall in the firewall farm, configure a probe to send ping packets that pass completely through the firewall, destined for the firewall load-balancing device on the other side. This tests both "inside" and "outside" interfaces of the firewall, requiring them to be active and operational so that the ping probe is reflected from the other side. Be sure that the firewall is configured to allow ICMP ping packets to pass through.

■ Allow load balancing to begin using the firewall:

```
(real-firewall) inserve
```

By default, the real firewall is not used by SLB unless it is placed in service. To remove a firewall from service, use **no inservice**.

c. *(Optional)* Define one or more flows that will be sent to the firewall farm:

```
(firewall-farm) access [source source-ip-address network-mask]
    [destination destination-ip-address network-mask]
```

When multiple firewall farms exist, traffic can be identified by address and sent through the appropriate firewall farm. A traffic flow is defined by its source and destination addresses and subnet masks. If either **source** or **destination** keywords are omitted, they default to 0.0.0.0 with a mask of 0.0.0.0, signifying all addresses and networks. This is the default behavior.

d. *(Optional)* Choose a firewall load-balancing method:

```
(firewall-farm) predictor hash address [port]
```

By default IOS SLB uses the source and destination IP addresses of a flow to select a destination firewall. Use the **port** keyword to use the source and destination addresses, and the source and destination TCP or UDP port numbers, in the selection decision.

e. *(Optional)* Use stateful backup to recover from a failure:

```
(firewall-farm) replicate casa listening-ip remote-ip port-number
    [interval] [password [0|7] password [timeout]]
```

The redundant load-balancing devices use CASA structure to exchange and replicate state information. This is sent from the *listening-ip* address (an interface on the local device) to the *remote-ip* address (an interface on the backup device), using *port-number* (1 to 65535). Replication messages are sent at *interval* seconds (1 to 300, default 10).

A *password* (text string; use **0** if unencrypted, the default; or **7** if encrypted) can be used for MD5 authentication with the backup device. The optional *timeout* (0 to 65,535 seconds; default 180 seconds) defines a time period when the password can be migrated from an old value to a new one. During this time, both old and new passwords are accepted.

f. *(Optional)* Adjust the TCP or UDP connection parameters.

- Enter the TCP or UDP configuration mode:

  ```
  (firewall-farm) {tcp|udp}
  ```

  You might need to make adjustments to both TCP and UDP. In this case, this command can be repeated to configure each independently.

- *(Optional; TCP only)* Hold connections open after they are terminated:

  ```
  (firewall-farm-protocol) delay duration
  ```

  After a TCP connection is terminated, the connection context can be maintained for *duration* (1 to 600 seconds, default 10 seconds). This can be useful when packets arrive out of sequence and the connection is reset before the last data packet arrives.

- *(Optional)* Hold connections open after no activity:

  ```
  (firewall-farm-protocol) idle duration
  ```

  When an absence of packets is detected for a connection, the connection is kept open for *duration* (10 to 65,535 seconds; default 3600 seconds or 1 hour) before an RST is sent.

- *(Optional)* Specify the maximum number of connections:

  ```
  (firewall-farm-protocol) maxconns number
  ```

  At any given time, the real server is limited to *number* (1 to 4,294,967,295; default 4,294,967,295) active connections.

- *(Optional)* Assign connections from the same IP address to the same firewall:

  ```
  (firewall-farm-protocol) sticky duration [netmask netmask]
  ```

  For a given IP address, connections are assigned to the last-used firewall for *duration* (0 to 65,535 seconds). A *netmask* can be given so that all source addresses within the mask are assigned to the same firewall.

g. *(IOS SLB only)* Allow firewall load balancing to begin using the firewall:

  ```
  (firewall-farm) inservice
  ```

  By default, the firewall is not used by firewall load balancing unless it is placed in service. To remove a firewall from service, use **no inservice**.

Firewall Load-Balancing Example

To perform firewall load balancing, two load-balancing devices are needed: one located externally and one located internally with respect to the firewall farm. Figure 10-4 shows a network diagram for this example.

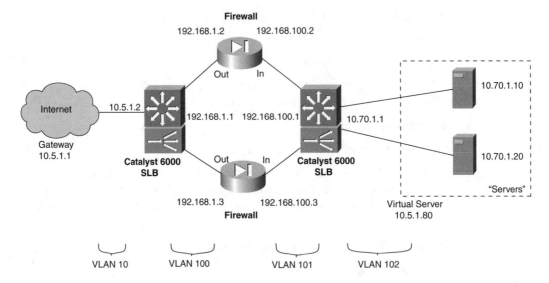

Figure 10-4 *Network Diagram for the Firewall Load-Balancing Example*

The firewall farm consists of two real firewalls. Their "outside" (unprotected) interfaces are at 192.168.1.2 and 192.168.1.3. Their "inside" (protected) interfaces are at 192.168.100.2 and 192.168.100.3. On the outside, the default gateway is 10.5.1.1, and the external SLB device is at 10.5.1.2.

The internal SLB device performs firewall load balancing for outbound traffic to the firewall farm. As well, it provides normal server load balancing for an internal server farm. The real servers are 10.70.1.10 and 10.70.1.20, and the virtual server appears as 10.5.1.80.

Ping probes are used by both external and internal SLB devices to test for firewall operation. An HTTP probe tests each of the real servers in the server farm. These use the default GET method and are sent every 240 seconds.

The configuration for the external load-balancing device is shown first:

```
(global) ip slb firewallfarm Outside
(firewall-farm) real 192.168.1.2
(real-firewall) weight 8
(real-firewall) probe Ping1
(real-firewall) inservice
(real-firewall) exit
(firewall-farm) real 192.168.1.3
(real-firewall) weight 8
(real-firewall) probe Ping2
(real-firewall) inservice
(real-firewall) exit
(firewall-farm) inservice
(firewall-farm) exit
```

```
(global) ip slb probe Ping1 ping
(probe) address 192.168.100.1
(probe) interval 10
(probe) faildetect 4
(global) ip slb probe Ping2 ping
(probe) address 192.168.100.1
(probe) interval 10
(probe) faildetect 4
(probe) exit
```

Now the configuration for the internal load-balancing device is shown:

```
(global) ip slb firewallfarm Inside
(firewall-farm) real 192.168.100.2
(real-firewall) weight 8
(real-firewall) probe Ping1
(real-firewall) inservice
(real-firewall) exit
(firewall-farm) real 192.168.100.3
(real-firewall) weight 8
(real-firewall) probe Ping2
(real-firewall) inservice
(real-firewall) exit
(firewall-farm) inservice
(firewall-farm) exit

(global) ip slb serverfarm Servers
(server-farm) nat server
(server-farm) probe HTTP1
(server-farm) real 10.70.1.10
(real-server) inservice
(real-server) exit
(server-farm) real 10.70.1.20
(real-server) inservice
(real-server) exit

(global) ip slb vserver Vservers
(virtual-server) serverfarm Servers
(virtual-server) virtual 10.5.1.80 tcp 0
(virtual-server) inservice
(virtual-server) exit

(global) ip slb probe Ping1 ping
(probe) address 192.168.1.1
(probe) interval 10
```

```
(probe) faildetect 4
(probe) exit
(global) ip slb probe Ping2 ping
(probe) address 192.168.1.1
(probe) interval 10
(probe) faildetect 4
(probe) exit
(global) ip slb probe HTTP1 http
(probe) port 80
(probe) interval 240
(probe) request
```

Displaying Information About Firewall Load Balancing

Table 10-2 lists some switch commands that you can use to display helpful information about SLB firewall load-balancing configuration and status.

Table 10-2   *Commands to Display SLB Firewall Load-Balancing Configuration and Status Information*

Display Function	Command
Status of firewalls in a farm	(exec) **show ip slb reals**
Firewall weight and connection counters	(exec) **show ip slb reals detail**
Firewall farm status	(exec) **show ip slb firewallfarm**
Load-balancing connections to firewalls	(exec) **show ip slb conns** [**firewall** *firewallfarm-name*] [**detail**]
Probes	(exec) **show ip slb probe** [**name** *probe_name*] [**detail**]
Sticky connections	(exec) **show ip slb sticky**

10-3: SLB Probes

■ Probes can be used to test for server or firewall connectivity and proper operation.

■ Probes can be defined to simulate requests for these protocols:

   ■ ICMP: Sends ICMP echo (ping) requests to a real server.

   ■ HTTP: Sends HTTP requests to a real server, using TCP port 80.

   ■ WSP: Requests and verifies the replies using Wireless Access Protocol (WAP), port 9201.

   ■ Telnet: Opens and closes a Telnet connection (TCP port 23) to a real server.

   ■ TCP: Establishes and resets TCP connections to a real server. This can be used to support any TCP port, including HTTPS or SSL, port 443.

- FTP: Opens and closes an FTP connection (TCP ports 20 and 21) to a real server.

- SMTP: Opens and closes an SMTP connection (TCP port 25) to a real server.

- DNS: Sends requests to and verifies the replies from a real DNS server.

Configuration

1. Define the probe:

    (global) **ip slb probe** name {**ping** | **http** | **wsp**}

    The probe is named *name* (text string up to 15 characters) and can be referenced by other SLB server and firewall farm commands. IOS SLB allows these probe types: **ping** (ICMP), **http**, or **wsp** (WAP port 9201). *(Optional)* Define the target address:

    (probe) **address** [ip-address]

    For a server farm, this command is not used. The *ip-address* used by the probe is inherited from each real server in the server farm. With IOS SLB, addresses are not inherited when the probe is used for a firewall farm. You must use this command to define the address of a target firewall.

2. Set the probe behavior:

    a. *(Optional)* Set the time between probes:

        (probe) **interval** seconds

        Probes are sent toward the target at intervals of *seconds* (IOS SLB: 1 to 65,535 seconds; default 1 second; CSM: 5 to 65,535 seconds; default 120 seconds).

    b. *(Optional)* Define the criteria for a failure:

        (probe) **faildetect** retry-count

        With IOS SLB, a server or firewall is considered to have failed if *retry-count* (1 to 255; default 10) consecutive ping probes are unanswered. With a CSM, the target has failed if *retry-count* (0 to 65,535; default 3) probes of any type are unanswered.

3. *(Optional; HTTP probe only)* Define the HTTP probe operation:

    a. *(Optional)* Set the port number:

        (probe) **port** port-number

        Usually, an HTTP probe uses *port-number* 80. If the *port-number* is unspecified, however, it is inherited from the virtual server. For a firewall probe, the *port-number* must be given (1 to 65,535). The target device must answer an HTTP request for the probe to work.

    b. *(Optional)* Define the HTTP probe method:

        (probe) **request** [**method** {**get** | **post** | **head** | **name** name}] [**url** path]

The probe requests information from the server using the **get** (the default), **post**, **head** (request a header data type), or **name** (request the data named *name*) method. A URL can also be given, specifying the server *path* (text string URL; default /).

c. *(Optional)* Specify the probe header information:

```
(probe) header field-name [field-value]
```

The probe header name is set to *field-name* (text string up to 15 characters), with a value of *field-value*. A colon is automatically inserted between the name and value. By default, the request contains these headers:

```
Accept: */*

Connection: close

User-Agent: cisco-slb-probe/1.0

Host: virtual-IP-address
```

d. *(Optional)* Specify the HTTP authentication values:

```
(probe) credentials username [password]
```

If HTTP authentication is required, a *username* (text string, up to 15 characters) and a *password* (text string up to 15 characters) can be given for the probe.

e. *(Optional)* Expect a specific status code to be returned:

```
(probe) expect [status status-code] [regex regular-expression]
```

A real server or a firewall is considered to have failed if it either does not respond to an HTTP probe or if it returns a *status-code* (100 to 599, default 200) other than the one specified. For firewalls, the *status-code* should be set to 401. For a CSM, the status code must be within the range *min-number* (default 0) and *max-number* (optional, default 999).

With IOS SLB, you can also expect a regular expression along with the status code. Use the **regex** keyword and specify a *regular-expression* (text string, no default). Only the first 2920 bytes of the probe reply are searched for a match.

4. (Optional; WSP probe only) Define the target URL:

```
(probe) url [path]
```

A URL can also be given, specifying the server *path* (text string URL; default /).

Displaying Information About SLB Probes

To display helpful configuration and status information about SLB probes, enter the following command:

```
(exec) show ip slb probe [name probe_name] [detail]
```

Chapter 11

Controlling Traffic and Switch Access

See the following sections for configuration information about these topics:

- **11-1: Broadcast Suppression:** Describes the method for preventing the switch from forwarding excessive broadcasts received on a port

- **11-2: Protocol Filtering:** Explains how to configure a port to prevent forwarding of flood packets of a particular protocol out a port

- **11-3: Port Security:** Provides the information required to configure a port for use only by a specified list of clients based on MAC addresses

- **11-4: VLAN Access Control Lists:** Describes how to control the traffic that passes through a Layer 2 switch using access control lists applied to a VLAN

- **11-5: Switch Authentication:** Explains how to configure the switch for use of a RADIUS, TACACS, or TACACS+ for authentication into the switch

- **11-6: Access Class:** Shows how to create a list of hosts that are permitted to access the switch for management purposes (Telnet, SNMP, and HTTP)

- **11-7: SSH Telnet Configuration:** Provides the information needed to configure the switch for Secure Shell Telnet logins

- **11-8: 802.1X Port Authentication:** Describes how to configure a port to require a login or certificate for user authentication before granting access to the network

- **11-9: Layer 2 Security:** Explains how to configure Layer 2 security features to prevent known security attacks

Note   Many of the traffic-control features covered in this chapter are dependent on the hardware and products. As you read through this chapter, note that many of the commands differ between the product lines and that some of the features discussed are not supported.

11-1: Broadcast Suppression

- A network protocol can create a large amount of broadcast traffic.

- In Layer 2 networks, broadcasts must be forwarded on all ports except the receiving port; because of this, a large or excessive number of broadcasts can have an impact on network and device performance.

- Broadcast suppression enables you to control how a receiving port handles excessive broadcast traffic.

- By configuring a threshold, a port can be configured to stop flooding broadcasts for a predefined period or until the broadcasts fall below a certain level.

- Suppressing these broadcasts can prevent them from being forwarded out other switch ports and limit the effect they have on the network.

- Suppression of the broadcasts does not have any effect on the multicast or unicast traffic received by the port.

- Broadcast suppression is supported on Catalyst IOS platforms.

- In addition to broadcast suppression, unicast and multicast suppression can also be configured for some platforms.

Configuring Broadcast Suppression

By default broadcast suppression is disabled on all platforms and on all operating systems. Broadcast suppression is applied to individual ports on a switch. When configuring broadcast suppression, keep in mind that it is the number of broadcasts received by a port. When the threshold is reached, the port stops passing broadcast packets to the backplane until the condition is corrected. To configure broadcast suppression, use the following steps.

1. Enable broadcast suppression:

   ```
   (interface) broadcast suppression threshold%
   ```

   Broadcast suppression prevents LAN interfaces from being disrupted by a broadcast storm. A broadcast storm occurs when multiple copies of broadcast or multicast frames flood the subnet, creating excessive traffic and degrading network performance. Errors in the protocol-stack implementation or in the network configuration can cause a broadcast storm.

   The broadcast suppression threshold numbers and the time interval combination make the broadcast suppression algorithm work with different levels of granularity. A higher threshold allows more broadcast packets to pass through. Broadcast suppression on the Cisco 6500 series switches is implemented in hardware. The suppression circuitry monitors packets passing from a LAN interface to the switching bus.

   Using the Individual/Group bit in the packet destination address, the broadcast suppression circuitry determines if the packet is unicast or broadcast, keeps track of the current count of broadcasts within the 1-second interval, and when a threshold is reached, filters out subsequent broadcast packets.

Because hardware broadcast suppression uses a bandwidth-based method to measure broadcast activity, the most significant implementation factor is setting the percentage of total available bandwidth that can be used by broadcast traffic. Because packets do not arrive at uniform intervals, the 1-second interval during which broadcast activity is measured can affect the behavior of broadcast suppression. The *threshold%* specifies the percentage of bandwidth limit that would have to be reached by broadcast traffic before action would be taken.

2. Specify action to be taken:

    (interface) **storm-control** {**broadcast level** *high level* [*lower level*]} |
        action {**shutdown** | **trap**}}

    When broadcast suppression occurs, the default action is to suppress or filter the packets. This means that packets are dropped and do not make it onto the backplane of the switch. You can, on some of the platforms, configure the switch to take another action. For the IOS devices, you can change the device from the default action of **trap** to the **shutdown** option. When the port is placed in shutdown mode, it remains there until an administrator has reenabled the port with the **no shutdown** command. Each time the threshold is crossed, the administrator must reenable the port. For the 2960 broadcast, frames are dropped unless the action has changed to **shutdown**. The 2960 default is to filter out the traffic and not to send traps. To revert to filtering the frames, the administrator must issue the command **no port storm-control broadcast action shutdown**. Another option that can be configured on the 2960 is for the switch to generate an SNMP **trap**. The action **trap** is not configurable for the Catalyst 6500 running Supervisor IOS.

Note   Because the action **trap** is not a configuration option for the Catalyst 6500 running Supervisor IOS 12.2.33SXH, one solution would be to have the Embedded Event Manager (EEM) to monitor for the syslog, and if it is seen then, the interface could be shut down and a syslog or trap generated to inform the network admin.

3. *(Optional)* Control unicast or multicast:

    (interface)**storm-control unicast** | **multicast level** *level*[*.level*]

    In addition to configuring the switch to control broadcast floods, you can also configure a port to drop frames or become disabled when it encounters a large number of unicast or multicast packets. To configure this option, use the **multicast** and **unicast** keywords in the commands to enable the control of the frames.

Verifying Configuration

After you configure broadcast suppression, use the following commands to verify the configuration and operation on the switch:

```
(privileged) show interfaces  switchport
(privileged) show interfaces  counters storm-control
(privileged) show interfaces counters storm-control [module slot_number]
```

Feature Example

For a 6500, this example shows how to enable one-quarter-percent broadcast suppression on interface FastEthernet 3/1 and verify the configuration: When enabling broadcast suppression, you can specify the threshold in hundredths of a percent:

- Enter 0.00 to suppress all broadcasts.

- Enter 0.01 for 0.01% (1/100th percent).

- Enter 0.50 for 0.50% (one-half percent).

- Enter 1 or 1.00 for 1% (one percent).

The threshold range is 0.00–100.00.

```
6500# configure terminal
6500(config)# interface fastethernet 3/1
6500(config-if)# broadcast suppression 0.25
6500(config-if)# end
6500# show running-config interface fastethernet 3/1 | include suppression
broadcast suppression 0.25
Router# copy running-config startup-config
```

11-2: Protocol Filtering

- Protocol filtering can be configured on Catalyst 4500 and 6500 series switches.

- Protocol filtering does not require any special feature cards on the switch to operate.

- Protocol filtering enables you to configure a port to filter or block flood (broadcast, multicasts, and unknown unicasts) traffic based on protocols.

- Protocol filtering is supported only on Layer 2 access ports and cannot be configured on trunk links or Layer 3 ports.

- Protocol filtering supports blocking of IP, IPX, AppleTalk, VINES, and DECnet traffic. All other protocols are not affected by protocol filtering.

- Administrative protocols such as *Spanning Tree Protocol (STP)*, *Cisco Discovery Protocol (CDP)*, and *VLAN Trunking Protocol (VTP)* are not blocked by protocol filtering.

Configuration

By configuring protocol filtering on a switch, you prevent the port from flooding traffic of that type received from other ports in the VLAN out the given port. This can be useful in controlling traffic from clients within the same VLAN running different and "chatty" protocols. To configure protocol filtering, use the following steps.

1. Enable protocol filtering for the switch:

   `(global)` **`protocol-filter`**

   Protocol filtering is disabled by default. For the ports to control the traffic, you must first enable protocol filtering for the switch. After enabling the process, you can set up the ports to react to a given protocol.

2. Enable protocol filtering on an access port:

   `(interface)` **`switchport protocol {ip | ipx | group} {on | off | auto}`**

For each port on which you want to control traffic, you must specify the protocol and how traffic is to be handled. The **protocol** option specifies the given type of protocol. You can choose from among the following options: **ip** (IP), **ipx** (IPX), and **group** (AppleTalk, DECnet, and Banyan VINES). The options specify how traffic is to be handled. The option **on** specifies that a port is to receive traffic for the protocol and forward flood traffic for that protocol. The option **off** specifies that the port cannot receive or flood traffic for a given protocol. The option **auto** indicates that the port will not flood traffic for a given protocol until it first receives a packet of that protocol on the port. Table 11-1 lists the default actions if the ports are not configured.

Verification

To verify the configuration of protocol filtering, use the following commands:

`(privileged)` **`show protocol-filtering`**

OR

`(privileged)` **`show protocol-filtering interface {type `** *slot/port* **`}`**

These **show** commands display the configuration for the specified ports. In IOS, the command **show protocol-filtering** without any port designations will show only ports that have at least one protocol that is in the nondefault mode.

Table 11-1 *Protocol Filtering Defaults*

Protocol	Mode
IP	on
IPX	auto
Group	auto

Feature Example

This example shows the configuration for protocol filtering. This example enables protocol filtering. It then sets the Fast Ethernet ports 5/1 through 5/6 to enable IP traffic to pass without being filtered and blocks all other traffic. This example also configures ports 5/7 to 5/8 to enable only IPX traffic. In the following example, ports 5/9 to 5/10 enable IP and IPX traffic only if the ports detect an IP or IPX client on the specific port and enable all other traffic to be forwarded:

```
Switch(config)# protocol-filter
Switch(config)# interface fastethernet 5/1
Switch(config-if)# switchport protocol ip on
Switch(config-if)# switchport protocol ipx off
Switch(config-if)# switchport protocol group off
Switch(config-if)# interface fastethernet 5/2
Switch(config-if)# switchport protocol ip on
Switch(config-if)# switchport protocol ipx off
Switch(config-if)# switchport protocol group off
Switch(config-if)# interface fastethernet 5/3
Switch(config-if)# switchport protocol ip on
Switch(config-if)# switchport protocol ipx off
Switch(config-if)# switchport protocol group off
Switch(config-if)# interface fastethernet 5/4
Switch(config-if)# switchport protocol ip on
Switch(config-if)# switchport protocol ipx off
Switch(config-if)# switchport protocol group off
Switch(config-if)# interface fastethernet 5/5
Switch(config-if)# switchport protocol ip on
Switch(config-if)# switchport protocol ipx off
Switch(config-if)# switchport protocol group off
Switch(config-if)# interface fastethernet 5/6
Switch(config-if)# switchport protocol ip on
Switch(config-if)# switchport protocol ipx off
Switch(config-if)# switchport protocol group off
Switch(config-if)# interface fastethernet 5/7
Switch(config-if)# switchport protocol ip off
Switch(config-if)# switchport protocol ipx on
Switch(config-if)# switchport protocol group off
Switch(config-if)# interface fastethernet 5/8
Switch(config-if)# switchport protocol ip off
Switch(config-if)# switchport protocol ipx on
Switch(config-if)# switchport protocol group off
Switch(config-if)# interface fastethernet 5/9
Switch(config-if)# switchport protocol ip auto
Switch(config-if)# switchport protocol ipx auto
Switch(config-if)# switchport protocol group off
```

```
Switch(config-if)# interface fastethernet 5/10
Switch(config-if)# switchport protocol ip auto
Switch(config-if)# switchport protocol ipx auto
Switch(config-if)# switchport protocol group off
Switch(config-if)# end
Switch(config)# copy running-config startup-config
```

11-3: Port Security

■ Port security enables you to configure a port to only allow a given device or devices access to the switch port.

■ Port security defines the allowed devices by MAC address.

■ MAC addresses for allowed devices can be manually configured and "learned" by the switch.

■ There are limits to how many MAC addresses can be secured on a port. These numbers vary between platforms.

■ When an unauthorized MAC attempts to access the port, the switch can suspend or disable the port.

■ Port security cannot be configured on a trunk port, a *Switched Port Analyzer (SPAN)* port, or a port that is dynamically assigned to a VLAN.

■ Port security is supported on the 6500, 4500, 3750, 3560, and 2960 series switches.

Configuration

When a port is active on a switch, any user can plug into the port and access the network. Because many networks use *Dynamic Host Configuration Protocol (DCHP)* to assign user addresses, it would be easy for someone with physical access to a network port to plug his own device, such as a laptop, into the port and become a user on the network. From there, a person could proceed to generate traffic or cause other problems within the network. Port security enables you to specify the MAC addresses of the devices that are allowed to connect to the port. Use the following steps to configure port security.

1. Enable port security:

   ```
   (interface) switchport port-security
   ```

   By default anyone can plug into a port and access network services. To protect a port, you must first enable port security on the individual port. Use the command that is appropriate for your device.

2. Specify the number of MAC addresses:

   ```
   (interface) switchport port-security maximum number_of_addresses vlan
      {vlan_ID | vlan_range}
   ```

After you enable port security, you need to determine how many different devices access the ports and how many addresses need to be secured. The *value* option specifies the number of addresses to be secured. The default value is one address. Each hardware platform has a limited number of addresses that can be secured, so if you expect to secure more than 250 total addresses on the switch, check the specific documentation for that hardware.

Note   When configuring the maximum number of secure MAC addresses on a port, note the following information:

■ With Release 12.2(18)SXE and later releases, the range for *number_of_addresses* is 1 to 4097.

■ With releases earlier than Release 12.2(18)SXE, the range for *number_of_addresses* is 1 to 1024.

■ With Release 12.2(18)SXE and later releases, port security supports trunks.

■ On a trunk, you can configure the maximum number of secure MAC addresses both on the trunk and for all the VLANs on the trunk.

■ You can configure the maximum number of secure MAC addresses on a single VLAN or a range of VLANs.

■ For a range of VLANs, enter a dash-separated pair of VLAN numbers.

■ You can enter a comma-separated list of VLAN numbers and dash-separated pairs of VLAN numbers.

3.   Manually enter MAC addresses to be secured:

```
(interface) switchport port-security mac-address mac_address
```

By default, the switches "learn" the MAC addresses of the devices that are plugged into that port. If you want to control which devices can access the switch, use these commands to specify which MAC addresses are secured on a port.

4.   Specify the action to be taken by the port:

```
(interface) switchport port-security violation {protect | restrict | shutdown}
```

When a violation occurs, the switch generally protects the port by dropping the traffic that comes from unauthorized MAC addresses. This means that the switch does not allow those frames through the device; if a frame comes from a device that is configured as secure, however, those frames are allowed through. This is the default configuration for each of the devices and is specified by the **protect** option. Another option that you can configure is for the interface to move to a **shutdown** state. If you configure this option, the port remains in the administratively down state until an administrator reenables the port with a **no shutdown** command. A third option is to generate an SNMP trap. If a violation occurs, the **restrict** option for IOS and the **trap** option for the 3500XL IOS perform this function.

Verification

To verify the configuration of port security on the switch, use the following command:

```
(privileged) show port security [interface interface-id] [address]
```

Feature Example

This example shows the configuration for port security. In this example, ports Fast Ethernet 2/1 are configured to enable a single MAC address 00-01-03-87-09-43 to have access to the port and will shut down if the security is violated. Ports 2/2 and 2/3 are configured to enable ten addresses each, which the switch will learn as devices plug into the ports and will drop unauthorized packets.

An example of IOS configuration follows:

```
Switch(config)# interface fastethernet 2/1
Switch(config-if)# switchport port-security
Switch(config-if)# switchport port-security mac-address 00-01-03-87-09-43
Switch(config-if)# switchport port-security violation shutdown
Switch(config-if)# interface fastethernet 2/2
Switch(config-if)# switchport port-security
Switch(config-if)# switchport port-security maximum 10
Switch(config-if)# interface fastethernet 2/3
Switch(config-if)# switchport port-security
Switch(config-if)# switchport port-security maximum 10
Switch(config-if)# end
Switch(config)# copy running-config startup-config
```

11-4: VLAN Access Control Lists

- *Access control lists* (ACL) define how traffic is to be handled as it passes through a network device.

- ACLs use addressing and port information to control conversations.

- ACLs are typically implemented in routers, but new hardware enables Layer 2 and Layer 3 switches to consult the list before passing the packet.

- ACLs enable users to configure any switch to control traffic based on Layer 3 and above of the OSI reference model.

- These ACLs are mapped to a VLAN or a Layer 2 port to control traffic flows.

- VACLs are controlled in hardware and are not supported on all platforms.

- Currently VACLs are supported on the 6500, 4500, 3560, and 3750 series switches.

Section 11-4

The *VLAN ACL* (VACL) is an ACL that specifies traffic parameters based on Layer 3 and above information that is applied to a Layer 2 VLAN or in some instances a Layer 2 interface. These lists offer a benefit over traditional router access lists of being applied in hardware and, therefore, being faster than traditional ACLs. They also add the capability to filter traffic within an IP subnet and beyond the IP subnet. Although the functionality is the same between operating systems, the configuration differs. This section is divided into two parts. The set of commands specifies the VACL configuration on IOS devices that support VACLs. Use the steps in each section to configure and apply VACLs on your switch. These steps apply to only IP VACLs because this is a protocol that is supported for all the platforms listed. It is possible to configure IPX VACLs for some platforms. Although the syntax and process are the same, the protocol options differ for IPX.

> **Note**   ACLs behave in the same manner on both routers and switches. This section does not discuss every option and configuration principal. For more on access list configuration, consult the Cisco Press title *Cisco Field Manual: Router Configuration*.

IOS VACL Configuration

IOS VACLs are configured as standard or extended IP access lists. Then those lists are mapped to a port or a VLAN. Currently, the 6500, 4500, 3750, and 3560 switches support VACLs. Use these commands to configure the VACL option.

1. Configure the access list.

   The first parameter that must be configured is the list, which identifies traffic to be controlled by the list. For IOS ACLs, the list is either a number or a name. There are also various types of ACLs, for example, standard lists that specify source information and extended lists that specify source and destination. Use the commands in these steps to configure the access lists.

   a. Configure a numbered standard access list:

      ```
      (global) access-list access-list-number {deny | permit | remark} {source
         source-wildcard | host source | any}
      ```

      The command creates a standard ACL. The number range for standard ACLs is 1 to 99 and 1300 to 1999. The parameter **permit** enables traffic, and **deny** drops traffic. The **remark** parameter enables you to insert remarks into the list that provide information about the list and why parameters are added. For the **permit** or **deny** option, the *address/mask* enables you to control traffic from specified source addresses. You can use the keyword **any** to specify all source addresses.

   b. Configure a numbered extended access list:

      ```
      (global) access-list access-list-number {deny | permit | remark} protocol
         {source source-wildcard | host source | any} [operator port]
         {destination destination-wildcard | host destination | any} [operator
         port]
      ```

The command creates a standard ACL. The number range for standard ACLs is 100 to 199 and 2000 to 2699. The parameter **permit** enables traffic, and **deny** drops traffic. The **remark** parameter enables you to insert remarks into the list that provide information about the list and why parameters are added.

The *protocol* parameter specifies which type of protocol within IP you are looking to match. Examples include **udp** or **tcp**. The protocol **ip** in this field would specify all IP traffic. The *address/mask* pair specifies the source and destination of the sending and receiving devices for which you are trying to control traffic. You can use the keyword **any** to specify all source or destination addresses. The operator and port options enable you to specify protocol- and application-specific ports.

c. Configure a named standard access list:

```
(global) ip access-list standard {name}

(std-acl) {deny | permit} {source source-wildcard | host source | any}
```

For a standard-named ACL, the command **ip access-list standard** *name* indicates that you want to enter a configuration mode on the list specified by the name given. From there the switch enters a mode that enables you to enter the options a line at a time until you exit the ACL configuration mode.

The parameter **permit** allows traffic, and **deny** drops traffic. For the **permit** or **deny** option, the *address/mask* pair specifies which source address will be controlled. You can use the keyword **any** to specify all source addresses.

d. Configure a named extended access list:

```
(global) ip access-list extended {name}

(extd-acl) {deny | permit} protocol {source source-wildcard | host source |
    any} [operator port] {destination destination-wildcard | host
    destination | any} [operator port]
```

For an extended-named ACL, the command **ip access-list extended** *name* indicates that you want to enter a configuration mode on the list specified by the name given. From there the switch enters a mode that enables you to enter the options a line at a time until you exit the ACL configuration mode.

The parameter **permit** allows traffic, and **deny** drops traffic. The *protocol* parameter specifies which type of protocol within IP you are looking to match. Examples include **udp** and **tcp**. The protocol **ip** in this field would specify all IP traffic. The *address/mask* pair specifies the source and destination of the sending and receiving devices for which you are trying to control traffic. You can use the keyword **any** to specify all source or destination addresses. The operator and port options enable you to specify protocol and application-specific ports.

Section 11-4

2. Create a VLAN map.

If the list you create is going to be mapped to a VLAN, you must configure a **vlan access-map** to specify an access map name and the action to be taken for a specific matched entry, as follows:

```
(global) vlan access-map name [number]

(vlan-map) match ip  address {aclname | aclnumber}

(vlan-map) action {drop | forward}
```

An *access map* is a list of map clauses that specify what action is to be taken for packets on the VLAN. When creating the access map, it is given a name, and then subsequent clauses are given numbers. Each clause is checked to find a match for the packets, and then the action specified for that clause is taken. If no clauses are found, the packets are dropped. To create an access map, use the **vlan access-map** command followed by a *name*. The *number* option is used for subsequent clauses in the access map.

After you enter a map name, you are placed in access map configuration mode, where you can specify an ACL name or number to identify the traffic to be acted upon for a clause. For ACLs that are included in this access map, a **permit** statement in the ACL is a match, and a **deny** is not a match for the given clause. After a match is identified by an ACL, the **action** command specifies whether to drop or permit the traffic. If none of the clauses match a given frame, the frame is dropped.

3. Apply the access lists.

After you create an access list, you need to apply the list to the VLAN:

```
(global) vlan filter mapname vlan-list list
```

To apply an access map to a VLAN for the IOS switches that support VACLs, use the **vlan filter** command. The *mapname* option specifies the name of the map created in Step 2. The **vlan-list** parameter is followed by a VLAN number or a list of VLAN numbers to which the ACL will be applied.

Verification

To verify configuration of IOS VACLs, use the following commands:

```
(privileged) show ip access-lists [number | name]
(privileged) show vlan access-map [mapname]
(privileged) show vlan filter [access-map name | vlan vlan-id]
(privileged) show ip interface type number
```

Feature Example

This example shows the configuration for VACL filtering. In the list configured on this switch, you want to meet the following conditions:

- Permit all IP traffic from subnet 10.101.0.0 to host 10.101.1.1.

- Permit ICMP echo request from all hosts.

- Permit ICMP echo reply from all hosts.

- Deny all other ICMP traffic.

- Permit all TCP traffic.

- Deny all UDP traffic not previously specified.

- Permit all other IP traffic.

You want to apply this list to VLAN 101 on the switch. An example of configuration follows:

```
Switch(config)# ip access-list extended ip_subnet2host
Switch(config-ext-acl)# permit ip 10.101.0.0 0.0.255.255 host 10.101.1.1
Switch(config)# ip access-list extended ping
Switch(config-ext-acl)# permit icmp any any echo
Switch(config-ext-acl)# permit icmp any any echo-reply
Switch(config-ext-acl)# exit
Switch(config)# ip access-list extended_icmp
Switch(config-ext-acl)# permit icmp any any
Switch(config-ext-acl)# exit
Switch(config)# ip access-list extended_tcp
Switch(config-ext-acl)# permit tcp any any
Switch(config-ext-acl)# exit
Switch(config)# ip access-list extended_udp
Switch(config-ext-acl)# permit udp any any
Switch(config-ext-acl)# exit
Switch(config)# vlan access-map watchlist
Switch(config-access-map)# match ip address ip_subnet2host
Switch(config-access-map)# action forward
Switch(config-access-map)# vlan access-map watchlist 10
Switch(config-access-map)# match ip address ping
Switch(config-access-map)# action forward
Switch(config-access-map)# vlan access-map watchlist 20
Switch(config-access-map)# match ip address ip_icmp
Switch(config-access-map)# action drop
Switch(config-access-map)# vlan access-map watchlist 30
Switch(config-access-map)# match ip address ip_tcp
Switch(config-access-map)# action forward
Switch(config-access-map)# vlan access-map watchlist 40
Switch(config-access-map)# match ip address ip_udp
Switch(config-access-map)# action drop
Switch(config-access-map)# vlan access-map watchlist 50
```

Section 11-4

```
Switch(config-access-map)# action forward
Switch(config-access-map)# exit
Switch(config)# vlan filter watchlist vlan-list 101
Switch(config)# end
Switch(config)# copy running-config startup-config
```

11-5: Switch Authentication

■ Switch authentication enables you to control how people access the switch.

■ By default switch authentication is controlled locally by the **user** password and the **enable** password.

■ You can configure the switch to use an authentication server, such as a RADIUS or TACACS+ server, for authentication.

■ After you configure RADIUS or TACACS+, it is important to have local authentication enabled to log in to the switch if the authentication server is down.

■ Configuration for authentication is sometimes required for options such as *Secure Shell (SSH)* Telnet and 802.1X port authorization.

Configuration

Switch authentication specifies how users are verified before being allowed to access the user or privileged mode command-line interface prompts. Authentication can be configured by local passwords on the switch, or it can be configured so users are authorized by a TACACS or RADIUS server. Use the following commands to control authentication of users on the switch.

1. Configure local authentication.

    Default authorization is handled by passwords on the switch. The commands listed in this section show how to enable or disable this default authentication. Local authentication should not be disabled even if you use a server for authentication because it provides a "back door," or a secondary option, for authentication if the server fails. A switch has two levels of authentication: user level and privileged level. These commands show how to control authentication for each level.

    a. Enable AAA Globally

    ```
    (global) aaa new-model
    ```

    ```
    (global) aaa authentication login {default | list-name} method1
      [method2...]
    ```

    Use this command to enable or disable user-level local authentication for the **console, telnet, http,** or **all** services on a switch.

b. Configure privileged-level authentication:

```
(global) line [aux | console | tty | vty] line-number [ending-line-number]

(global) login authentication {default | list-name}
```

Use this command to enable or disable privileged-level local authentication for the **console**, **telnet**, **http**, or **all** services on a switch.

2. Configure TACACS authentication.

It is also possible to configure the switch to authenticate users from a database on a TACACS server. For this to work, a username and password must be configured on the TACACS server. After the server has been configured, you use the following commands to provide TACACS authentication.

a. Configure the TACACS server:

```
(global)tacacs-server host hostname [single-connection] [port integer]
   [timeout integer] [key string]
```

This command specifies the address of the TACACS server. This assumes that the switch has been configured for an IP address and has a gateway if necessary to reach the server. You can specify multiple servers if one of the devices is not functioning.

b. Enable TACACS authentication for user level:

```
(global) aaa authentication login {default | group | tacacs+ | local}
```

After you specify the server address, you set the user-level authentication process to use the **tacacs** option for the **console**, **telnet**, **http**, or **all** services. If that fails, other authentication methods, such as local login, are attempted.

c. Specify the TACACS key:

```
(global) tacacs-server key key
```

Because the information between the TACACS device and the switch is encrypted, you must also supply the TACACS process with the *key* that is used by the server. This command specifies the key used.

3. Configure RADIUS authentication.

In addition to local or TACACS, you can configure the switch to authenticate users from a database on a RADIUS server. For this to work, a username and password must be configured on the RADIUS server. After the server has been configured, you use the following commands to provide RADIUS authentication.

a. Configure the RADIUS server:

```
(global) radius-server host {hostname | ip_address}
```

This command specifies the address of the RADIUS server. This assumes that the switch has been configured for an IP address and has a gateway if necessary to reach the server. You can specify multiple servers in case one of the devices is not functioning.

b. Enable RADIUS authentication for user level:

`(global)` **`aaa authentication login {default | group | radius}`**

After you specify the server address, you set the user-level authentication process to use the **radius** option for the **console**, **telnet**, **http**, or **all** services. The **primary** option for this command specifies that RADIUS is the first authentication method. If that fails, other authentication methods, such as local login, are attempted.

c. Specify the RADIUS key:

`(global)` **`radius-server host`** `{hostname | ip-address}` `[auth-port port-number]` `[acct-port port-number]`

`radius-server key` `string`

Because the information between the RADIUS device and the switch is encrypted, you must also supply the RADIUS process with the *key* that is used by the server. This command specifies the key used.

Verification

To verify configuration of authentication, use the following commands:

```
show radius statistics
show tacacs
```

Feature Example

This example shows the configuration for a switch that uses a RADIUS server with the address 192.168.1.10 as the primary authentication method for Telnet users and a TACACS server with the address 192.168.1.8 for the primary authentication method for console users. The TACACS key will be abc123, and the radius key will be 789xyz.

An example of the configuration follows:

```
Switch# conf t
Switch (config)# aaa new-model
Switch (config)# ip radius source-interface Interface Gig1/1/1
Switch (config)# radius-server host 192.168.1.10
Switch (config)# radius-server key 789xyz
Switch (config)# aaa authentication login default group radius
Switch (config)# line con 0
```

```
Switch (config-line)# login authentication consoleport
Switch (config-line)# aaa authentication login consoleport tacacs+ enable
Switch (config-line)# exit
Switch (config)# tacacs-server host 192.168.1.8
Switch (config)# tacacs-server key abc123
```

11-6: Access Class

■   To restrict incoming and outgoing connections between a particular virtual terminal line.

■   By applying an access list to an inbound vty, you can control who can access the lines to a router.

■   By applying an access list to an outbound vty, you can control the destinations that the lines from a router can reach.

Configuration

To control inbound access to vty, perform this task when you want to control access to a vty coming into the router by using an access list.

1.   Add addresses to the access list:

    (global) **access-list** *access-list-number* **deny** {*source* [*source-wildcard*] | **any**}
    [**log**]

    To control which devices are allowed to access the switch, you must first configure the access list. The *address* parameter specifies the IP address of the device that is allowed to access the network. The *mask* parameter is an option. The mask is in dotted-decimal format, where a 1 means match the address and a 0 means ignore the address. For example, the address 172.16.101.1 with a mask of 0.0.0.255 would match all the addresses that start with 172.16.101. The address of 172.16.101.1 with a mask of 0.0.0.0 would match only the host 172.16.101.1. If you do not specify a mask, a mask of all 0s or the host mask is used.

2.   Assign access class to the Telnet Virtual Terminal Line:

    line vty *line-number* [*ending-line-number*]

    access-class *access-list-number* **in**

    After you configure a list of devices that are permitted, use this command to enable the permit list.

3. Enable HTTP access control:

```
(global) ip http access-class {access-list-number | name}
```

Verification

Use the following command to verify the configuration of the access class:

```
show line [line-number | summary]
```

Feature Example

The following example shows an access class configuration. This list enables any user from the network 172.168.5.0 to access the device for Telnet. This example also enables any user from the 172.168.1.0 subnet to access the device via Telnet:

```
switch# configure terminal
switch (config)# access-list 1 permit 172.168.5.0 0.0.0.255
switch (config)# line vty 5 10
switch (config-line)# access-class 1 in
switch (config-line)# exit
```

11-7: SSH Telnet Configuration

- Telnet connections to the switch take place over TCP port 23 and are transmitted in plain text.

- If someone with a network analyzer captures packets going to a server, he can see the data transmitted in plain text, including the passwords.

- *Secure Shell (SSH)* is a method of communicating through Telnet that encrypts packets before they are transmitted between devices.

- SSH runs on TCP port 22 between an SSH-compatible client and a device configured to accept SSH connections.

- Cisco switches support SSH.

- To implement SSH on your switch, it must be Crypto-compatible code.

- By default SSH is disabled on the switch and must be enabled before clients can connect.

Configuration

To provide secure Telnet communications between the switch and an SSH Telnet client, you must configure the switch to enable SSH connectivity. The following commands outline the configuration steps to activate SSH.

1. Set the Crypto key:

    ```
    (global) crypto key generate rsa
    ```

    Before you can configure SSH, you must enable the switch to generate a key for encoding the data. The **crypto key rsa** command generates that key. For IOS you are prompted for a value. The greater the length, the stronger the encryption. The recommended modulus is 1024 or greater.

2. Enable SSH:

    ```
    (global) ip ssh
    ```

Verification

To verify configuration of SSH, use the following commands:

```
show ip ssh
show ip permit
```

Feature Example

This example shows the configuration that enables any device to access the switch using SSH. The RSA modulus for the switch will be set to 1024.

An example configuration follows:

```
Switch(config)# crypto key generate rsa
Enter modulus:1024
Switch(config)# ip ssh
Switch(config)# end
Switch(config)# copy running-config startup-config
```

11-8: 802.1X Port Authentication

■   On most switches, ports are enabled by default, and anyone who can plug into the port gains access to the network.

■   Port security using MAC addresses can control which devices can access a network on a given port but must be reconfigured if a device is moved.

■   802.1X provides a standard method for authorizing ports using client certificates or usernames.

■   802.1X uses a RADIUS server to provide authorization of a port for use.

■   Until an 802.1X port is authorized, it cannot be used to pass user traffic.

■   In 802.1X, the switch acts as a proxy between the client and the server to pass authentication information.

Configuration

To configure 802.1X port authentication, use the following steps.

1. The 802.1X authentication is enabled automatically.

2. Specify the RADIUS server and key:

    `(global)` **`radius-server host`** *`address`* **`key`** *`string`*

    Because the 802.1X process relies on a RADIUS server, you must configure the switch with the address of the RADIUS server and the key used on the server.

3. Create an authentication, authorization, accounting (AAA) model:

    `(global)` **`aaa new-model`**

    `(global)` **`aaa authentication dot1x default group radius`**

    You will enable 802.1X authentication by creating a AAA model using the commands listed.

4. Enable 802.1x on the port:

    `(interface)` **`dot1x port-control {auto | force-authorized | force-unauthorized}`**

    After completing the previous steps, you can configure a port for 802.1X authorization. When a port is configured for 802.1X authentication, it does not pass user traffic until a RADIUS server sends authorization for the port.

Feature Example

The following example shows the configuration for Ethernet port 3/6 to provide 802.1X authentication for a client using the RADIUS server 10.1.1.1 with a key string of **funhouse**:

```
Switch(config)# radius-server host 10.1.1.1 key funhouse
Switch(config)# aaa new-model
Switch(config)# aaa authentication dot1x default group radius
Switch(config)# interface fastethernet 3/6
Switch(config-if)# dot1x port-control auto
Switch(config-if)# end
Switch(config)# copy running-config startup-config
```

11.9: Layer 2 Security

There are different security requirements for networking devices; switches are susceptible to network attacks in different ways. These attacks include the following along with solutions to mitigate these type of attacks:

■ Switches have MAC address table sizes that are limited in size. Typically, a network intruder floods the switch with a large number of invalid source Media Access Control (MAC) addresses until the CAM table fills up. When that occurs, the switch floods all ports with incoming traffic because it cannot find the port number for a particular MAC address in the MAC table; table overflow attack can be mitigated by configuring or implementing port security on the switch. Port security provides a mechanism to specify the number of MAC addresses on a particular switch port or specify of the number of MAC addresses that can be learned by a switch port.

■ MAC spoofing attacks involve the use of a known MAC address of another host to attempt to make the target switch forward frames destined for the remote host to the network attacker; use the port security feature to mitigate MAC spoofing attacks. Port security provides the capability to specify the MAC address of the system connected to a particular port.

■ ARP is used to map IP addressing to MAC addresses in a LAN segment where hosts of the same subnet reside. Normally, a host sends out a broadcast ARP request to find the MAC address of another host with a particular IP address, and an ARP response comes from the host whose address matches the request. The requesting host then caches this ARP response. Within the ARP protocol, another provision is made for hosts to perform unsolicited ARP replies. The unsolicited ARP replies are called Gratuitous ARP (GARP), which can be exploited maliciously by an attacker to spoof the identity of an IP address on a LAN segment. This is typically used to spoof the identity between two hosts or all traffic to and from a default gateway in a "man-in-the-middle" attack. Dynamic ARP inspection determines the validity of an ARP packet based on the valid MAC address to IP address bindings stored in a DHCP snooping database. Additionally, dynamic ARP inspection can validate ARP packets based on user-configurable access control lists (ACL). This allows for the inspection of ARP packets for hosts that use statically configured IP addresses. Dynamic ARP inspection allows for the use of per-port and VLAN Access Control Lists (PACL) to limit ARP packets for specific IP addresses to specific MAC addresses.

■ A DHCP starvation attack works by the broadcast of DHCP requests with spoofed MAC addresses. If enough requests are sent, the network attacker can exhaust the address space available to the DHCP servers for a period of time. The network attacker can then set up a rogue DHCP server on his system and respond to new DHCP requests from clients on the network. DHCP snooping can be used to help guard against a DHCP starvation attack. DHCP snooping is a security feature that filters untrusted DHCP messages and builds and maintains a DHCP Snooping binding table. The binding table contains information such as the MAC address, IP address, lease time, binding type, VLAN number, and the interface information that corresponds to the local untrusted interfaces of a switch.

Port Security

You can use the port security feature to limit and identify MAC addresses of the stations allowed to access the port. This restricts input to an interface. When you assign secure MAC addresses to a secure port, the port does not forward packets with source addresses outside the group of defined addresses. If you limit the number of secure MAC addresses to one and assign a single secure MAC address, the workstation attached to that port is assured the full bandwidth of the port. If a port is configured as a secure port and the maximum number of secure MAC addresses is reached, when the MAC address of a station that attempts to access the port is different from any of the identified secure MAC addresses, a security violation occurs. Also, if a station with a secure MAC address configured or learned on one secure port attempts to access another secure port, a violation is flagged. By default, the port shuts down when the maximum number of secure MAC addresses is exceeded.

Feature Example

The port security feature is shown configured on the FastEthernet 1/0/2 interface; we allow only mac-address 0011.858D.9AF9 on interface FastEthernet 1/0/2. By default, the maximum number of secure MAC addresses for the interface is one. You can issue the **show port-security interface** command to verify the port security status for an interface:

```
switch(config)# interface fastEthernet 1/0/2
switch(config-if)# switchport mode access
switch(config-if)# switchport port-security
switch(config-if)# switchport port-security mac-address 0011.858D.9AF9
switch(config-if)# switchport port-security violation shutdown
```

Verification

Now we connect a different device into the FastEthernet 1/0/2 interface:

```
00:22:51: %PM-4-ERR_DISABLE: psecure-violation error detected on Fa1/0/2,
          putting Fa1/0/2 in err-disable state
00:22:51: %PORT_SECURITY-2-PSECURE_VIOLATION: Security violation occurred,
          caused by MAC address 0011.8565.4B75 on port FastEthernet1/0/2.
00:22:52: %LINEPROTO-5-UPDOWN: Line protocol on Interface FastEthernet1/0/2,
          changed state to down
00:22:53: %LINK-3-UPDOWN: Interface FastEthernet1/0/2, changed state to down
```

Note   With the **show error-disable** command, you can use the **errdisable recovery cause psecure-violation** global configuration command, or you can manually reenable it by entering the **shutdown** and **no shutdown** interface configuration commands.

```
switch# show port-security interface fastEthernet 1/0/2
Port Security               : Enabled
Port Status                 : Secure-shutdown
Violation Mode              : Shutdown
Aging Time                  : 0 mins
Aging Type                  : Absolute
SecureStatic Address Aging  : Disabled
Maximum MAC Addresses       : 1
Total MAC Addresses         : 1
Configured MAC Addresses    : 1
Sticky MAC Addresses        : 0
Last Source Address:Vlan    : 0011.8565.4B75:1
Security Violation Count    : 1
```

Note   Port security can only be configured on static access ports or trunk ports.

DHCP Snooping

DHCP Snooping acts like a firewall between untrusted hosts and DHCP servers. You use DHCP Snooping to differentiate between untrusted interfaces connected to the end user and trusted interfaces connected to the DHCP server or another switch. When a switch receives a packet on an untrusted interface and the interface belongs to a VLAN that has DHCP Snooping enabled, the switch compares the source MAC address and the DHCP client hardware address. If the addresses match (the default), the switch forwards the packet. If the addresses do not match, the switch drops the packet.

Tip   For DHCP Snooping to function properly, all DHCP servers must be connected to the switch through trusted interfaces.

To ensure that the lease time in the database is accurate, Cisco recommends that you enable and configure NTP.

Feature Example

The DHCP server connects to interface Fastethernet 1/0/3; all interfaces on the switch are in VLAN 1:

1.   Enable DHCP Snooping on the switch:

```
switch(config)# ip dhcp snooping vlan 1
```

Note   DHCP Snooping is not active until it is enabled on a VLAN.

2. Configure the interface connected to the DHCP server as trusted:

```
switch(config)# interface fastEthernet 1/0/3

switch(config-if)# ip dhcp snooping trust
```

Verification

1. Display the DHCP Snooping configuration for the switch:

```
switch# show ip dhcp snooping

Switch DHCP snooping is enabled

DHCP snooping is configured on following VLANs:1

Insertion of option 82 is disabled

Option 82 on untrusted port is not allowed

Verification of hwaddr field is enabled

Interface               Trusted      Rate limit (pps)

– – – – – – – – – – –    – – –·      – – – – – – – –

FastEthernet1/0/3         yes         unlimited
```

2. Display the DHCP Snooping binding entries for the switch:

```
switch# show ip dhcp snooping binding

MacAddress          IpAddress    Lease   Type          VLAN Interface
                                 (sec)

– – – – – – – – –    – – – – –    – – –   – – – – – –·   – –  – – – – – –

00:11:85:A5:7B:F5    10.0.0.2     86391   dhcp-snooping  1   FastEthernet1/0/1

00:11:85:8D:9A:F9    10.0.0.3     86313   dhcp-snooping  1   FastEthernet1/0/2

Total number of bindings: 2
```

Note   DHCP servers connected to the untrusted port cannot assign IP addresses to the clients.

Dynamic ARP Inspection

Dynamic ARP inspection is a security feature that validates ARP packets in a network. It intercepts, logs, and discards ARP packets with invalid IP-to-MAC address bindings. This capability protects the network from certain man-in-the-middle attacks. Dynamic ARP inspection ensures that only valid ARP requests and responses are relayed. The switch performs these activities:

- Intercepts all ARP requests and responses on untrusted ports

- Verifies that each of these intercepted packets has a valid IP-to-MAC address binding before it updates the local ARP cache or before it forwards the packet to the appropriate destination

- Drops invalid ARP packets

Dynamic ARP inspection determines the validity of an ARP packet based on valid IP-to-MAC address bindings stored in a trusted database, the DHCP Snooping binding database. This database is built by DHCP Snooping if DHCP Snooping is enabled on the VLANs and on the switch. If the ARP packet is received on a trusted interface, the switch forwards the packet without any checks. On untrusted interfaces, the switch forwards the packet only if it is valid. In non-DHCP environments, dynamic ARP inspection can validate ARP packets against user-configured ARP ACLs for hosts with statically configured IP addresses. You can issue the **arp access-list** global configuration command to define an ARP ACL. ARP ACLs take precedence over entries in the DHCP Snooping binding database. The switch uses ACLs only if you issue the **ip arp inspection filter vlan** global configuration command to configure the ACLs. The switch first compares ARP packets to user-configured ARP ACLs. If the ARP ACL denies the ARP packet, the switch also denies the packet even if a valid binding exists in the database populated by DHCP Snooping.

Feature Example

1. Enable dynamic ARP inspection on the VLAN:

   ```
   switch(config)# ip arp inspection vlan 1
   ```

2. Configure the interface connected to the DHCP server as trusted:

   ```
   switch(config)# interface fastEthernet 1/0/3

   switch(config-if)# ip arp inspection trust
   ```

Verification

```
switch# show ip arp inspection vlan 1
Source Mac Validation      : Disabled
Destination Mac Validation : Disabled
IP Address Validation      : Disabled
   Vlan    Configuration    Operation    ACL Match            Static ACL
   ――      ――――――.          ――――.        ――――.                ――――
     1      Enabled          Active


   Vlan    ACL Logging      DHCP Logging
   ――      ――――.            ―――――
     1      Deny             Deny
```

Further Reading

Refer to the following recommended sources for further information about the topics covered in this chapter.

Clark, Kennedy and Kevin Hamilton. *Cisco LAN Switching*. Cisco Press, ISBN 157870-094-9.

Froom, Richard, Balaji Sivasubramanian, and Erum Frahim. *Building Cisco Multilayer Switched Networks (BCMSN) (Authorized Self-Study Guide)*, Fourth Edition. Cisco Press, ISBN 158705-273-3.

Hucaby, Dave. *CCNP BCMSN Official Exam Certification Guide*, Fourth Edition. Cisco Press, ISBN 1-58720-171-2.

Hucaby, Dave and Steve McQuerry. *Cisco Field Manual: Router Configuration*. Cisco Press, ISBN 1-58705-024-2.

Chapter 12

Switch Management

See the following sections to configure and use these topics:

- **12-1: Logging:** Covers the steps needed to configure a variety of methods to log messages from a switch

- **12-2: Simple Network Management Protocol:** Presents information on how to configure a switch to use network management protocols

- **12-3: Switched Port Analyzer:** Explains how to mirror switch traffic for network analysis, either locally or from a remote switch

- **12-4: Power Management:** Covers the commands for managing power to the chassis and modules

- **12-5: Environmental Monitoring:** Covers the commands for displaying switch temperature information

- **12-6: Packet Tracing:** Discusses several methods for tracing both Layer 2 and Layer 3 packets through a network. From a switch, you can test connectivity to a remote host

12-1: Logging

- Logging is used by the switch to send system messages to a logging facility.

- Logging messages can be sent to any of four different facilities: the switch console, a file on the switch, Telnet sessions, or a syslog server.

- Logging history can be maintained in a file to ensure that a record of the messages sent to *Simple Network Management Protocol (SNMP)* or syslog servers are kept in case a packet is lost or dropped.

- Logging displays all error and debug messages by default. The logging level can be set to determine which messages should be sent to each of the facilities.

- Timestamping logging messages or setting the syslog source address can help in real-time debugging and management. If the time and date are set on a switch, the switch can provide timestamps with each syslog message. The clocks in all switches can be synchronized so that it becomes easier to correlate syslog messages from several devices.

- System messages are logged with the following format:

    - `timestamp %function-severity-MNEMONIC:description`

    where the `timestamp` denotes the time of the event, `%function` is the switch function (also called facility) generating the event, `severity` is the severity level (0 to 7, lower is more severe) of the event, and `MNEMONIC` is a text string that briefly describes the event. A more detailed `description` text string completes the message.

    An example of a severity level 3 Supervisor IOS system message follows:

    - `11w1d: %LINK-3-UPDOWN: Interface FastEthernet0/10, changed state to up`

    An example of a severity level 5 Catalyst OS system message is as follows:

    - `2001 Dec 20 11:44:19 %DTP-5-NONTRUNKPORTON:Port 5/4 has become non-trunk`

Note   Logging to a syslog server uses UDP port 514.

Configuration

1. *(Optional)* Enable or disable logging:

   `(global) [no] logging on`

   Logging is enabled by default. Use the **no** keyword to disable all logging on the switch, except for logging to the console.

2. *(Optional)* Log messages to a syslog server.

   a. Identify the syslog server:

   `(global) logging syslog-host`

   Text messages are sent to the syslog server at *syslog-host* (hostname or IP address). The messages are captured and can be reviewed on the syslog server.

   b. Send messages to a syslog facility:

   `(global) logging facility facility-type`

When the syslog server receives a message, it forwards the message to a log file or destination based on the originating system facility. In this fashion, syslog servers can collect and organize messages by using the facility as service area or type. All syslog messages from switches can be collected together if the facility is set identically in each switch.

Syslog servers are based around UNIX operating system concepts and have facility types that are named after various system services. The facility used in switch syslog messages is defined as *facility-type*, given as one of **local0**, **local1**, **local2**, **local3**, **local4**, **local5**, **local6**, **local7** (the default), which all represent locally defined services. Usually, one or more local facilities are used for messages from network devices.

The Supervisor IOS also allows these additional facility types: **auth** (user authentication services), **cron** (job scheduling services), **daemon** (system background or daemon services), **kern** (system kernel services), **lpr** (line printer spooler services), **mail** (system mail services), **news** (Usenet newsgroup services), **syslog** (syslog services), **sys9**, **sys10**, **sys11**, **sys12**, **sys13**, **sys14** (all reserved for system services), **user** (system user processes), or **uucp** (UNIX-to-UNIX copy file transfer services).

c. Limit the severity of the logged messages:

(global) **logging trap** *level*

System messages are assigned a severity level based on the type and importance of the error condition. Only messages that are less than or equal to (at least as severe as) the severity level are sent to the syslog server. Table 12-1 defines the level, which is a number (0 to 7, default 6).

Table 12-1 *Message Logging Level Keywords*

Level Keyword	Level	Description	Syslog Definition
emergencies	0	System unstable	LOG_EMERG
alerts	1	Immediate action needed	LOG_ALERT
critical	2	Critical conditions	LOG_CRIT
errors	3	Error conditions	LOG_ERR
warnings	4	Warning conditions	LOG_WARNING
notifications	5	Normal but significant condition	LOG_NOTICE
informational	6	Informational messages only	LOG_INFO
debugging	7	Debugging messages	LOG_DEBUG

The Supervisor IOS also enables you to enter the *level* as a name. Most physical state transitions (ports and modules up or down) are logged at level 5, whereas hardware or software malfunctions are reported at level 3.

d. *(Optional; IOS only)* Use a specific source address for syslog messages:

```
(global) logging source-interface type number
```

An IOS switch can use the IP address of a specific interface as the source address in syslog packets. This can be useful if there are many interfaces, but you want to see all syslog messages from a switch appear as a single switch address.

e. *(Optional)* Limit the messages logged to the SNMP history table:

```
(global) logging history level
```

```
(global) logging history size number
```

Messages sent as traps to an SNMP management station can be lost. Therefore, messages that are less than or equal to the specified severity level can also be saved to a history table for future review. The *level* is a number (0 to 7) defined in Table 12-1. By default, only one message is kept in the history table. You can change this by specifying the **size** keyword with the *number* of message entries (1 to 500).

3. *(Optional)* Log messages to the switch buffer:

```
(global) logging buffered [size]
```

All system messages are saved in a section of switch memory. The message buffer remains intact until the switch is powered off or the buffer is cleared with the **clear logging** command. The maximum buffer size can be given as *size*; Supervisor IOS: 4096 to 2,147,483,647 bytes, default 4096 bytes.

Caution   The buffer size varies between Catalyst switch platforms. By logging to a buffer on a Supervisor IOS switch, you can use system resources that can also be needed for the operational aspects of the switch. Be prudent when setting the maximum buffer size so that you don't waste system memory.

4. *(Optional; IOS only)* Log messages to a file on the switch:

```
(global) logging file [flash:]filename [max-file-size] [min-file-size] level
```

System messages are stored to a file named *filename* (text string) located on the system **flash:** device. The file can be constrained to a maximum size *max-file-size* (4096 to 2,147,483,647 bytes, default 4096) and a minimum size *min-file-size* (1024 to 2,147,483,647 bytes, default 2048). Messages with a severity level less than or equal to *level* (0 to 7 or a name from Table 12-1, default 7 or **debugging**) are appended to the file.

5. *(Optional)* Log messages to terminal sessions.

    a. *(Optional)* Log messages to the switch console:

```
(global) logging console level
```

       By default, system messages are logged to the console. You can disable logging with the **disable** keyword. On an IOS switch, only messages with a severity level less than or equal to *level* (0 to 7 or a name from Table 12-1, default 7 or **debugging**) are sent to the console.

    b. *(Optional)* Log messages to a Telnet or line session:

```
(global) logging monitor level
```

       By default system messages are logged to all Telnet and terminal line sessions. Only messages with a severity level less than or equal to *level* (0 to 7 or a name from Table 12-1, default 7 or **debugging**) are sent to the session.

Note   To view system messages during a Telnet or SSH session to a vty line on a switch, you must issue the **terminal monitor** EXEC command.

    c. *(Optional)* Control the output of messages to terminal sessions:

```
(line) logging synchronous [level level | all] [limit buffers]
```

       When synchronous logging is enabled, logging messages are queued until solicited output (regular output from **show** or configuration commands, for example) is displayed. When a command prompt is displayed, logging output will be displayed. Synchronization can be used on messages at or below a specific severity *level* (0 to 7 or a name from Table 12-1; default 2) or **all** levels. With the **limit** keyword, the switch can queue up to *buffer* (default 20) messages before they are dropped from the queue.

Tip   Although synchronous logging keeps switch messages from interfering with your typing or reading other displayed text, it can also be confusing. When synchronous logging is enabled on the switch console line and no one is currently logged in to the switch, for example, the switch queues all messages until the next person logs in. That person sees a flurry of messages scroll by, possibly from hours or days before.

6. *(Optional)* Record a timestamp with each system message:

```
(global) service timestamps log {uptime | datetime}
```

    By default, a switch records the system uptime. To use the date and time, use the **datetime** keyword. This can prove useful if you need to reference an error condition to the actual time that it occurred.

Tip   You should configure and set the correct time, date, and time zone on the switch before relying on the message logging timestamps. Refer to section "3-8: Time and Calendar" in Chapter 3, "Supervisor Engine Configuration," for further information.

7.   *(Optional)* Control the rate of system message generation:

(global) `logging rate-limit` *number* [`all` | `console`] [`except` *level*]

To avoid flooding system messages to a logging destination, you can limit the rate that the messages are sent to *number* (1 to 10,000 messages per second, no default). The **all** keyword rate limits all messages, whereas the **console** keyword rate limits only messages that are sent to the console. You can use the **except** keyword to rate-limit messages at or below the specified *level* (0 to 7 as given in Table 12-1).

Logging Example

A switch is configured for logging to a syslog server at 192.168.254.91. By default, the local7 facility is used, with messages that are at level 6, or informational, or less. The switch buffers up to 64 Kb characters of message text.

The switch prepends date and time timestamps to each logged message:

(global) `logging 192.168.254.91`
(global) `logging buffered 65536`
(global) `service timestamps log datetime`

Displaying Information About Logging

Table 12-2 lists some switch commands that you can use to display helpful information about system logging.

12-2: Simple Network Management Protocol

- Simple Network Management Protocol (SNMP) is a protocol that enables the monitoring of information about and management of a network device.

- A Management Information Base (MIB) is a collection of variables stored on a network device. The variables can be updated by the device or queried from an external source.

Table 12-2   *Switch Commands to Display System Logging Information*

Display Function	Command
Logging configuration	(exec) **show logging**
System messages	(exec) **show logging**

- MIBs are structured according to the SNMP MIB module language, which is based on the Abstract Syntax Notation One (ASN.1) language.

- An SNMP agent runs on a network device and maintains the various MIB variables. Any update or query of the variables must be handled through the agent.

- An SNMP agent can also send unsolicited messages, or traps, to an SNMP manager. Traps alert the manager of changing conditions on the network device.

- An SNMP manager is usually a network management system that queries MIB variables, can set MIB variables, and receives traps from a collection of network devices.

- SNMP agents can send either traps or inform requests. Traps are sent in one direction and are unreliable. Inform requests are reliable in the sense that they must be acknowledged or be re-sent.

- SNMP version 1 (SNMPv1) is the original version. It is based on RFC 1157 and has only basic clear text community strings for security. Access can also be limited to the IP address of the SNMP manager.

- SNMP version 2 (SNMPv2) is an enhanced version, based on RFCs 1901, 1905, and 1906. It improves on bulk information retrieval and error reporting but uses the clear-text community strings and IP addresses to provide security.

- SNMP version 3 (SNMPv3) is based on RFCs 2273 to 2275 and offers robust security. Data integrity and authentication can be provided through usernames, Message Digest 5 (MD5), and Security Hash Algorithm (SHA) algorithms, and encryption through Data Encryption Standard (DES).

Note SNMP requests and responses are sent using UDP port 161. Notifications or traps are sent using UDP port 162.

- Remote Monitoring (RMON) provides a view of traffic flowing through a switch port. IOS switches can also provide RMON alarms and events. RMON support provides nine management groups as defined in RFC 1757: Statistics (group 1), History (group 2), Alarms (group 3), Hosts (group 4), hostTopN (group 5), Matrix (group 6), Filter (group 7), Capture (group 8), and Event (group 9). RMON2 support, in RFC 2021, adds two groups: UsrHistory (group 18) and ProbeConfig (group 19).

- When RMON is enabled, a switch collects data internally. Therefore, the RMON data cannot be viewed from the switch command-line interface (CLI) but must be polled through a network management system (NMS).

Configuration

1. Configure the SNMP identity.

   a. Define the contact information:

   ```
   (global) snmp-server contact contact-string
   ```

The *contact-string* contains text information that the router can provide about the network administrator. If the string is omitted, it is cleared.

b. Define the device location:

```
(global) snmp-server location location-string
```

The *location-string* is text information that the router can provide about its physical location. If the string is omitted, it is cleared.

c. Define the device serial number:

```
(global) snmp-server chassis-id id-string
```

The *id-string* is text information that the router can provide about its own serial number. If the hardware serial number can be read by Cisco IOS Software, this number is the default chassis ID.

2. Configure SNMP access.

a. *(Optional)* Define SNMP views to restrict access to MIB objects:

```
(global) snmp-server view view-name oid-tree {included | excluded}
```

If necessary, an SNMP manager can be limited to view only specific parts of the switch's MIB tree. You can define a view with the name *view-name*. The *oid-tree* value is the object identifier of the MIB subtree in ASN.1 format. This value is a text string with numbers or words representing the subtree, separated by periods (that is, *system*, *cisco*, *system.4*, *1.*.2.3*). You can use wildcards (asterisks) with any component of the subtree. Viewing access of the subtree is either permitted or denied with the **included** and **excluded** keywords.

Multiple views can be defined, each applied to a different set of users or SNMP managers.

The view can be stored in either **volatile** or **nonvolatile** (preserved across power cycles) memory.

b. Define access methods for remote users.

- *(SNMPv1 or SNMPv2c only)* Define community strings to allow access:

```
(global) snmp-server community string [view view] [ro | rw] acc-list
```

A community string value *string* permits access to SNMP information on the switch. Any SNMP manager that presents a matching community string is permitted access. You can specify an optional view with the **view** keyword. Access is then limited to only the MIB objects permitted by the view definition.

Access is granted as read-only or read-write with the **ro** / **read-only** (default community, "public," can't read the community strings), **rw** / **read-write** (default community, "private," can write any MIB object except community strings), and **read-write-all** (default community, "secret," can write any MIB object) keywords.

Optional standard IP access list *acc-list* can be given to further limit access only to SNMP managers with permitted IP addresses. Access can be defined for read-only and read-write SNMP modes. Refer to section "11-6: Access Class" in Chapter 11, "Controlling Traffic and Switch Access," for more information about the IP permit command.

Section 12-2

> **Tip**   You should strongly consider changing the default SNMP community strings on all switches. Leaving the default values active can make it easier for unauthorized people to gain access to your switch's activity and configuration. After you change the community strings to unique values, restrict SNMP access to only the IP addresses of the network management hosts under your control.

- *(SNMPv3 only)* Define names for the engine IDs.

  To specify the local engine ID name, enter the following commands:

  ```
  (global) snmp-server engineID [local id-string] | [remote ip-address
     udp-port port id-string]
  ```

  SNMPv3 uses authentication and encryption based on several parameters. Each end of the SNMP trust relationship must be defined, in the form of engine ID text strings, *id-string*. These values are 24-character strings but can be specified with shorter strings that are filled to the right with zeros. The local switch running SNMP must be defined with the **local** keyword and *id-string*.

- To specify the remote SNMP engine ID name, enter the following command:

  ```
  (global) snmp-server engineID remote ip-address [udp-port port] id-string
  ```

  The remote SNMP engine (an SNMP instance on a remote host or management station) is defined with an *ip-address* and a text string name *id-string*. An optional UDP port to use for the remote host can be given with the **udp-port** keyword (default 161).

> **Note**   If either local or remote engine ID names change after these commands are used, the authentication keys become invalid, and users must be reconfigured. MD5 and SHA keys are based on user passwords and the engine IDs.

- *(Optional)* Define a group access template for SNMP users:

  ```
  (global) snmp-server group [groupname {v1 | v2c | v3 {auth | noauth}}] [read
     readview] [write writeview] [notify notifyview] [access acc-list]
  ```

  The template *groupname* defines the security policy to be used for groups of SNMP users. The SNMP version used by the group is set by the **v1**, **v2c**, and **v3** keywords. For SNMPv3, the security level must also be specified as **auth** (packet authentication, no encryption), **noauth** (no packet authentication), or **priv** (packet authentication with encryption).

You can also specify SNMP views to limit MIB access for the group, using the keywords **read** (view *readview* defines readable objects; defaults to all Internet 1.3.6.1 OID space), **write** (view *writeview* defines writeable objects; no default write access), and **notify** (view *notifyview* defines notifications that can be sent to the group; no default). You can use an optional standard IP access list *acc-list* to further limit SNMP access for the group.

■ *(Optional)* Define SNMP users and access methods.

For SNMPv1 or SNMPv2c, apply a user to a group by entering the following:

```
(global) snmp-server user username groupname [remote ip-address] {v1|v2c}
[access acc-list]
```

A user *username* is defined to belong to the group template *groupname*. The IP address of the remote SNMP manager where the user belongs can be specified with the **remote** keyword. The version of SNMP must be specified with the **v1** or **v2c** keywords. You can use a standard IP access with the **access** keyword to enable only specific source addresses for the SNMP user.

For SNMPv3, apply a user to a group and security policies by entering the following:

```
(global) snmp-server user username groupname [remote ip-address] v3
[encrypted] [auth {md5|sha} auth-password] [access acc-list]
```

A user *username* is defined to belong to the group template *groupname*. The IP address of the remote SNMP manager where the user belongs can be specified with the **remote** keyword. SNMP version 3 must be specified with the **v3** keyword. You can use a standard IP access list with the **access** keyword to enable only specific source addresses for the SNMP user.

By default passwords for the user are input as text strings. If the **encrypted** keyword is given, passwords must be input as MD5 digests (already encrypted). An authentication password for the user is specified with the **auth** keyword, the type of authentication as keywords **md5** (HMAC-MD5-96 Message Digest 5) or **sha** (HMAC-SHA-96), and a text string *auth-password* (up to 64 characters).

c. *(Optional)* Limit the switch operations controlled by SNMP.

■ Enable use of the SNMP reload operation:

```
(global) snmp-server system-shutdown
```

By default, you cannot use SNMP to issue a reload operation to the switch. If this function is desired, you can use this command to enable reload control.

- Specify the TFTP server operations controlled by SNMP:

  `(global) snmp-server tftp-server-list` *acc-list*

  You can use SNMP to cause the switch to save or load its configuration file to a TFTP server. You can use the standard IP access list *acc-list* to permit only a limited set of TFTP server IP addresses.

3. *(Optional)* Configure SNMP notifications.

   a. Define a global list of notifications to send:

      `(global) snmp-server enable {traps [`*type*`] [`*option*`] | informs}`

      Notifications (both traps and informs) are enabled for the types specified. Because only one type can be given with this command, you can issue the command as many times as necessary. If the *type* keyword is not specified, all available notifications are enabled. In addition, if this command is not issued at least once, none of the notifications that it controls are enabled.

      The possible choices for *type* are **c2900** (notifications based on the Catalyst 2900 series), **cluster** (cluster management changes), **config** (configuration changes), **entity** (entity MIB changes), **hsrp** (HSRP state changes), **vlan-membership** (changes in a port's VLAN membership), and **vtp** (VLAN Trunking Protocol events). For the *type* **snmp** (basic router status changes), the *option* keyword can also be given as **authentication** (authentication failures), **linkup** (interface has come up), **linkdown** (interface has gone down), or **coldstart** (router is reinitializing). If none of these keywords are given, all of them are enabled.

   b. Define recipients of notifications:

      `(global) snmp-server host` *host* `[traps | informs] [version {1 | 2c | 3 [auth | noauth]}]` *community-string* `[udp-port` *port*`] [`*type*`]`

      A single host (*host* is either IP address or hostname) is specified to receive SNMP notifications (either **traps** or **informs**). The SNMP version can optionally be given as SNMPv1 (**1**, the default), SNMPv2c (**2c**), or SNMPv3 (**3**). If SNMPv3, a keyword can be given to select the type of security: **auth** (use MD5 and SHA authentication) or **noauth** (no authentication or privacy; the default).

      The *community-string* keyword specifies a "password" that is shared between the SNMP agent and SNMP manager. The UDP port used can be given as *port* (default 162).

      The possible choices for *type* are **c2900** (notifications based on the Catalyst 2900 series), **cluster** (cluster management changes), **config** (configuration changes), **entity** (entity MIB changes), **hsrp** (HSRP state changes), **vlan-membership** (changes in a port's VLAN membership), and **vtp** (VLAN Trunking Protocol events). For the *type* **snmp** (basic switch status changes), the *option* keyword can also be given as **authentication** (authentication failures), **linkup** (interface has come up), **linkdown** (interface has gone down), or **coldstart** (switch is reinitializing). If none of these keywords are given, all of them are enabled.

c. *(Optional)* Tune notification parameters.

- Specify trap options:

  (global) **snmp-server trap-timeout** *seconds*

  (global) **snmp-server queue-length** *length*

  SNMP traps are not sent reliably because no acknowledgment is required. Traps can be queued and re-sent only when no route to the trap recipient is present. In that case, the router waits *seconds* (default 30 seconds) before retransmitting the trap. In addition, ten traps can be queued for each recipient by default. You can use the **queue-length** command to set the queue size to *length* traps each.

- Specify the source address to use for notifications:

  (global) **snmp-server trap-source** *interface*

  SNMP traps can be sent from any available switch interface. To have the switch send all traps using a single source IP address, specify the *interface* to use. In this way, traps can be easily associated with the source switch.

d. *(Optional)* Enable SNMP link traps on specific interfaces:

(interface) **[no] snmp trap link-status**

By default, generate SNMP link traps on all interfaces when they go up or down. If this is not desired, use the **no** keyword to disable traps on specific interfaces. The default for IOS switches is to **disable** traps on all ports.

4. *(Optional)* Enable RMON support.

a. *(Optional)* Collect RMON statistics:

(interface) **rmon collection stats** *index* [*owner name*]

A switch collects RMON statistics only on the configured interfaces. Statistics are gathered in "collections," each uniquely identified by a collection number or *index* (1 to 65535). An optional owner *name* (text string) can be given to associate a username with the collection.

b. *(Optional)* Collect RMON history statistics:

(interface) **rmon collection history** *index* [**owner** *name*] [**buckets** *nbuckets*] [**interval** *seconds*]

A switch can collect history statistics on the configured interfaces. Statistics are gathered in "collections," each uniquely identified by a collection number or *index* (1 to 65535). An optional owner *name* (text string) can be given to associate a username with the collection. The **buckets** keyword defines the number of collection buckets to be used (default 50). The **interval** keyword specifies the number of seconds (default 1800 seconds) during the polling cycle.

c. *(Optional)* Define an RMON alarm:

```
(global) rmon alarm number object interval {delta | absolute} rising-
   threshold rise [event] falling-threshold fall [event] [owner string]
```

An alarm indexed by *number* (1 to 65535) is configured to monitor a specific MIB variable *object*. The object is given as a dotted-decimal value, in the form of *entry.integer.instance*. The *interval* field specifies the number of seconds (1 to 4294967295) that the alarm monitors the object. The **delta** keyword watches a change between MIB variables, whereas **absolute** watches a MIB variable directly. You can configure the alarm to test the object against a **rising-threshold** and a **falling-threshold**, where *rise* and *fall* are the threshold values that trigger the alarm. The *event* field specifies an event number in an event table to trigger for the rising and falling thresholds. An optional **owner** text string can be given, as the owner of the alarm.

d. *(Optional)* Define an RMON event:

```
(global) rmon event number [description string] [owner name] [trap
   community] [log]
```

An RMON event is identified by an arbitrary *number* (1 to 65535). The **description** keyword gives the event a descriptive *string* (text string). An optional event **owner** can be assigned as *name* (text string). If the **trap** keyword is given, an SNMP trap is generated with the *community* string (text string). The **log** keyword causes the event to generate an RMON log entry on the switch.

SNMP Example

A switch is configured for SNMP, using community *public* for read-only access and community *noc-team* for read-write access. SNMP access is limited to any host in the 172.30.0.0 network for read-only, and to network management hosts 172.30.5.91 and 172.30.5.95 for read-write access. (This is possible with access lists.)

SNMP traps are sent to an SNMP agent machine at 172.30.5.93, using community string *nms*. All possible traps are sent, except for switch configuration change traps. Also SNMP link up/down traps are disabled for port 3/1:

```
(global) snmp-server contact John Doe, Network Operations
(global) snmp-server location Building A, closet 123
(global) snmp-server community public ro 5
(global) snmp-server community noc-team rw 6

(global) snmp-server host 172.30.5.93 traps nms
(global) snmp-server enable traps
(global) no snmp-server enable config

(global) access-list 5 permit 172.30.0.0 0.0.255.255
```

```
(global) access-list 6 permit host 172.30.5.91
(global) access-list 6 permit host 172.30.5.95

(global) interface gig 3/1
(interface) no snmp trap link-status
```

Displaying Information About SNMP

Table 12-3 lists some switch commands that you can use to display helpful information about SNMP.

Table 12-3　*Switch Commands to Display SNMP Information*

Display Function	Command
SNMP configuration	(exec) **show snmp**
RMON collections	(exec) **show rmon** [**alarms**|**events**|**history**|**statistics**]

12-3: Switched Port Analyzer

- *Switched Port Analyzer (SPAN)* mirrors traffic from one or more source switch ports or a source VLAN to a destination port. This allows a monitoring device such as a network analyzer to be attached to the destination port for capturing traffic.

- SPAN source and destination ports must reside on the same physical switch.

- Multiple SPAN sessions can be configured to provide several simultaneous monitors.

- *Remote SPAN* (RSPAN) provides traffic mirroring from a source on one switch to a destination on one or more remote switches.

- RSPAN is carried from source to destination over a special RSPAN VLAN.

Note　What happens if a speed mismatch occurs between the SPAN source and destination ports? During a SPAN session, a switch merely copies the packets from the source and places them into the output queue of the destination port. If the destination port becomes congested, the SPAN packets are dropped from the queue and are not seen at the destination. Traffic from the SPAN source then is not affected by any congestion at the SPAN destination.

SPAN Configuration

1.　Create a SPAN session.

- *(Catalyst 2900/3500 only)* Select the source and destination:

```
(global) interface dest-interface

(interface) port monitor [src-interface | vlan src-vlan]
```

The source of traffic for the SPAN session can be either switch ports or VLANs. If switch ports are to be monitored, they are identified as *src-interface* (only a single interface type and number).

If a VLANs is to be monitored, it is identified as *src-vlan*.

The SPAN destination port, where the monitoring device is connected, is selected by the **interface** *dest-interface* command before the **port monitor** command is applied. The destination port must belong to the same VLAN as the source.

Switches inherently monitor traffic in both directions.

- Select the source and destination.

a. Select the session source:

```
(global) monitor session session {source {interface interface} | {vlan
vlan-id}} [, | - | rx | tx | both]
```

The SPAN session is uniquely identified by *session* (**1** or **2**). The source can be an *interface* (an interface type and number or a port-channel number) or a VLAN number *vlan-id* (1 to 1005). Multiple source VLANs can be given by using the **vlan** keyword followed by *vlan-id* numbers separated by commas (,). To specify a range of VLAN numbers, use the **vlan** keyword followed by the first and last *vlan-id* numbers, separated by a dash (-).

- Source traffic to be monitored can be one of **rx** (traffic received at the source), **tx** (traffic transmitted from the source), or **both** (the default).

b. Select the session destination:

```
(global) monitor session session {destination {interface interface} [, |
-] | {vlan vlan-id}}
```

The destination for the SPAN *session* (session number **1** or **2**) can be an *interface* (interface type and number) or a VLAN number *vlan-id* (1 to 1005). Multiple destinations can also be specified, if needed. These can be given with the **interface** keyword, followed by a list of *interface* numbers separated by commas (,). To specify a range of interfaces, use the **interface** keyword followed by the first and last *interface* numbers, separated by a dash (-).

c. *(Optional)* Filter VLANs on a trunk source:

```
(global) monitor session session filter vlan vlan-id} [, | -]
```

If a trunk is used as a source port, you can filter the trunk to select specific VLANs to be monitored. A VLAN number is identified as *vlan-id* (1 to 1005). Multiple source VLANs can be given with the **vlan** keyword, followed by a list of *vlan-id* numbers separated by commas (,). To specify a range of VLANs, use the **vlan** keyword followed by the first and last *vlan-id* numbers, separated by a dash (-).

Section 12-3

2. *(Optional)* Disable a SPAN session:

    `(global) no monitor session session`

    SPAN sessions can be disabled individually, referenced by by *session* number.

RSPAN Configuration

1. Create one or more VLANs to be used by RSPAN:

    `(config)vlan vlan_ID{[-vlan_ID]|[,vlan_ID])`

    `(config-vlan) remote-span`

    The VLAN number *vlan-id* (1 to 1000, 1025 to 4094) should be created on all
    switches from the RSPAN source to the RSPAN destination. As well, the RSPAN
    VLAN should be trunked end-to-end because it carries the remotely monitored traf-
    fic. Create a different RSPAN VLAN for each RSPAN session that you will be using.
    See Chapter 6, "VLANs and Trunking," for more configuration information related
    to VLANs and VTP.

Note   Notice the use of the **rspan** keyword when the RSPAN VLAN is created. This must
be used so that the VLAN can correctly carry the RSPAN traffic. An RSPAN-capable
switch floods the RSPAN packets out all its ports belonging to the RSPAN VLAN to send
them toward the RSPAN destination. This is because a switch participating in RSPAN has
no idea where the destination is located.

Otherwise, if the switch were using a regular VLAN, it would try to forward the RSPAN
packets on ports where the packet destination addresses were detected, something quite
different from RSPAN altogether! This is why all switches involved in the end-to-end
RSPAN path must be RSPAN-capable.

Tip   Create and maintain the RSPAN VLAN for the special monitoring purpose. Don't
allow any normal hosts to join the RSPAN VLAN.

Ideally, all the switches belong to a common VTP domain so that the VLAN can be created
on a VTP server and propagated to all other switches. VTP pruning also prunes the RSPAN
VLAN from unnecessary trunks, limiting the traffic impact in unrelated areas of the network.

Be aware that RSPAN traffic can increase the traffic load on a trunk, even though RSPAN
is restricted to one special VLAN in the trunk. If the additional load is significant, the normal and monitored traffic contends with each other for available bandwidth, and both
could suffer.

2. *(Source switches only)* Select the monitor sources:

```
(config) monitor session session_number source {{single_interface |
interface_list | interface_range | mixed_interface_list | single_vlan |
vlan_list | vlan_range | mixed_vlan_list} [rx | tx | both]} | {remote vlan
rspan_vlan_ID}}
```

The RSPAN source is identified as one or more physical switch ports *src-mod/src-ports*, as one or more VLAN numbers *vlans*. This is performed only on the switch where the source is connected. The RSPAN VLAN number to be used is *rspan-vlan* (1 to 1000, 1025 to 4094). The direction of the monitored traffic can be **rx** (traffic received at the source), **tx** (traffic transmitted from the source), or **both** (the default).

By default multicast traffic is monitored as it exits from the source. To disable this behavior, use the **multicast disable** keywords.

If a trunk is used as a source port, you can filter the trunk to select specific VLANs to be monitored by using the **filter** *vlans* (one or a range of VLAN numbers) keywords.

Tip   You can configure more than one active RSPAN session at the source switch. The first session is created as previously shown. To create subsequent sessions, use the **create** keyword. If **create** is omitted, the newly configured session overwrites the first session. You should use a different RSPAN VLAN for each session.

3. (Destination switches only) Select the destinations:

```
monitor session session_number destination {single_interface | interface_list
| interface_range | mixed_interface_list} | {remote vlan rspan_vlan_ID}}
```

The RSPAN destination port, where the monitoring device is connected, is identified as *mod/port*. This is performed only on the switch where the destination port resides.

The destination port is normally used for a traffic-capturing device, so inbound traffic on the destination port is not allowed by default. If needed, you can enable normal switching of inbound traffic at the destination with the **inpkts enable** keywords.

Note   RSPAN differs from SPAN in that the destination port always has the STP enabled. This prevents bridging loops from accidentally forming if other network devices are connected to the destination port. However, this also means that you can't monitor STP BPDUs with RSPAN.

By default the MAC addresses from inbound packets on the destination port are learned because they are on any switch port. You can disable address learning on the destination with the **learning disable** keywords.

> **Tip**   You also can configure more than one active RSPAN session at the destination switch. The first session is created as shown previously. To create subsequent sessions, use the **create** keyword. If **create** is omitted, the newly configured session overwrites the first session. You should use a different RSPAN VLAN for each session.

   4.   *(Intermediate switches only)* No further configuration is needed.

   The switches in the path from RSPAN source to destination do not need to know about any specific RSPAN configuration. After all the RSPAN VLANs have been created end-to-end, the intermediate switches flood the RSPAN traffic correctly toward the destinations. Remember that all the intermediate switches must be RSPAN-capable.

   5.   *(Optional)* Disable an RSPAN session:

   ```
   (config)no monitor session {session_number | all | local | range
   session_range[[,session_range],...] | remote}
   ```

   You can disable an RSPAN session when it is no longer needed. Source sessions are identified by the *rspan-vlan* (VLAN number) or the **all** keyword. Destination sessions are identified by the destination port as *mod/port* or the **all** keyword.

SPAN Examples

Network analyzer A (a "sniffer") is connected to a Catalyst switch port 5/1 and monitors all traffic on VLAN 58.

A PC connects to port 4/39 and a file server to port 2/4 of a Catalyst switch. Network analyzer B connects to port 5/48. The switch is configured for a SPAN session that allows the analyzer to capture all traffic to and from the server. Figure 12-1 shows a network diagram of the two SPAN sessions with the configuration following.

```
(global) monitor session 1 source vlan 58 both
(global) monitor session 1 destination interface fast 5/1
(global) monitor session 2 source interface fast 5/48 both
(global) monitor session 2 destination interface fast 2/4
```

Figure 12-2 shows a network of three switches. A file server is connected to Catalyst B port 3/1. A network analyzer connects to Catalyst C port 5/48. Catalyst A connects Catalysts B and C by two trunk ports. RSPAN VLAN 901 carries all the RSPAN traffic from the source to the destination. (Assume for this example that Catalyst B is the VTP server for the domain of three switches.)

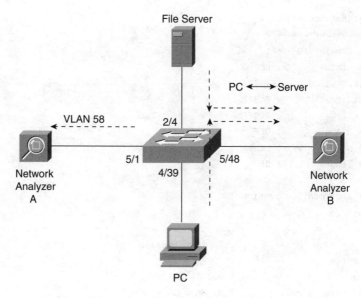

Figure 12-1   *Network Diagram for the SPAN Example*

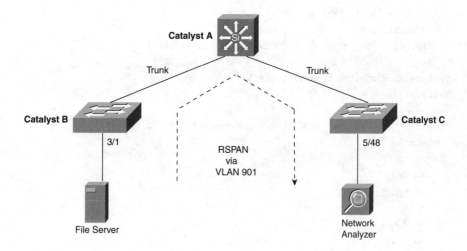

Figure 12-2   *Network Diagram for the RSPAN Example*

Displaying Information About SPAN

Use the following command to display helpful information about SPAN.

```
Router#show monitor session[session-number]
Router# show monitor capture
```

```
Capture instance [1] :
=======================
Capture Session ID   : 1
Session status       : up
rate-limit value     : 10000
redirect index       : 0x807
buffer-size          : 2097152
capture state        : OFF
capture mode         : Linear
capture length       : 68


Router# show monitor session 1
Session 1
— — —·
Type                        : Capture Session
Source Ports                :
    Both                    : Gi3/1-3,Gi3/5
Capture buffer size         : 32 KB
Capture filters             : None


Egress SPAN Replication State:
Operational mode            : Centralized
Configured mode             : Distributed (default)


Router# show monitor session 1 detail
Session 1
— — —·
Type                        : Capture Session
Description                 : -
Source Ports                :
    RX Only                 : None
    TX Only                 : None
    Both                    : Gi3/1-3,Gi3/5
Source VLANs                :
    RX Only                 : None
    TX Only                 : None
    Both                    : None
Source RSPAN VLAN           : None
Destination Ports           : None
Filter VLANs                : None
Dest RSPAN VLAN             : None
Source IP Address           : None
Source IP VRF               : None
Source ERSPAN ID            : None
Destination IP Address      : None
```

```
Destination IP VRF          : None
Destination ERSPAN ID       : None
Origin IP Address           : None
IP QOS PREC                 : 0
IP TTL                      : 255
Capture dst_cpu_id          : 1
Capture vlan                : 0
Capture buffer size         : 32 KB
Capture rate-limit
              value         : 10000
Capture filters             : None


Egress SPAN Replication State:
Operational mode            : Centralized
Configured mode             : Distributed (default)
```

12-4: Power Management

■ Power supplies can be put into a redundancy mode so that multiple supplies share the total power load. If one supply fails, another supply carries the entire system load.

■ Power supplies not in redundancy mode can combine their capacities to power the system. This proves useful when the total load of all switch modules is greater than the capacity of a single power supply. If one power supply fails and the other supply does not have the capacity to carry the entire system load, some switch modules are powered down to reduce the load.

Configuration

1. *(Catalyst 6500 only)* Configure power-supply redundancy:

   (global) **power redundancy-mode {combined | redundant}**

   Power-supply redundancy (**enable** or **redundant**) is enabled by default.

2. *(Catalyst 6500 only)* Control power-supply operation:

   (global) [**no**] **power enable power-supply** *number*

   By default power is enabled to all power supplies. Supplies are identified by *number* (1 or 2). Use the **no** keyword to disable a power supply.

3. *(Catalyst 6500 only)* Control power to switch modules:

   (global) [**no**] **power enable module** *mod*

   By default all switch modules receive power. To disable power to a module, use the **no** (IOS) keyword with the module number *mod* (1 to the maximum number of slots in the chassis).

Table 12-4   *Switch Commands to Display Power Management Information*

Display Function	Command
System power	(exec) `show power`
Module power state	(exec) `show power status all`

Displaying Information About Power Management

Table 12-4 lists some switch commands that you can use to display helpful information about power management.

12-5: Environmental Monitoring

A switch command that you can use to display helpful information about environmental monitoring is as follows:

(exec) `show environment temperature`

The output from the **show environment temperature** command lists the temperatures measured at the intake and exhaust of each module, with the warning and critical alarm temperatures in parentheses. To operate normally, a switch temperature should not exceed the levels shown within the parentheses.

"Device 1" and "Device 2" temperatures refer to additional sensors within the modules. "VTT" modules are located on the chassis backplane.

12-6: Packet Tracing

- The **ping** (Packet Internet Groper) command tests end-to-end connectivity from a switch to a remote host. The IP ping uses ICMP type 8 requests and ICMP type 0 replies.

- The **traceroute** or Layer 3 traceroute command discovers the routers along the path that packets take to a destination. An IP traceroute uses UDP probe packets on port 33434.

- The **l2trace** or Layer 2 traceroute command discovers the physical path that a packet takes through a switched network.

- **l2trace** looks up the destination in the forwarding table and then contacts the next neighboring switch via CDP. Each switch hop is queried in a similar fashion.

Configuration

1. Use ping packets to check reachability:

```
(exec) ping [host]
```

The IP ping sends ICMP type 8 (echo request) packets to the target *host* (IP address or hostname), and ICMP echo replies are expected in return. The ping packet size, *packet-size* (bytes), and the number of packets, *packet-count*, can also be specified.

A switch sends five ping packets toward the destination by default. Each ping is displayed by one of these characters: ! (successful reply packet received), . (no reply seen within the timeout period, 2 seconds), U (a destination unreachable error was received), M (a could-not-fragment message was received), C (a congestion-experienced packet was received), I (the ping test was interrupted on the switch), ? (an unknown packet type was received), or & (the packet lifetime or *time-to-live* [TTL] was exceeded).

When the test completes, the success rate is reported along with a summary of the round-trip minimum, average, and maximum in milliseconds.

Note   For the regular **ping** command, only the destination address can be given. The source address used in the ping packets comes from the switch management interface.

The switch also provides a more flexible echo test called an *extended ping*. The EXEC-level command **ping** is given, with no options. You will be prompted for all available **ping** options, including the source address to be used. You can specify the following options:

- Protocol (default **ip**).

- Target address.

- Repeat count (default 5 packets): The number of echo packets to send.

- Datagram size (default 100 bytes): The size of the echo packet; choose a size larger than the *maximum transfer unit* (MTU) to test packet fragmentation.

- Timeout (default 2 seconds): The amount of time to wait for a reply to each request packet.

- Extended commands:

  - Source address or interface: Any source address can be given; however, the address must be the address of the management interface on the switch if the reply packets are to be seen.

  - Type of service (default 0).

- Set DF bit in IP header (default no): If set, the packet is not fragmented for a path with a smaller MTU; you can use this to detect the smallest MTU in the path.

- Validate reply data (default no): The data sent in the echo request packet is compared to the data echoed in the reply packet.

- Data pattern (default 0xABCD): The data pattern is a 16-bit field that is repeated throughout the data portion of the packet; this can prove useful for testing data integrity with CSU/DSUs and cabling.

- Loose, strict, record, timestamp, verbose (default none): **loose** (loose source route with hop addresses), **strict** (strict source route with hop addresses), **record** (record the route with a specified number of hops), **timestamp** (record time stamps at each router hop), and **verbose** (toggle verbose reporting). The **record** option can be useful to see a record of the router addresses traversed over the round-trip path.

- Sweep range of sizes (default no): Sends echo requests with a variety of packet sizes:

  - Sweep min size (default 36)

  - Sweep max size (default 18024)

  - Sweep interval (default 1)

2. *(Optional)* Use Layer 3 traceroute to discover routers along a path:

   ```
   (exec) traceroute [protocol] [host]
   ```

   The **traceroute** command sends successive probe packets to *host* (either a network address or a hostname).

   For IP, the first set of packets (default 3) is sent with a TTL of one. The first router along the path decrements the TTL, detects that it is zero, and returns ICMP TTL-exceeded error packets. Successive sets of packets are then sent out, each one with a TTL value incremented by one. In this fashion, each router along the path responds with an error, allowing the local router to detect successive hops.

   The following fields are output as a result of traceroute probes:

   - Probe sequence number: The current hop count.

   - Hostname of the current router.

   - IP address of the current router.

   - Round-trip times (in milliseconds) of each of the probes in the set.

   - *: The probe timed out.

   - U: Port unreachable message was received.

   - H: Host unreachable message was received.

- P: Protocol unreachable message was received.

- N: Network unreachable message was received.

- ?: An unknown packet type was received.

- Q: Source quench was received.

The traceroute probes continue to be sent until the maximum TTL value (30 by default for IP) is exceeded or until you interrupt the router with the escape sequence (**Ctrl-Shift-6**).

You can also invoke traceroute with no options. This enables the switch to prompt for the parameters from the following list:

- **Protocol (default IP).**

- **Target address.**

- **Source address:** An IP address of a router interface; if not specified, the interface closest to the destination is used.

- **Numeric display (default no):** By default, both the hostname and IP address of each hop display; if set to yes, only the IP addresses display. This is handy if DNS is not available.

- **Timeout in seconds (default 3):** The amount of time to wait for a response to a probe.

- **Probe count (default 3):** The number of probes to send to each TTL (or hop) level.

- **Minimum TTL (default 1):** The default of one hop can be overridden to begin past the known router hops.

- **Maximum TTL (default 30):** The maximum number of hops to trace; **traceroute** ends when this number of hops or the destination is reached.

- **Port number (default 33434):** The UDP destination port for probes.

- **Loose, strict, record, timestamp, verbose (default none): loose** (loose source route with hop addresses), **strict** (strict source route with hop addresses), **record** (record the route with a specified number of hops), **timestamp** (record time stamps at each router hop), and **verbose** (toggle verbose reporting). The **record** option can be useful to see a record of the router addresses traversed over the round-trip path.

Note   Some routers do not respond to traceroute probes correctly. In this case, some or all the probes sent are reported with asterisks (*) in the display.

3. *(Optional)* Use Layer 2 traceroute to discover switches along a path:

```
Switch# traceroute mac
```

Section 12-6

```
[interface type interface_number] source_mac_address

[interface type interface_number]

destination_mac_address [vlan vlan_id] [detail]
```

Layer 2 traces are performed from the source MAC address *src-mac* (in dash-separated hexadecimal pairs) to the destination MAC address *dest-mac*. Both source and destination must be present in the address table on the switch. As well, both source and destination must be in the same VLAN. If the hosts belong to more than one VLAN, you can specify the desired VLAN number as *vlan*. The **detail** keyword displays additional information about the switch port media at each hop along the path.

If the MAC addresses are not readily known, you can give the source and destination as IP addresses *src-ip* and *dest-ip*. However, both hosts must be present in the switch's ARP table so that their MAC addresses can be found.

Packet-Tracing Example

On a Catalyst 6500 switch, a Layer 2 trace is performed from source 00-b0-d0-40-01-d1 to destination 00-10-a4-c6-b4-b7. These two hosts are on the same VLAN and are both present in the switch's address table.

The source address is found on port 2/12 of the local switch. The first Layer 2 hop is at IP address 192.168.1.16, where the destination address is found in the address table for port 3/1 on that switch.

Notice that the second Layer 2 hop is the switch at 192.168.1.253, which was identified via CDP. However, either the switch model or its OS does not support the l2trace protocol. As a result, the Layer 2 traces time out, and no response is returned from the neighboring switch at 192.168.1.253:

```
Switch#traceroute mac 00b0.d040.01d1 0010.a4c6.b4b7 detail
Source 00b0.d040.01d1 found on WS-C6509 (192.168.1.16)
1 192.168.1.16 :
Gi2/12 [full, 1000M] => Gi3/1 [auto, auto]
2 no response from neighbor 192.168.1.253
3 no response from neighbor 192.168.1.253
4 Error in trace
```

Further Reading

Refer to the following recommended sources for further information about the topics covered in this chapter.

Clark, Kennedy and Kevin Hamilton. *Cisco LAN Switching*. Cisco Press, ISBN 157870-094-9.

Froom, Richard, Balaji Sivasubramanian, and Erum Frahim. *Building Cisco Multilayer Switched Networks (BCMSN) (Authorized Self-Study Guide)*, Fourth Edition. Cisco Press, ISBN 157870-273-3.

Hucaby, Dave. *CCNP BCMSN Official Exam Certification Guide*, Fourth Edition. Cisco Press, ISBN 1-58720-171-2.

Maggiora, Elliott, Pavone, Phelps, and Thompson. *Performance and Fault Management*. Cisco Press, ISBN 1-57870-180-5.

Chapter 13

Quality of Service

See the following sections to configure and use these features:

- **13-1: QoS Theory:** Discusses the various operations and mechanisms that make up *quality of service (QoS)* as a whole

- **13-2: QoS Configuration:** Explains the sequence of steps necessary to configure and monitor QoS on a Catalyst switch

- **13-3: QoS Data Export:** Presents the configuration steps needed to gather and send QoS statistics information to external collection devices

13-1: QoS Theory

- QoS defines policies on how switches and routers deliver different types of traffic. A *QoS domain* is the entire collection of network devices that are administered so that they adhere to the QoS policies.

- To guarantee that QoS policies are met, QoS must be configured on all switches and routers end-to-end across the network.

- Traffic should be classified at the edges of the QoS domain. Where this isn't possible, classify traffic as close as possible to the source. Classification can occur at Layer 2 or Layer 3, depending on the network functions available at the edge.

- The top portion of Figure 13-1 shows QoS operations on a Catalyst switch, including the following:

  - **Classification:** Selects specific traffic to which a QoS policy can be applied. The priority values of inbound frames can also be trusted or reclassified.

  - **Policing:** Limits the bandwidth used by a traffic flow. Policers can control aggregate or individual flows and can also mark or drop traffic.

- **Marking:** Assigns a value to either the Layer 3 *Differentiated Services Code Point (DSCP)*, the Layer 2 *class of service* (CoS), or both for each frame.

- **Scheduling:** Assigns traffic to a specific switch port queue for either ingress or egress traffic.

- **Congestion Avoidance:** Reserves bandwidth in the switch port queues. Traffic that exceeds a threshold can be dropped or reduced in priority, making space for other traffic in the queues.

- All Catalyst QoS operations are based around the concept of an *internal DSCP* value. This value is determined by an ingress port's trust state and is carried throughout the QoS process with each frame. Upon egress, the internal DSCP can be used to mark other QoS values within the frame. The bottom portion of Figure 13-1 shows the internal DSCP operations.

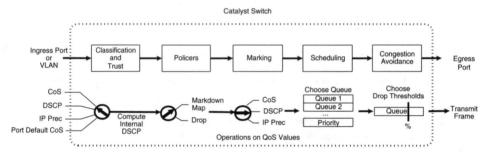

Figure 13-1 *Catalyst Switch QoS Operations and Internal DSCP*

Layer 2 QoS Classification and Marking

At Layer 2, individual frames have no mechanism for indicating the priority or importance of their contents. Therefore, the delivery of Layer 2 frames must be on a "best effort" basis.

When *virtual LANs (VLAN)* are trunked over a single link, however, the trunk provides a means to carry priority information along with each frame. Layer 2 CoS is transported as follows:

- **IEEE 802.1Q trunk:** Frames are tagged with a 12-bit VLAN ID. The CoS is contained in the three 802.1p priority bits in the User field. Frames in the native VLAN are not tagged at all; they are given the default CoS or priority for the switch port. Figure 13-2 shows the format of the 802.1Q encapsulation tag.

0	1	2	3
Tag Protocol ID (0x8100)		User	VLAN ID (12 bits)

Figure 13-2 *802.1Q Trunk Encapsulation Format*

■ **Inter-Switch Link (ISL) trunk:** Frames are tagged with a 15-bit VLAN ID. The CoS is contained in the lower three bits of the User field. Although this is not standardized, Catalyst switches copy the 802.1p CoS bits from a frame in an 802.1Q trunk into the User field of frames in an ISL trunk. Figure 13-3 shows the format of the ISL tag.

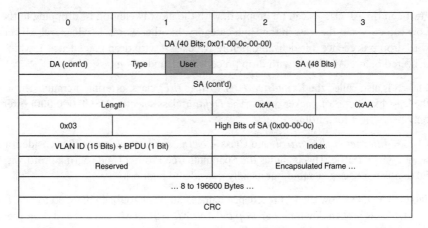

Figure 13-3 *ISL Trunk Encapsulation Format*

Layer 3 QoS Classification and Marking

QoS is also built around the concept of *Differentiated Service* (DiffServ), where the QoS specification is carried within each Layer 3 packet. IP packets have a *type of service (ToS)* byte that is formatted according to the top row of Figure 13-4. Bits P2, P1, and P0 form the IP precedence value. Bits T3, T2, T1, and T0 form the ToS value.

For DiffServ, the same byte is called the *Differentiated Services (DS)* byte and is also formatted according to the bottom row of Figure 13-4. Bits DS5 through DS0 form the *Differentiated Services Code Point (DSCP)*. The DSCP is arranged to be backward compatible with the IP precedence bits because the two quantities share the same byte in the IP header.

ToS Byte:	P2	P1	P0	T3	T2	T1	T0	Zero
DS Byte:	DS5	DS4	DS3	DS2	DS1	DS0	ECN1	ECN0
	(Class Selector)			(Drop Precedence)				

Figure 13-4 *ToS and DSCP Byte Formats*

Bits DS5, DS4, and DS3 form the DSCP class selector. Classes 1 through 4 are termed the *Assured Forwarding (AF)* service levels. Higher class numbers indicate higher-priority traffic. Each class or AF service level has three *drop precedence* categories:

- Low (1)

- Medium (2)

- High (3)

Traffic in the AF classes can be dropped, with the most likelihood of dropping in the Low category and the least in the High category. In other words, service level AF class 4 with drop precedence 3 is delivered before AF class 4 with drop precedence 1, which is delivered before AF class 3 with drop precedence 3, and so on.

Class 5 is also called the *Expedited Forwarding (EF)* class, offering premium service and the least likelihood of packet drops. The *Default* class selector (DSCP 000 000) offers only best-effort forwarding.

Class 6, *Internetwork Control*, and Class 7, *Network Control*, are both set aside for network control traffic. This includes the Spanning Tree Protocol and routing protocols, traffic that is not user-generated but usually considered high-priority.

Table 13-1 shows how the IP precedence names and bits have been mapped to DSCP values. DSCP is broken down by *per-hop behavior (PHB)*, class selector, and drop precedence. Many times, DSCP values are referred to by the codepoint name (AF23, for example), which are also listed in the table. The DSCP bits are shown along with their decimal equivalent. In many DSCP-related commands, you need to enter a decimal DSCP value, even though it is difficult to relate the decimal numbers with the corresponding DSCP service levels and PHBs. Use this table as a convenient cross-reference.

Table 13-1   *Mapping of IP Precedence and DSCP Fields*

IP Precedence (3 Bits)			DSCP (6 Bits)				
Name	Value	Bits	Per-Hop Behavior	Class Selector	Drop Precedence	Codepoint Name	DSCP Bits (Decimal)
Routine	0	000	Default	—	—	Default	000 000 (0)
Priority	1	001	AF	1	1: Low	AF11	001 010 (10)
					2: Medium	AF12	001 100 (12)
					3: High	AF13	001 110 (14)

Table 13-1   *Mapping of IP Precedence and DSCP Fields (Continued)*

IP Precedence (3 Bits)			DSCP (6 Bits)				
Name	Value	Bits	Per-Hop Behavior	Class Selector	Drop Precedence	Codepoint Name	DSCP Bits (Decimal)
Immediate	2	010	AF	2	1: Low	AF21	010 010 (18)
					2: Medium	AF22	010 100 (20)
					3: High	AF23	010 110 (22)
Flash	3	011	AF	3	1: Low	AF31	011 010 (26)
					2: Medium	AF32	011 100 (28)
					3: High	AF33	011 110 (30)
Flash Override	4	100	AF	4	1: Low	AF41	100 010 (34)
					2: Medium	AF42	100 100 (36)
					3: High	AF43	100 110 (38)
Critical	5	101	EF	N/A	N/A	EF	101 110 (46)[1]
Internetwork Control	6	110	N/A	N/A	N/A	N/A	N/A[2]
Network Control	7	111	N/A	N/A	N/A	N/A	N/A[2]

[1]IP precedence value 5 (DSCP EF) corresponds to the range of DSCP bits 101000 through 101111, or 40 to 47. However, only the value 101110 or 46 is commonly used and is given the EF designation.

[2]IP precedence values 6 and 7 consume the DSCP ranges 48 to 55 and 56 to 63, respectively. However, these values are normally used by network control traffic and are not shown in the table for simplicity.

Tip   Layer 2 CoS and Layer 3 DSCP/ToS are completely independent concepts. As such, the two QoS values do not intermingle or automatically translate to each other. A switch must map between CoS and DSCP values at a Layer 2 and Layer 3 boundary.

The Layer 3 DSCP/ToS is carried within each IP packet, allowing the QoS information to be propagated automatically. The Layer 2 CoS is not contained in Layer 2 frames, however, and can only be carried across a trunk. To propagate the CoS values, you must use a trunk between switches.

Catalyst Switch Queuing

Catalyst switch ports have both ingress and egress queues. These buffer frames as they are received or before they are transmitted. Each port usually has multiple queues, each configured for a relative traffic priority. For example, the lowest-priority queue is serviced only after the higher-priority queues.

Most switch platforms have a strict-priority queue that is used for time-critical traffic. This queue is always serviced before any other queue on the port.

Each port queue usually has one or more thresholds that indicate when traffic can or cannot be dropped. When the queue is less full than a threshold, frames are not dropped. If the queue is filled over a threshold, the likelihood that frames can be dropped increases.

During QoS configuration, you must reference the queues by number. The lowest-priority standard queue is always queue 1. The next-higher priority standard queues follow, beginning with 2. The strict-priority queue always receives the highest queue index number.

Cisco Catalyst switch ports are described with the following queue type notation: x**p**y**q**z**t**, where the notations indicate the following:

- **p:** The number of strict-priority queues, given by x

- **q:** The number of standard queues, given by y

- **t:** The number of configurable thresholds per queue, given by z

For example, a switch port of type **1p1q4t** has one strict-priority queue, one standard queue, and four thresholds per queue. The low-priority standard queue is called queue 1, whereas the strict-priority queue is called queue 2.

13-2: QoS Configuration

- QoS operations and policies can be applied as follows:

  - **Port-based:** All data passing through a specific port. This is usually used on a switch with a Layer 3 switching engine.

  - **VLAN-based:** All data passing through a specific VLAN on the switch. This is usually used on a switch with a Layer 2 switching engine or when QoS policies are common for all traffic on a VLAN.

■ Classification can be performed at ingress switch ports. Inbound CoS, IP precedence, or DSCP values can be trusted by accepting the values that were assigned by an attached device. This is acceptable when the source of the values is known and under administrative control. If these values cannot be trusted as they enter a switch, they can be mapped to new values. An internal DSCP value is derived from the classification for each frame.

■ Ingress switch port queues and scheduling can be tuned to support advanced QoS needs.

■ Policers can be used to control ingress traffic:

   ■ Policers use a *token bucket* algorithm to monitor the bandwidth utilization of a traffic flow. The lengths of inbound frames are added to the token bucket as they arrive. Every 0.25 ms (1/4000th of a second), a value of the *committed information rate* (CIR) or average policed rate is subtracted from the token bucket. The idea is to keep the token bucket equal to zero for a sustained data rate.

   ■ The policer allows the traffic rate to burst a certain amount over the average rate. Valid burst amounts are allowed as the token bucket rises up to the level of the burst value (in bytes). This is also called *in-profile traffic*.

   ■ When the token bucket size exceeds the burst value, the policer considers the traffic flow to be "excessive." With a PFC2 module, a *peak information rate (PIR)* can be defined. When traffic flows exceed the maximum burst size over the PIR, the policer considers the flow to be "in violation." This type of traffic is also called *out-of-profile traffic*.

   ■ Aggregate policers monitor and control a cumulative flow that travels through one or more ingress ports or a VLAN. Up to 1023 aggregate policers can be defined on a Catalyst 6500 switch.

   ■ Microflow policers monitor and control one specific traffic flow, or a *microflow*. An IP microflow is defined by source and destination IP addresses, Layer 4 protocol, and source and destination port numbers. An IPX microflow has common source and destination networks and a common destination node. A MAC layer microflow has a common protocol and common source and destination MAC addresses. Up to 63 microflow policers can be defined on a Catalyst 6000 switch.

■ *Access control entries (ACE)* match traffic based on address and Layer 4 port information. ACEs are grouped into *access control lists (ACL)* or QoS policies that are applied to specific switch ports.

■ Congestion avoidance is configured by assigning thresholds to the various egress queues. Traffic is dropped when the queue level rises above the appropriate threshold, reserving queue space for other traffic.

■ Egress switch port queue scheduling can be tuned to assign classes of traffic to queues and thresholds with relative service priorities.

Catalyst 2000/3000 Configuration

> **Tip** The QoS operations on a Catalyst 2900XL or 3500XL switch are limited to QoS trust and fixed-queue scheduling. Therefore, these switches are presented here separately.

1. *(Optional)* Classify traffic based on a port.

    a. *(Optional)* Set the default ingress CoS value:

    ```
    (interface) switchport priority default cos
    ```

    Frames that are untagged receive CoS value *cos* (0 to 7).

    b. *(Optional)* Don't trust any inbound information:

    ```
    (interface) switchport priority override
    ```

    For a Catalyst 200/3000, the CoS value is set to the default CoS value configured in Step 1a. By default, all switch ports override inbound untagged or static access CoS values with 0.

    c. *(Optional)* Instruct a connected appliance to handle CoS:

    ```
    (interface) switchport priority extend {cos cos | none | trust}
    ```

    CoS trust can be extended to a Cisco IP Phone or other appliance that is connected to a Catalyst switch port. The switch can instruct the appliance on how to trust CoS values from other devices connected to it. CoS trust can be **cos** (override the CoS in frames from other devices with value *cos*, 0 to 7), **none** (the appliance doesn't do anything with the CoS, the default), or **trust** (the appliance trusts and forwards the CoS in frames from other devices). See Chapter 14, "Voice," for more IP Phone configuration information.

2. Port queue scheduling:

    ■ Catalyst 2000/3000 switches have a single ingress queue. This queue cannot be configured.

    ■ These switches have 2q0t egress ports. Frames with a CoS 0 to 3 are assigned to the lower-priority queue (queue 1). Frames with CoS 4 to 7 are assigned to the higher-priority queue (queue 2).

    ■ The egress queue scheduling is not configurable. As well, the congestion-avoidance thresholds are fixed at 100 percent.

All Other Catalyst Configuration

1. Enable QoS functionality:

    ```
    (global) mls qos
    ```

    By default, QoS is disabled. All traffic is switched in a "pass-through" mode, where only "best effort" delivery is offered.

2. Apply QoS to ports or VLANs:

`(interface)` **`mls qos vlan-based`**

By default, QoS is **port-based** (**no mls qos vlan-based**) or applied to individual Layer 2 ports. QoS policies can be applied to a port's VLAN instead. When the application is changed, any port-based QoS policies are detached from the port.

3. Classify traffic based on a port.

Tip   A switch port can be configured to always trust selected inbound QoS parameters in this step. Otherwise, a QoS policy can be defined to trust QoS parameters conditionally. This is done in Step 6 (COS) and Step 8 (IOS). On an IOS switch, the trust state can be set only on physical switch ports and not on VLAN interfaces.

a. *(Optional)* Set the default ingress CoS value:

`(interface)` **`mls qos cos`** *`cos-value`*

The CoS value is set to *cos-value* (0 to 7, default 0) for frames received on untrusted ports and for unmarked frames received on trusted ports (frames in the 802.1Q native VLAN).

b. *(Optional)* Don't trust any inbound information:

`(interface)` **`no mls qos trust`**

The inbound CoS, DSCP, and IP precedence values are not trusted. All these values are reclassified based on any matching QoS policies or maps. If no policies are present, both the CoS and DSCP are set to 0.

When QoS is enabled, the default state for each port is **untrusted**.

c. *(Optional)* Trust the inbound CoS value by default.

■   Map CoS values to internal DSCP values:

`(global)` **`mls qos map cos-dscp`** *`dscp1 ... dscp8`*

The CoS values (0 to 7) from inbound frames are mapped to the corresponding 8 *dscp1* through *dscp8* values (0 to 63). The resulting internal DSCP values are then used by the QoS processes in the switch. The default mapping is as follows:

CoS	DSCP
0	0 ("best effort")
1	8 (AF class 1 "best effort")
2	16 (AF class 2 "best effort")
3	24 (AF class 3 "best effort")
4	32 (AF class 4 "best effort")
5	40 (EF "best effort")
6	48 (Internetwork control "best effort")
7	56 (Network control "best effort")

Note that no drop precedences are used by default. This gives DSCP values that differ slightly from those shown in Table 13-2 because the drop precedence bits are all 000. When you need to map CoS to DSCP values in a switch, alter the default mapping so that distinct drop precedences are used instead. To return to the default mapping, use the **clear qos cos-dscp-map** or **no mls qos map cos-dscp** command.

■ Enable CoS trust on one or more ports:

```
(interface) mls qos trust cos
```

Trust only the inbound CoS value, from which the ToS or DSCP values will be derived.

d. *(Optional)* Trust the inbound IP precedence value by default.

■ Map IP precedence to internal DSCP values:

```
(global) mls qos map ip-prec-dscp dscp1 ... dscp8
```

The IP precedence values (0 through 7, or **routine**, **priority**, **immediate**, **flash**, **flash-override**, **critical**, **internet**, and **network**) from inbound packets are mapped to the corresponding 8 *dscp1* through *dscp8* values (0 to 63; defaults are 0, 8, 16, 24, 32, 40, 48, and 56). The resulting internal DSCP values are then used by QoS. The following table shows the default mapping.

ToS	DSCP
0 (routine)	0 ("best effort")
1 (priority)	8 (AF class 1 "best effort")
2 (immediate)	16 (AF class 2 "best effort")
3 (flash)	24 (AF class 3 "best effort")
4 (flash-override)	32 (AF class 4 "best effort")
5 (critical)	40 (EF "best effort")
6 (internet)	48 (Internetwork control "best effort")
7 (network)	56 (Network control "best effort")

Note that no drop precedences are used by default. This gives DSCP values that differ slightly from those shown in Table 13-2 because the drop precedence bits are all 000. When you need to map CoS to DSCP values in a switch, alter the default mapping so that distinct drop precedences are used instead. To return to the default mapping, use the **clear qos ipprec-dscp-map** or **no mls qos map ip-prec-dscp** command.

■ Enable IP precedence trust on one or more ports:

```
(interface) mls qos trust ip-precedence
```

Trust only the inbound IP precedence value (ToS), from which the DSCP values will be derived.

e. *(Optional)* Trust the inbound DSCP value by default:

```
(interface) mls qos trust dscp
```

You can choose to trust only the inbound DSCP value, keeping the ToS and DSCP values intact. No other mapping derives the internal DSCP values.

f. *(Optional)* Map DSCP values between QoS domains.

- Create a DSCP mutation map:

```
(global) mls qos map dscp-mutation dscp-mutation-name in-dscp to
    out-dscp
```

When a switch port is at the boundary of a QoS domain, the inbound DSCP values can be mapped to a set of different DSCP values. The mutation map named *dscp-mutation-name* (text string) contains the inbound values *in-dscp* (up to 8 values 0 to 63 separated by spaces) that are mapped to corresponding new values *out-dscp* (up to 8 values 0 to 63 separated by spaces). The command can be repeated if more than eight DSCP values need to be mapped.

- Apply a mutation map to an interface:

```
(interface) mls qos dscp-mutation dscp-mutation-name
```

By default, no DSCP mutation occurs on an interface. Otherwise, the mutation map named *dscp-mutation-name* (text string) is used. Each Gigabit Ethernet interface can have a different mutation map, whereas only one map can be used on each group of 12 10/100 Ethernet interfaces.

4. *(Optional)* Tune the ingress port queues.

> **Tip** By default, the ingress ports use the congestion avoidance and scheduling in Table 13-2.

Table 13-2 *Congestion Avoidance/Scheduling for Ingress Ports*

Queue Type	Threshold Number (Standard Queue)							
	CoS: Percentage Tail-Drop or Low%/High% WRED							
	T1	T2	T3	T4	T5	T6	T7	T8
1q4t	0,1: 50%	2,3: 60%	4,5: 80%	6,7: 100%	—	—	—	—
1p1q4t	0,1: 50%	2,3: 0%	4: 80%	6,7:100%	—	—	—	—
1p1q8t	0: 40%/70%	1: 40%/70%	2: 50%/80%	3: 50%/80%	4: 60%/90%	6: 60%/90%	7: 70%/100%	—

Tip   All port types assign frames with CoS 5 to their strict-priority queues (except 1q4t, which has none). The 1p1q0t ports have no thresholds; all frames with CoS values other than 5 are assigned to the standard queue and dropped when the queue is 100 percent full.

a.   *(Optional)* Tune the ingress queue ratio:

```
(interface) rcv-queue queue-limit queue1 queue2
```

By default, the standard queue (queue 1) receives 80 percent of the available space, whereas the strict-priority queue (queue 2) receives 20 percent of the space. If QoS is disabled, the standard queue receives 100 percent of the space.

Estimate the ratio of normal and priority traffic coming into a switch port. Use the *queue1* and *queue2* values to set the percentage (1 to 99) for the two receive queues. These values must total 100 percent.

Caution   When using this command, all ports cycle through a link-down and link-up process. In a production network, this causes a network outage while the ports are down and while they progress through the spanning-tree states again.

b.   *(Optional)* Set the congestion-avoidance thresholds.

■   *(Optional)* Use standard tail-drop receive queues:

```
(interface) rcv-queue threshold queue-id threshold-percent-1 ...
    threshold-percent-n
```

OR

```
(interface) wrr-queue threshold queue-id threshold-percent-1 ...
    threshold-percent-n
```

For most switch port receive queues (1q4t, 1p1q4t, 2q2t, and 1p1q0t), standard tail-drop congestion avoidance can be used. By default, frames with a CoS 5 are assigned to the strict-priority queue. All other frames are assigned to the standard queue.

The number of queue thresholds available is the number preceding the **t** in the queue type. For each threshold, you can assign the percentage of the buffer that is available to receive frames. The *threshold-percentage-n* values (1 to 100 percent) are given in sequential order. When the buffer rises above the threshold level, new inbound frames are dropped.

> **Tip** On an IOS switch, the 1q4t queue is serviced by a *weighted round-robin* (WRR) algorithm. Therefore, the thresholds must be set with the **wrr-queue threshold** command.

- (Optional) Use *weighted random early detection* (WRED) receive queues:

  ```
  (interface) rcv-queue random-detect min-threshold queue-id thr1-min
      thr2-min ...
  ```

  ```
  (interface) rcv-queue random-detect max-threshold queue-id thr1-max
      thr2-max ...
  ```

  For 1p1q8t port types, WRED is used. The *queue-id* is **1** (standard queue) or **2** (priority queue). Two limits are used for each of the eight queue thresholds: a minimum *thr1-min* (1 to 100 percent) and a maximum *thr1-max* (1 to 100 percent).

  When the buffer is below the minimum level, no frames are dropped. As the buffer rises above the minimum but below the maximum, the chances that frames will be dropped increases. Above the maximum level, all frames are dropped.

> **Tip** The IOS 1p1q8t receive queues also require the **wrr-queue random-detect** *queue-id* command to enable the WRED drop thresholds.

c. *(Optional)* Tune ingress scheduling and congestion avoidance:

```
(interface) rcv-queue cos-map queue-id threshold-id cos-list
```

OR

```
(interface) wrr-queue cos-map queue-id threshold-id cos-list
```

If the inbound CoS values are trusted from Step 3c or a QoS policy, frames with certain CoS values can be mapped and sent to specific ingress queues and thresholds. The *cos-list* can be a single value (0 to 7), multiple values separated by commas, or a hyphenated range of values. This mapping is set for all switch ports (COS switch) or per-interface (IOS switch).

The *port-type* is the type of queuing available, as seen by the **show queueing interface** command. The *queue-id* (**1** for standard or **2** for strict priority) and the *threshold-id* (1 to 4) identify the specific queue and threshold where inbound frames will be queued. The range of values is dependent upon the switch port hardware.

By default when QoS is enabled, CoS 0 through 7 are mapped to the standard ingress queue (queue 1). If a strict-priority queue (queue 2) is supported (queue type begins with **1p...**), CoS 5 is mapped there.

5. *(Optional; Layer 3 only)* Create a policer to control inbound packet flow.

    a. *(Optional)* Use an aggregate policer:

```
(global) mls qos aggregate-policer aggregate-name rate burst [max-burst]
  [pir peak-rate] [conform-action action] [exceed-action action]
  [violate-action action]
```

On an IOS switch, set the CIR *rate* (32,000 to 4,000,000,000 in bps) and the *burst* size (1000 to 512,000,000 bytes). With a PFC2 module, you can also specify a PIR with the **pir** keyword and a *peak-rate* (32,000 to 4,000,000,000 in bps) and a maximum burst size *max-burst* (1000 to 512,000,000 bytes).

The policer can take the following actions, based on how it measures the traffic rate:

- **Conforming (in-profile, less than the CIR):** Forwarded by default. An IOS switch allows a **conform-action** to be taken instead: **drop** (the frame is dropped and not forwarded), **policed-dscp-transmit** (the internal DSCP value is marked down by a mapping), or **transmit** (the frame is forwarded as is).

- **Exceeding (out-of-profile, exceeds the CIR):** Dropped by default. A switch allows an **exceed-action** to be taken: **drop** (the frame is dropped and not forwarded), **policed-dscp-transmit** (the internal DSCP value is marked down by a mapping), or **transmit** (the frame is forwarded as is).

- **Violating (out-of-profile, exceeds the PIR):** By default, the action is the same as the Exceeding action. A switch allows a **violate-action** to be taken: **drop** (the frame is dropped and not forwarded), **policed-dscp-transmit** (the internal DSCP value is marked down by a mapping), or **transmit** (the frame is forwarded as is).

    b. *(Optional)* Use a microflow policer.

On a switch, microflow policers are configured as a part of a policy map. See the second bullet point in Step 8d for more information.

The policer can take the following actions, based on how it measures the traffic rate:

- **Conforming (in-profile, less than the CIR):** Forwarded by default.

- **Exceeding (out-of-profile, exceeds the CIR):** Dropped by default. A COS switch allows **drop** (frame is not forwarded) or **police-dscp** (the internal DSCP value is marked down by a mapping).

Tip   The *rate* value you specify for a CIR might be different from the value that is actually used. The QoS hardware uses values that are the specified *rate* rounded to the nearest multiple of the rate granularity as shown in Table 13-3.

Table 13-3 *Granularity of CIR Rate Values*

CIR/PIR *rate* Range	Granularity of Actual Value
1–1,048,576 (1 mbps)	32,768 (32 kbps)
1,048,577–2,097,152 (2 mbps)	65,536 (64 kbps)
2,097,153–4,194,304 (4 mbps)	131,072 (128 kbps)
4,194,305–8,388,608 (8 mbps)	262,144 (256 kbps)
8,388,609–1,677,216 (16 mbps)	524,288 (512 kbps)
1,677,217–33,554,432 (32 mbps)	1,048,576 (1 mbps)
33,554,433–67,108,864 (64 mbps)	2,097,152 (2 mbps)
67,108,865–134,217,728 (128 mbps)	4,194,304 (4 mbps)
134,217,729–268,435,456 (256 mbps)	8,388,608 (8 mbps)
268,435,457–536,870,912 (512 mbps)	1,677,216 (16 mbps)
536,870,913–1,073,741,824 (1 gbps)	33,554,432 (32 mbps)
1,073,741,825–2,147,483,648 (2 gbps)	67,108,864 (64 mbps)
2,147,483,649–4,294,967,296 (4 gbps)	134,217,728 (128 mbps)
4,294,967,297–8,589,934,592 (8 gbps)	268,435,456 (256 mbps)

Tip   As a rule of thumb, the *burst* size should be set to 32 kilobits or greater. Because the *burst* size operates the token bucket, use caution when choosing a value. Packets that arrive and cause the token bucket to exceed the burst value can potentially be dropped.

Therefore, you should choose a *burst* value that is greater than the *rate* value divided by 4000 and also greater than the size of the largest frame you expect to receive. If you choose a *burst* that is too small, frames that are larger than the burst value will be out-of-profile and can be dropped. Be aware that the QoS hardware uses values that are the specified *burst* rounded to the nearest multiple of the burst granularity as shown in Table 13-4.

c. *(Optional; Layer 3 only)* Allow microflow policing of bridged traffic:

`(interface) mls qos bridged`

Microflow policing is normally allowed only on Layer 3 switched traffic or on traffic that is switched between VLANs. However, you can use microflow policers for bridged (intra-VLAN) traffic on specific VLANs. Specify a *vlan-list* (COS) or use this command on the VLAN interfaces.

Table 13-4   *Granularity of CIR Burst Values*

CIR/PIR *burst* Range	Granularity of Actual Value
1–32,768 (32 Kb)	1024 (1 Kb)
32,769–65,536 (64 Kb)	2048 (2 Kb)
65,537–131,072 (128 Kb)	4096 (4 Kb)
131,073–262,144 (256 Kb)	8192 (8 Kb)
262,145–524,288 (512 Kb)	16,384 (16 Kb)
524,289–1,048,576 (1 Mb)	32,768 (32 Kb)
1,048,577–2,097,152 (2 Mb)	65,536 (64 Kb)
2,097,153–4,194,304 (4 Mb)	131,072 (128 Kb)
4,194,305–8,388,608 (8 Mb)	262,144 (256 Kb)
8,388,609–16,777,216 (16 Mb)	524,288 (512 Kb)
16,777,217–33,554,432 (32 Mb)	1,048,576 (1 Mb)
33,554,433–67,108,864 (64 Mb)	2,097,152 (2 Mb)
67,108,865–134,217,728 (128 Mb)	4,194,304 (4 Mb)
134,217,729–268,435,456 (256 Mb)	8,388,608 (8 Mb)
268,435,457–536,870,912 (512 Mb)	16,777,216 (16 Mb)

   d.   *(Optional)* Define a DSCP markdown mapping:

   ```
   (global) mls qos map policed-dscp internal-dscp to policed-dscp
   ```

   The internal DSCP values *internal-dscp* are marked down to *policed-dscp* values. Internal DSCP values can be specified as single values, multiple values separated by commas, or as a hyphenated range. A COS switch requires a colon (:) between the internal and policed DSCP values, whereas an IOS switch requires the **to** keyword. More mappings can be given on a COS switch by separating them with spaces, and on an IOS switch by repeating this command.

6.   Define matching traffic for a QoS policy.

> **Tip**   In the following steps, source and destination addresses are given by *source-ip* and *destination-ip*, along with masks for wildcard matching (0-bit matches, 1-bit is wildcard). If any address is to be matched, you can replace the address and mask fields with the keyword **any**. If a specific host address is to be matched, you can replace the address and mask fields with the keyword **host** followed by its IP address.

The *dscp* value can be given as a number (6 bits, 0 to 63) or as a text string name. Available names are **default** (000000), **ef** (101110), (Assured Forwarding, AF) **af11** (001010), **af12** (001100), **af13** (001110), **af21** (010010), **af22** (010100), **af23** (010110), **af31** (011010), **af32** (011100), **af33** (011110), **af41** (100010), **af42** (100100), **af43** (100110), (Class Selector, CS) **cs1** (precedence 1, 001000), **cs2** (precedence 2, 010000), **cs3** (precedence 3, 011000), **cs4** (precedence 4, 100000), **cs5** precedence 5, 101000), **cs6** (precedence 6, 110000), and **cs7** (precedence 7, 111000).

The switch also allows the **tos** keyword to match the ToS level (0 to 15). Available values are **max-reliability**, **max-throughput**, **min-delay**, **min-monetary-cost**, and **normal**.

a. *(Optional)* Match IP traffic by source address:

```
(global) access-list acc-list-number {permit | deny} ip source-ip
    source-mask
```

OR

```
(global) ip access-list standard  acl-name
```

```
(access-list) {permit | deny} source-ip [source-mask]
```

The access list is referenced by its name *acl-name* (text string) or by its number *acc-list-number* (1 to 99 or 1300 to 1999).

b. *(Optional)* Match IP traffic by source, destination, and port number:

```
(global) access-list acc-list {permit | deny} protocol source-ip source-
mask [operator [source-port]] destination-ip destination-mask [operator
[dest-port]] [precedence precedence] [dscp dscp] [tos tos]
```

OR

```
(global) ip access-list extended acl-name
```

```
(access-list) {permit | deny} protocol source-ip source-mask [operator
[source-port]] destination-ip destination-mask [operator [dest-port]]
[precedence precedence] [dscp dscp] [tos tos]
```

The access list is referenced by its name *acl-name* (text string) or by its number *access-list-number* (100 to 199 or 2000 to 2699).

An IP *protocol* can be specified. The protocol can be one of **ip** (any IP protocol), **tcp**, **udp**, **eigrp** (EIGRP routing protocol), **gre** (Generic Routing Encapsulation), **icmp** (Internet Control Message Protocol), **igmp** (Internet Group Management Protocol), **igrp** (IGRP routing protocol), **ipinip** (IP-in-IP tunnel), **nos**, **ospf** (OSPF routing protocol), or an IP protocol number (0 to 255).

An **operator** can be specified to determine how the source and destination port numbers are to be matched. You can use the operators **lt** (less than), **gt** (greater than), **eq** (equal to), **neq** (not equal to), or **range** (within a range given by two port number values). The source and destination ports are given as a number (0 to 65535) or as a text string port name.

Available TCP names are **bgp, chargen, daytime, discard, domain, echo, finger, ftp, ftp-data, gopher, hostname, irc, klogin, kshell, lpd, nntp, pop2, pop3, smtp, sunrpc, syslog, tacacs-ds, talk, telnet, time, uucp, whois,** and **www.** In addition, you can use the **established** keyword to match packets from established connections or packets that have either the RST or ACK bits set.

Available UDP names are **biff, bootpc, bootps, discard, dns, dnsix, echo, mobile-ip, nameserver, netbios-dgm, netbios-ns, ntp, rip, snmp, snmptrap, sunrpc, syslog, tacacs-ds, talk, tftp, time, who,** and **xdmcp.**

c. *(Optional)* Match ICMP traffic:

```
(global) access-list acc-list {permit | deny} icmp source-ip source-mask
destination-ip destination-mask [icmp-type [icmp-code] | icmp-message]
[precedence precedence] [dscp dscp] [tos tos]
```

OR

```
(global) ip access-list extended  acl-name

(access-list) {permit | deny} icmp source-ip source-mask destination-ip
destination-mask [icmp-type [icmp-code] | icmp-message] [precedence
precedence] [dscp dscp] [tos tos]
```

The access list is referenced by its name *acl-name* (text string) or by its number *acc-list-number* (100 to 199 or 2000 to 2699).

One or more of *icmp-type*, *icmp-type icmp-code*, or *icmp-message* can be added to the command line. The *icmp-type* field is the ICMP message type (0 to 15), and the *icmp-code* is an optional ICMP message code (0 to 255). The *icmp-message* field is a text string name, chosen from the following: **administratively-prohibited, alternate-address, conversion-error, dod-host-prohibited, dod-net-prohibited, echo, echo-reply, general-parameter-problem, host-isolated, host-precedence-unreachable, host-redirect, host-tos-redirect, host-tos-unreachable, host-unknown, host-unreachable, information-reply, information-request, mask-reply, mask-request, mobile-redirect, net-redirect, net-tos-redirect, net-tos-unreachable, net-unreachable, network-unknown, no-room-for-option, option-missing, packet-too-big, parameter-problem, port-unreachable, precedence-unreachable, protocol-unreachable, reassembly-timeout, redirect, router-advertisement, router-solicitation, source-quench, source-route-failed, time-exceeded, timestamp-reply, timestamp-request, traceroute, ttl-exceeded,** and **unreachable.**

d. *(Optional)* Match IGMP traffic:

```
(global) access-list acc-list {permit | deny} igmp source-ip source-mask
destination-ip destination-mask [igmp-type] [precedence precedence] [dscp
dscp] [tos tos]
```

OR

```
(global) ip access-list extended  acl-name
```

```
(access-list) {permit | deny} igmp source-ip source-mask destination-ip
destination-mask [igmp-type] [precedence precedence] [dscp dscp] [tos tos]
```

The access list is referenced by its name *acl-name* (text string) or by its number *acc-list-number* (100 to 199 or 2000 to 2699).

When the protocol is **igmp**, an additional IGMP message type field can be added for further filtering, chosen from the following: **dvmrp**, **host-query**, **host-report**, **pim**, and **trace**.

e. *(Optional)* Match MAC layer traffic:

```
(global) mac access-list extended acl-name
```

```
(access-list) {permit | deny} {source-mac source-mask | any} {dest-
  mac_dest-mask | any} ether-type
```

The access list is referenced by its name *acl-name* (text string).

Both source and destination MAC addresses (*source* and *destination*) and masks (*source-mask* and *destination-mask*) are specified for matching. The addresses are 48-bit MAC addresses written as three groups of four hex digits separated by dots (that is, 0000.1111.2222). The mask fields specify masks to use for matching multiple addresses. A 1 bit in the mask causes that address bit to be ignored.

For COS switches, the *ether-type* field can be one of these values: **Ethertalk** (0x809b), **AARP** (0x8053), **dec-mop-dump** (0x6001), **dec-mop-remote-console** (0x6002), **dec-phase-iv** (0x6003), **dec-lat** (0x6004), **dec-diagnostic-protocol** (0x6005), **dec-lavc-sca** (0x6007), **dec-amber** (0x6008), **dec-mumps** (0x6009), **dec-lanbridge** (0x8038), **dec-dsm** (0x8039), **dec-netbios** (0x8040), **dec-msdos** (0x8041), **banyan-vines-echo** (0x0baf), **xerox-ns-idp** (0x0600), and **xerox-address-translation** (0x0601).

For IOS switches, the *ether-type* field can be one of these values: **aarp** (0x80f3), **amber** (0x6008), **appletalk** (0x809b), **diagnostic** (0x6005), **decnet-iv** (0x6003), **dec-spanning** (0x8038), **dsm** (0x8039), **etype-6000** (0x6000), **etype-8042** (0x8042), **lat** (0x6004), **lavc-acm** (0x6007), **mop-console** (0x6002), **mop-dump** (0X6001), **msdos** (0X8041), **mumps** (0x6009), **netbios** (0x8040), **vines-ip** (0x0bad), **vines-echo** (0x0baf), or **xns-idp** (0x0600).

7. Group matching traffic into a class map.

a. Create the class map:

```
(global) class-map class-name [match-all | match-any]
```

For the class map *class-name* (text string), one or more matching conditions is specified. You can match against all of them (**match-all**, the default) or against any of them (**match-any**).

b. *(Optional)* Use an access list for matching candidate traffic:

(cmap) **match access-group name** *acc-list*

The class map matches traffic that is permitted by the access list *acc-list* (named or numbered). This access list is configured in Step 6.

c. *(Optional)* Match against IP precedence values:

(cmap) **match ip precedence** *ipprec1* [...*ipprecN*]

Up to eight IP precedence *ipprec* (0 to 7) values can be given to match against. Separate the values by spaces. Available values are **critical** (5), **flash** (3), **flash-override** (4), **immediate** (2), **internet** (6), **network** (7), **priority** (1), and **routine** (0).

d. *(Optional)* Match against DSCP values:

(cmap) **match ip dscp** *dscp1* [...*dscpN*]

Up to eight DSCP values can be given to match against. These values should be separated by spaces.

The *dscp* values can be given as a number (6 bits, 0 to 63) or as a text string name. Available names are **default** (000000), **ef** (Express Forwarding, EF, 101110), (Assured Forwarding, AF) **af11** (001010), **af12** (001100), **af13** (001110), **af21** (010010), **af22** (010100), **af23** (010110), **af31** (011010), **af32** (011100), **af33** (011110), **af41** (100010), **af42** (100100), **af43** (100110), (Class Selector, CS) **cs1** (precedence 1, 001000), **cs2** (precedence 2, 010000), **cs3** (precedence 3, 011000), **cs4** (precedence 4, 100000), **cs5** (precedence 5, 101000), **cs6** (precedence 6, 110000), and **cs7** (precedence 7, 111000).

8. Define a QoS policy.

a. Create the policy:

(global) **policy-map** *policy-name*

b. Use one or more class maps to find matching traffic.

- *(Optional)* Use an existing class map:

    (pmap) **class** *class-name*

    If a class map is already defined, it can be referenced by its name *class-name* (text string).

- *(Optional)* Create a new class map:

    (pmap) **class** *class-name* {**access-group** *acc-list* | **dscp** *dscp1*
    [...*dscpN*] | **precedence** *ipprec1* [...*ipprecN*]}

    A class map can also be created while the policy is defined. This offers a more efficient way to define class maps.

c. *(Optional)* Set the QoS trust state:

(pmap-class) **trust** {**cos** | **dscp** | **ip-precedence**}

IOS switches can selectively choose the source for the internal DSCP values from ingress traffic. For frames matching the class map, the DSCP value can be derived from **cos** (using the CoS-to-DSCP mapping), **dscp** (using the inbound DSCP as is), or **ip-precedence** (using the ToS-to-DSCP mapping).

d. Use a policer to control the bandwidth of matching traffic.

■ *(Optional)* Use a named aggregate policer:

```
(pmap-class) police aggregate policer-name
```

■ The policer named *policer-name* (text string) controls the aggregate traffic from all the ingress ports to which it is assigned.

■ *(Optional)* Define a per-interface policer for controlling one interface:

```
(pmap-class) police [aggregate policer-name] [flow] rate burst [max-
    burst] [pir peak-rate] [conform-action action] [exceed-action
    action] [violate-action action]
```

When a policer is defined as a part of the policy, it operates only on the aggregate traffic from the ingress port where the policy is assigned. Use the **aggregate** keyword to define an aggregate policer or the **flow** keyword to define a microflow policer.

Tip   To use microflow policers on an IOS switch, you must first enable the microflow functionality with the **mls qos flow-policing** command. In addition, microflow policing of bridged traffic must also be enabled on a PFC2 or to police multicast traffic. This is done with the **mls qos bridged** VLAN interface command.

Set the CIR *rate* (32,000 to 4,000,000,000 in bps) and the *burst* size (1000 to 512,000,000 bytes). With a PFC2 module, you can also specify a PIR with the **pir** keyword and a *peak-rate* (32,000 to 4,000,000,000 in bps) and a maximum burst size *max-burst* (1000 to 512,000,000 bytes).

Tip   The *rate* value you specify for a CIR or PIR might differ from the value that is actually used. See the *rate* and *burst* ranges and actual granularities shown in Step 5b.

As a rule of thumb, the *burst* size should be set to 32 kilobits (4096 bytes for IOS) or greater. Because the *burst* size operates the token bucket, use caution when choosing a value. Packets that arrive and cause the token bucket to exceed the burst value can potentially be dropped.

Therefore, choose a *burst* value that is greater than the *rate* value divided by 4000 and also greater than the size of the largest frame you expect to receive. If you choose a *burst* that is too small, frames that are larger than the burst value will be out-of-profile and can be dropped.

The policer can take the following actions based on how it measures the traffic rate:

- **Conforming (in-profile, less than the CIR):** Forwarded by default. An IOS switch allows a **conform-action** to be taken instead: **drop** (the frame is dropped and not forwarded), **set-dscp-transmit** *new-dscp* (the DSCP is set to *new-dscp*), **set-prec-transmit** *new-precedence* (the IP precedence is set to *new-precedence*) or **transmit** (the frame is forwarded as is).

- **Exceeding (out-of-profile, exceeds the CIR):** Dropped by default. An IOS switch enables an **exceed-action** to be taken: **drop** (the frame is dropped and not forwarded), **policed-dscp-transmit** (the internal DSCP value is marked down by a mapping), or **transmit** (the frame is forwarded as is).

- **Violating (out-of-profile, exceeds the PIR):** By default, the action is the same as the Exceeding action. An IOS switch enables a **violate-action** to be taken: **drop** (the frame is dropped and not forwarded), **policed-dscp-transmit** (the internal DSCP value is marked down by a mapping), or **transmit** (the frame is forwarded as is).

e. Attach the policy to the port:

```
(interface) service-policy input policy-name
```

The policy (COS: *acl-name*; IOS: *policy-name*) is attached to the switch port for immediate use on ingress traffic. If the policy will be used for VLAN QoS, it is attached to the VLAN number *vlan* or the VLAN interface.

9. *(Optional)* Tune the egress port queues.

Tip   By default, the egress ports use the congestion avoidance and scheduling, as listed in Table 13-5.

All port types assign frames with CoS 5 to their strict-priority queues (except 2q2t, which has none).

a. *(Optional)* Tune the egress queue ratio:

```
(interface) wrr-queue queue-limit queue1 queue2 [queue3] queue-priority
```

Caution   When this command is used, all ports cycle through a link-down and link-up process.

Table 13-5 *Queue Scheduling and Congestion-Avoidance Thresholds*

Queue Type	Threshold Number CoS: Percentage Tail-Drop or Low%/High% WRED					
	Standard Queue 1		Standard Queue 2		Standard Queue 3	
	T1	T2	T1	T2	T1	T2
2q2t	01: 80%	2,3: 100%	4,5: 80%	6,7: 100%	—	—
1p2q2t	0,1: 50%	2,3: 60%	4: 80%	6,7: 100%	—	—
1p3q1t	0,1: 100%	—	2,3,4: 100%	—	6,7: 100%	—
1p2q1t	0,1,2,3: 70%/100%	—	4,6,7: 70%/100%	—	—	—

Estimate the ratio of normal (low and high priority) and strict-priority traffic to the total amount of traffic going out of a switch port. Use the *queue1*, *queue2*, and optionally *queue3* values to set the percentages (1 to 100) for the standard transmit queues. Use the *queue-priority* value to set the percentage (1 to 100) of the strict-priority queue. These values must total 100 percent.

Table 13-6 lists how the switch port buffers are divided by default.

b. *(Optional)* Adjust the weighting of transmit queue servicing:

```
(interface) wrr-queue bandwidth weight1 weight2 [weight3]
```

For *port-type* **2q2t**, **1p2q2t**, **1p3q1t**, and **1p2q1t**, the standard queues are serviced in a WRR fashion. The strict-priority queue is always serviced, regardless of any other queue. Then each standard queue is serviced in turn, according to its *weight* value; each queue's weight is relative to the others.

By default, ports with two queues have a ratio of 4:255, and ports with three queues have a ratio of 100:150:200. (When QoS is disabled, all queues are equally weighted at 255.)

Table 13-6 *Switch Port Buffer Division Defaults*

Port Type	Low Priority	Medium Priority	High Priority	Strict Priority
2q2t	80% (queue1)	—	20% (queue2)	—
1p2q2t	70% (queue1)	—	15% (queue2)	15% (queue3)
1p3q1t	25% (queue1)	25% (queue2)	25% (queue3)	25% (queue4)
1p2q1t	50% (queue1)	—	30% (queue2)	20% (queue3)

> **Tip**   The *weight* value for a queue specifies how many bytes are transmitted before moving to the next queue. A whole frame is always transmitted, even if you choose a *weight* value that is smaller. Therefore, make sure you choose a value for *weight1* (the lowest priority queue) that is at least as large as the MTU (the largest frame that can be sent). Then scale the other weight values proportionately.
>
> The larger the weights for higher priority queues, the more time elapses before lower-priority queues are serviced. This increases the latency for lesser-priority queues.
>
> After setting the weights for a port, confirm that the hardware is using an appropriate value. Use the **show qos info runtime** *mod/port* command and look at the transmit queue ratio information. The ratio and number of bytes are shown.

10. *(Optional)* Map internal DSCP values to egress CoS values:

    (global) **mls qos map dscp-cos** *dscp-list* **to** *cos-value*

    The internal DSCP generates a final CoS value for each frame. The final CoS is written into the CoS fields of egress trunks and is also used to control egress scheduling and congestion avoidance.

    DSCP values *dscp-list* can be a single value (0 to 63), a hyphenated range of values, or multiple values and ranges separated by commas. The CoS value is given by *cos-value* (0 to 7).

    Table 13-7 shows the default DSCP-to-CoS map.

    The IOS command can be repeated several times until all the CoS mappings are defined.

11. *(Optional)* Tune egress scheduling and congestion avoidance.

    a. *(Optional)* Set the congestion-avoidance thresholds.

        (Optional) Use standard tail-drop receive queues:

        (interface) **wrr-queue threshold** *queue-id threshold-percent-1 threshold-percent-2*

        For 2q2t switch ports, standard tail-drop congestion avoidance can be used. For each threshold, you can assign the percentage of the buffer that is available to transmit frames. The *threshold-percentage-n* values (1 to 100 percent) are given in sequential order. When the buffer rises above the threshold level, new outbound frames are dropped. By default, threshold 1 is set to 100 percent, and threshold 2 is set to 60 percent.

Table 13-7   *DSCP-to-CoS Map Default*

DSCP	0–7	8–15	16–23	24–31	32–39	40–47	48–55	56–63
CoS	0	1	2	3	4	5	6	7

■   *(Optional)* Use WRED receive queues:

```
(interface) wrr-queue random-detect min-threshold queue-id thr1-min
    thr2-min ...
```

```
(interface) wrr-queue random-detect max-threshold queue-id thr1-max
    thr2-max ...
```

For 1p2q2t, 1p3q1t, and 1p2q1t port types, WRED is used. The *queue-id* is
1 (standard low-priority queue) or **2** (standard high-priority queue)—except
1p3q1t ports, which add **3** (standard highest-priority queue). Two limits are
used for each of the queue thresholds: a minimum *thr1-min* (1 to 100 percent) and a maximum *thr1-max* (1 to 100 percent).

When the buffer is below the minimum level, no frames are dropped. As the
buffer rises above the minimum but below the maximum, the chances that
frames will be dropped increases. Above the maximum level, all frames are
dropped.

Tip The IOS 1p3q1t and 1p2q1t transmit queues also require the **wrr-queue random-
detect** *queue-id* command to enable the WRED drop thresholds.

b. *(Optional)* Tune egress scheduling.

```
(interface) wrr-queue cos-map queue-id threshold-id cos-list
```

Outbound frames with certain CoS values can be mapped and sent to specific
egress queues and thresholds. The *cos-list* can be a single value (0 to 7), multiple
values separated by commas, or a hyphenated range of values. This mapping is
set for all switch ports (COS switch) or per-interface (IOS switch).

The *port-type* is the type of queuing available, as seen by the **show port capabilities** (COS) or **show queueing interface** (IOS) command. The *queue-id* (**1** for
standard or **2** for strict priority) and the *threshold-id* (1 to 4) identify the specific queue and threshold where outbound frames are queued. The range of values
depends on the switch port hardware.

The default mappings are shown in Table 13.6.

Displaying Information About QoS

Table 13-8 documents some switch commands that you can use to display helpful information about QoS configuration and operation.

Table 13-8   *Commands to Display QoS Configuration and Operation Information*

Display Function	Command
QoS port information	(exec) **show mls qos** {*type number* | **port-channel** *number* | **vlan** *vlan-id*]
Port queue scheduling and congestion avoidance	(exec) **show queueing interface** {*type number* | **Null** *interface-number* | **vlan** *vlan-id*}
QoS mapping	(exec) **show mls qos maps**
Policers	(exec) **show mls qos aggregate policer** [*aggregate-name*]
QoS policies	(exec) **show class-map** [*class-name*] OR (exec) **show policy-map** *policy-map-name*
Policy activity on an interface	(exec) **show policy-map interface** [*type number* | **null** *interface-number* | **Vlan** *vlan-id*] [**input** | **output**]

13-3: QoS Data Export

■ QoS statistics data can be gathered from sources within a switch and sent to a data collection device.

■ QoS data export is limited to the Catalyst 6000 family.

■ Statistics data is exported using a specific UDP port or a syslog facility.

■ The sources of QoS data can be one of the following. The data fields shown are separated by a delimiter character when data is exported:

   ■ **Switch port:** Data export type 1, slot/port, number of ingress packets, ingress bytes, egress packets, egress bytes, and a time stamp.

   ■ **Aggregate policer:** Data export type 3, policer name, number of in-profile packets, out-of-profile packets exceeding the CIR, out-of-profile packets exceeding the PIR, and a time stamp.

   ■ **QoS policy class map:** Data export type 4, class map name, port, VLAN, or port-channel number, number of in-profile packets, out-of-profile packets exceeding the CIR, out-of-profile packets exceeding the PIR, and a time stamp.

Configuration

1. Specify how to send QoS statistics.

   a. Select a destination for statistic collection:

   (global) **mls qos statistics-export destination** {*host-name* \| *host-ip-address*}

By default, no statistics are sent to the destination. Statistics can be sent to the destination *host* (either IP address or hostname) using a specific UDP *port* or through syslog (UDP port 514). If the **syslog** keyword is used, the syslog *facility-name* can be given as **kern, user, mail, daemon, auth, lpr, news, uucp, cron, local0, local1, local2, local3, local4, local5, local6** (the default), or **local7**. The syslog *severity* is one of **emerg, alert, crit, err, warning, notice, info,** or **debug** (the default). See section "12-1: Logging" in Chapter 12, Switch Management," for more information about syslog.

b. *(Optional)* Set the data export interval:

```
(global) mls qos statistics-export interval interval
```

QoS statistics are sent to the destination every *interval* seconds (30 to 65,535 seconds; COS default 30 seconds, IOS default 300 seconds).

> **Tip**   Be careful when choosing an interval value. If the time is too long, the QoS statistics counters could reach their maximum values and wrap back to 0. If the time chosen is too short, the switch CPU load increases significantly. Begin with the default and make adjustments, taking notice of the effects on both CPU and counters.

Section 13-3

c. *(Optional)* Set the statistics delimiter:

```
(global) mls qos statistics-export delimiter character
```

QoS statistics can be separated by a specific *character* (default pipe or |) if desired.

2. Enable data gathering on the switch:

```
(global) mls qos statistics-export
```

By default, no QoS statistics are gathered or exported.

3. Gather QoS statistics from one or more sources.

a. *(Optional)* Select a switch port:

```
(interface) mls qos statistics-export
```

b. *(Optional)* Select an aggregate policer:

```
(global) mls qos statistics-export aggregate-policer policer-name
```

QoS statistics are gathered from the aggregate policer named *policer-name* (text string). The policer must be configured as described in section "13-2: QoS Configuration."

c. *(Optional)* Select a QoS class map:

```
(global) mls qos statistics-export class-map classmap-name
```

You can gather statistics about a specific portion of a more complex QoS policy if needed. Statistics are gathered from the QoS class map named *classmap-name* (text string). The class map must be configured as described in section "13-2: QoS Configuration."

QoS Data Export Example

QoS statistics are gathered on a switch and are sent to a collection host at 192.168.111.14 using the *local6* syslog facility and *debug* severity (the defaults). Data is collected and sent every 300 seconds. Statistics are gathered only for ports 3/1, 3/2 and the aggregate policer named *MyPolicer*:

```
(global) mls qos statistics-export destination  192.168.111.14 syslog
(global) mls qos statistics-export interval 300
(global) mls qos statistics-export
(global) interface gig 3/1
(interface) mls qos statistics-export
(global) interface gig 3/2
(interface) mls qos statistics-export
(global) mls qos statistics-export aggregate-policer MyPolicer
```

Displaying Information About QoS Data Export

You can use the following switch commands to display QoS statistic sources:

```
(exec) show mls qos statistics-export info
```

Further Reading

Refer to the following recommended sources for further information about the topics covered in this chapter.

Definition of Differentiated Services (DiffServ) IETF RFC 2474 at http://www.ietf.org/rfc/rfc2474.txt.

QoS Policing on Catalyst 6500/6000 Series Switches at http://www.tinyurl.com/2599l.

QoS Output Scheduling on Catalyst 6500/6000 Series Switches Running Cisco IOS System Software at http://www.tinyurl.com/egcmd.

The COPS Protocol, RFC 2748 at http://www.faqs.org/rfcs/rfc2748.html.

The RSVP Protocol at http://www.isi.edu/div7/rsvp/rsvp.html.

Vegesna, Srinivas. *IP Quality of Service*. Cisco Press, ISBN 1-57870-116-3.

Chapter 14

Voice

See the following sections to configure and use these features:

- **14-1: Voice Ports:** Covers the commands necessary to configure switched Ethernet ports for IP telephony

- **14-2: Voice QoS:** Presents guidelines and configuration suggestions that provide end-to-end *quality of service* (QoS) in a campus network

14-1: Voice Ports

- Inline power is provided to a powered device as follows:

  - A phantom-powered device can be detected as a switch port becomes active.

  - A powered device loops the transmit and receives pairs back so that the switch detects its own 340 kHz test tone.

  - Power is applied to the port if the device is present; no power is applied if a normal Ethernet device is connected.

  - Inline power is provided over pairs 2 and 3 (RJ-45 pins 1,2 and 3,6) at 48V DC.

  - Inline power is available on a variety of Catalyst switch products.

  - Powered devices can connect to a wall power adapter and the power patch panel. The devices use the patch panel as a backup power source.

  - Power is provided over pairs 1 and 4 (RJ-45 pins 4,5 and 7,8) at 48V DC.

- A Catalyst switch can send instructions to a Cisco IP Phone on how to present frames from its voice and data ports. This is done through *Cisco Discovery Protocol (CDP)* messages.

- The switch and phone can communicate over an 802.1Q trunk, with voice traffic in a separate *voice VLAN ID (VVID)*. Voice *class of service (CoS)* information can be propagated across the trunk.

- A Cisco IP Phone performs the following steps during initialization:

    1. Inline power is detected by the switch, if needed.

    2. The phone triggers a CDP exchange. The actual amount of required power is sent to the switch, while the VVID number is sent to the phone. The phone can also receive instructions on how to extend the QoS trust boundary.

    3. A special 802.1Q trunk is negotiated between the phone and the switch, if a VVID is to be supported. On Catalyst 4000 and 6000 switches, the trunk is negotiated through *Dynamic Trunk Protocol (DTP)* messages.

    4. A DHCP request is made.

    5. A DHCP reply is sent to the phone, containing the IP address and TFTP server address (DHCP option 150).

    6. The TFTP server is contacted for a phone configuration file. A list of Cisco Unified Communications Manager (CUCM) servers is also obtained.

    7. Registration with a CallManager server is performed. A *directory number (DN)* is obtained so that calls can be placed and received.

Configuration

1. *(Optional)* Detect an inline-powered device:

    `(interface) power inline {auto | never}`

    By default, the switch attempts to discover an inline-powered device on a switch port (**auto**). Use the **off** (COS) or **never** (IOS) keyword to disable inline power detection.

Caution   After a powered device has been detected and power has been applied to a switch port, the switch waits four seconds to see that the device has initialized and the link is established. If not, power is removed from the switch port.

If you unplug the powered device within the four-second delay and plug a regular Ethernet device in its place, power will still be applied, and the device could be damaged. Wait at least ten seconds before swapping devices on a switch port.

Tip   A Cisco IP Phone can use an 802.1Q trunk to transport packets from two VLANs: the voice VLAN (voice packets) and the native VLAN (data packets, untagged). By default, a Cisco IP Phone transports both its voice packets and the data packets from a connected device over the native VLAN. All data is untagged.

After a switch has been configured to instruct an IP Phone to support a VVID number, the switch and phone must use an 802.1Q trunk between them.

For Catalyst switches, a special-case 802.1Q trunk is negotiated with the IP Phone using CDP and the DTP. When the phone is detected, the switch port becomes a *vlan2-access port*, supporting only the two voice and data VLANs. The port won't be shown in trunking mode from the **show trunk** command. In fact, it doesn't matter which trunking mode (*auto, desirable, on, or off*) is configured on the port—the special trunk will be negotiated through the DTP. Be sure that the trunk is not configured using the **nonegotiate** keyword because DTP messages will not be sent or received, and the trunk will not be automatically established.

The *Spanning Tree Protocol (STP)* is automatically supported over the IP Phone trunk as well. The **show spantree** command displays the STP state for both of the VLANs on the trunk.

2. Establish VLANs with the IP Phone.

   a. *(Optional)* Use a VLAN for data.

   ■ *(Optional)* Identify the switch-port access VLAN:

   ```
   (interface) switchport access vlan vlan-id
   ```

   ■ You can configure switch ports to support both PCs and IP Phones. For the case when a regular host (not an IP Phone) is connected to a switch port, the access VLAN should be set to *vlan-id* (1 to 1000 or 1025 to 4094). When a PC is connected, only the access VLAN is supported, and no special trunking negotiations take place. See section "6-1: VLAN Configuration" in Chapter 6, "VLANS and Trunking," for more information.

   ■ Identify the switch-port native VLAN:

   ```
   (interface) switchport trunk native vlan vlan-id
   ```

   ■ Data from the access switch port on an IP Phone is carried over the native VLAN (untagged) of the special 802.1Q trunk. Therefore, you should identify the native VLAN number as *vlan-id* (1 to 1000 or 1025 to 4094).

   b. *(Optional)* Instruct the phone to transport data and voice.

   ■ *(Optional)* Use an 802.1Q trunk with a voice VLAN:

   ```
   (interface) switchport voice vlan vlan-id
   ```

   The IP Phone is instructed to use an 802.1Q trunk. Voice frames are tagged with VLAN *vlan-id* (1 to 4096 COS or 1 to 1001 IOS), whereas frames from the phone's data port are sent untagged (the native VLAN). The CoS value of the voice frames are carried in the 802.1p priority field.

- *(Optional)* Use an 802.1Q trunk with no voice VLAN:

  `(interface) `**`switchport voice vlan dot1p`**

  The IP Phone is instructed to use an 802.1Q trunk and the 802.1p CoS priority field, but all voice frames are placed in the null VLAN (VLAN 0). Frames from the phone's data port are sent untagged (the native VLAN). This enables the voice priority information to be propagated without requiring a separate voice VLAN.

- *(Optional)* Use an 802.1Q trunk with no VLAN information:

  `(interface) `**`switchport voice vlan untagged`**

  The IP Phone is instructed to send all voice frames untagged, over the native VLAN. As a result, no 802.1Q encapsulation is used, and no 802.1p CoS priority information can be propagated.

- *(Optional)* Don't instruct the phone at all:

  `(interface) `**`switchport voice vlan none`**

- The switch will not provide the IP Phone with a VVID to use. This is the default configuration. The phone will have no knowledge of a voice VLAN, and both voice and data frames are sent to the switch port over the same access VLAN.

3. *(Optional)* Optimize the switch port for an IP Phone.

> **Tip**   A switch can perform the actions of the following configuration steps with a single command: **switchport host** at the interface configuration prompt.
>
> Note that this command effectively disables trunking on the switch port; however, the switch port and the IP Phone still use a special form of 802.1Q trunking regardless.

a. Turn off EtherChannel support:

   `(interface) `**`no channel-group`**

   Support for dynamic EtherChannel configuration using *Port Aggregation Protocol (PAgP)* is disabled, saving about 10 seconds of port startup time. See section "4-3: EtherChannel" in Chapter 4, "Layer 2 Interface Configuration," for more information.

b. Enable Spanning Tree PortFast:

   `(interface) `**`spanning-tree portfast`**

   The switch port is tuned for a faster STP startup time by bypassing the *listening* and *learning* STP states. The port can be moved into the *forwarding* state immediately. See section "7-3: STP Convergence Tuning" in Chapter 7, "Spanning Tree Protocol (STP)," for more information.

Example

A Catalyst switch is configured to support an IP Phone on a port. The switch supports inline power, but the switch port might connect to a regular PC or to a Cisco IP Phone.

The port is set to automatically detect a device that supports inline power. The access or port VLAN ID (PVID) is set to VLAN number 55. If a PC is directly connected to the switch port, all data frames are transported over the access VLAN. If an IP Phone is connected, a two-VLAN 802.1Q trunk is negotiated. Data frames from a PC connected to the phone are carried untagged over the native VLAN 55 on the trunk. Voice frames to and from the phone are tagged and carried over the voice or auxiliary VLAN (VVID) 200 on the trunk.

The switch port is also configured to minimize the port-initialization delays due to PAgP and STP. This is optional but can keep the IP Phones from waiting for switch-port delays before phone configuration data is downloaded:

```
(global)    interface fastethernet 0/1
(interface) power inline auto
(interface) switchport access vlan 55
(interface) switchport trunk native vlan 55
(interface) switchport voice vlan 200
(interface) switchport trunk encapsulation dot1q
(interface) switchport mode trunk
(interface) no channel-group
(interface) spanning-tree portfast
```

Displaying Information About Voice Ports

Table 14-1 lists some switch commands that you can use to display helpful information about voice ports.

Table 14-1 *Switch Commands to Display Voice Port Information*

Display Function	Command
Inline power status	(exec) **show power inline** [*interface-id*] [**actual** | **configured**]
	OR
	(exec) **show cdp neighbor** [*interface-id*] **detail**
Access, native, and voice VLANs	(exec) **show interface** [*interface-id*] **switchport**
Discovered device	(exec) **show cdp neighbor** [*interface-id*] [**detail**]

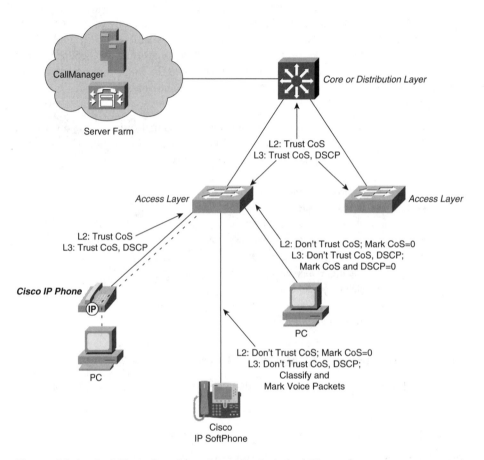

14-2: Voice QoS

To support proper delivery of voice traffic in a hierarchical switched network, follow several QoS rules of thumb. See the basic network diagram in Figure 14-1.

Figure 14-1 *QoS Trust Considerations in a Switched Network*

- Access layer
- A QoS trust boundary should be established as close to the end devices (at the access layer) as possible.
- Let the IP Phone handle the trust boundary for attached PCs; the IP Phone should be trusted.
- PCs running Cisco SoftPhone should be untrusted. Instead, the inbound voice traffic should be classified and the CoS and *differentiated services code point* (DSCP) values marked.

- Normal PCs with no voice capability should be untrusted (CoS and *type of service* [ToS] set to 0).

- On Catalyst 6000 switches, port trust can be VLAN-based and applied to the voice VLAN on all trusted ports.

- Modify the CoS and ToS to DSCP maps so that 3 maps to DSCP 26 (AF31) and 5 maps to DSCP 46 (EF), where possible.

- Uplinks into the distribution and core layers should trust DSCP values, if possible.

- Schedule egress voice frames with CoS 3 to be assigned to the higher-priority queue. Frames with CoS 5 are automatically assigned to the strict-priority egress queue.

- Distribution and core layers.

- If the DSCP values can be controlled by the access layer switches, trust them on those ports.

- If the access layer switches are Layer 2-only and cannot classify or mark frames based on DSCP, set the DSCP values for voice frames in the higher-layer switches. This can be done on a voice VLAN for ports that are configured for VLAN-based trust.

- Modify the CoS and ToS to DSCP maps so that 3 maps to DSCP 26 (AF31) and 5 maps to DSCP 46 (EF), where possible.

- Schedule egress voice frames with CoS 3 to be assigned to the higher-priority queue. Frames with CoS 5 are automatically assigned to the strict-priority egress queue.

You can use several voice protocols within a network:

- **Voice control protocols:** Protocols that are used to register and set up calls:

  - Skinny Client Control Protocol (SCCP), also known as Simple Client Control Protocol

  - H.323

  - Session Initiation Protocol (SIP)

  - Media Gateway Control Protocol (MGCP)

  - Megaco or H.248

- **Real-Time Transport Protocol (RTP):** The UDP encapsulation of the actual voice-bearer packets. All voice protocols use RTP as the transport mechanism after a call has been established.

These voice protocols use the UDP or TCP port numbers shown in Table 14-2. These values can come in handy when you need to classify voice traffic for QoS in a Catalyst switch. Each of the voice-call control protocols should be marked as CoS 3 or DSCP 26 (AF31). The RTP voice-bearer packets should *always* be marked as CoS 5 or DSCP 46 (EF) to ensure timely delivery. RTP packet marking is usually done at the source by definition.

Table 14-2 *Voice Protocol Port Numbers*

Voice Protocol	Port	Description
Skinny	TCP 2000	Skinny Client Control Protocol (SCCP)
	TCP 2001	Skinny Station Protocol (SSP)
	TCP 2002	Skinny Gateway Protocol (SGP)
H.323	TCP 1718	Gatekeeper messages
	TCP 1719	Gatekeeper RAS
	TCP 1720	H.225 call control
	TCP 11000 to 11999	H.245
SIP	UDP/TCP 5060	Default server ports; can also be arbitrarily chosen
MGCP	TCP 2427	Call agents to gateway
	TCP 2727	Gateway to call agents
Megaco	UDP/TCP 2944	Text call control messages
H.248	UDP/TCP 2945	Binary call control messages
RTP	UDP port negotiated by voice-call signaling protocol	Voice payload transport

Access Layer Configuration

1. *(Optional)* Establish a trust boundary at the access layer.

   a. *(Optional)* Trust QoS from a Cisco IP Phone:

      IOS L3 (interface) `mls qos vlan-based`
                (interface) `mls qos trust cos`

      IOS L2 (interface) `mls qos trust cos`

      A single QoS policy can be applied to all voice traffic from IP Phones on a common voice VLAN. This is only possible on Layer 3 switches. Otherwise, the inbound CoS values can be trusted when IP Phones classify and mark CoS from their own voice and data access ports. The IP Phone is instructed to control QoS trust with the configuration in Step 3.

> **Tip** A Cisco IP Phone marks its SCCP voice control packets with CoS 3, ToS 3, and DSCP 26 (AF31). The RTP voice bearer packets are marked with CoS 5, ToS 5, and DSCP 46 (EF). These are carried over the frames in the voice VLAN (VVID) of the 802.1Q trunk.
>
> The IP Phone also marks traffic from its access switch port if instructed to do so. By default, these frames are carried untagged over the native VLAN of the 802.1Q trunk and have their ToS and DSCP values set to 0.

    b. *(Optional)* Don't trust QoS from a PC running Cisco SoftPhone:

IOS L3	`(interface) mls qos cos 0`
	`(interface) no mls qos trust`
IOS L2	`(interface) mls qos cos 0`
	`(interface) no mls qos trust`

Although a SoftPhone PC produces voice control and bearer data packets, other applications running can attempt to mark the CoS in nonvoice packets. Because of this, you should not trust the QoS information coming from the PC. Set these switch ports to an untrusted state and configure Layer 3 switches in your QoS domain to classify and mark the voice control and bearer packets appropriately.

> **Tip** The Cisco SoftPhone application marks its SCCP voice control packets with CoS 0, ToS 0, and DSCP 0 (default). The RTP voice bearer packets are marked with CoS 5, ToS 5, and DSCP 46 (EF). These are carried over the access VLAN untagged because no inherent trunk is used.

    c. *(Optional)* Don't trust QoS from a regular data-only host:

IOS L3	`(interface) mls qos cos 0`
	`(interface) no mls qos trust`
IOS L2	`(interface) mls qos cos 0`
	`(interface) no mls qos trust`

Frames that are untagged or that do not match any QoS-classifying *access control lists (ACL)* will be marked with CoS value 0. This also causes the ingress DSCP values to be mapped to 0 by the CoS-to-DSCP mapping. (See the next step.)

2. *(Optional; Layer 3 only)* Adjust the ingress QoS-to-DSCP mappings:

```
(global) mls qos map cos-dscp 0 8 16 26 32 46 48 56
(global) mls qos map ip-prec-dscp 0 8 16 26 32 46 48 56
```

You can make minor adjustments to the mappings so that CoS 3 maps to DSCP 26 (AF31) and CoS 5 maps to DSCP 46 (EF). The default values are slightly different and are not the standard values expected for voice traffic.

3. *(Optional)* Extend QoS trust into the IP Phone.

a. Set the phone access-port trust:

```
(interface) switchport priority extend {trust |none}
```

A Cisco IP Phone has its own access layer switch port, where a PC can be connected. This port is **untrusted** (IOS **none**) by default, causing the CoS and IP Precedence values for inbound frames to be set to 0. To allow the PC to mark its own packets with IP Precedence values, set the mode to **trusted** (IOS **trust**).

b. Set the default phone access-port CoS value:

```
(interface) switchport priority  extend cos cos-value
```

■   When the phone's access port is set to untrusted mode, the CoS value for all inbound data frames is set to *cos-value* (0 to 7, default 0) by the phone.

4. *(Layer 3 only)* Trust DSCP information on the uplink ports:

```
(interface) mls qos trust dscp
```

Because the distribution and core layer switches are also within the QoS domain and are properly configured to follow the QoS requirements, you can safely assume that any QoS information coming from them has been examined and adjusted to conform to the QoS policies. As such, this information can be trusted over the uplink ports on an access layer switch.

5. *(Optional; Layer 3 only)* Apply a QoS policy to the voice traffic.

a. Define matching traffic with an ACL:

```
(global) ip access-list extended acl-name

(access-list) permit tcp any any range 2000 2002 dscp 26

(access-list) exit
```

In this case, SCCP voice control TCP ports 2000, 2001, and 2002 are matched. These frames are given a DSCP value of 26 (AF31), even if this value was already set. This matching ACL is also necessary so that the CoS trust can be established on switch ports configured with the **set port qos trust trust-cos** command.

If other voice protocols are used, you can change the ACL to match against the appropriate port numbers.

b. *(Layer 3 IOS only)* Define the QoS policy:

```
(global) policy-map policy-name

(pmap) class class-name access-group acl-name

(pmap-class) trust cos
```

The policy uses a class to match traffic from the ACL. CoS values are then trusted for matching traffic.

c. Apply the QoS policy to the voice VLAN:

```
(global) interface vlan voice-vlan

(interface) service-policy input policy-name
```

You can apply the QoS policy to all ports carrying the voice VLAN. This is an efficient way to use a QoS policy on one specific VLAN within a trunk.

6. Configure voice scheduling on the egress ports.

```
IOS L3   (interface) no mls qos vlan-based
         (interface) wrr-queue cos-map 2 1 3

IOS L2   (interface) wrr-queue cos-map 2 1 3
```

By default, all frames with CoS 5 are sent to the strict-priority queue. Frames with CoS 3 are sent to the lowest-priority queue. The scheduling map makes sure that the voice control frames (CoS 3) are sent to a higher-priority queue, serviced ahead of other traffic.

Distribution and Core Layer Configuration

1. Establish a trust boundary.

a. *(Optional; Layer 3 only)* Trust VLAN-based QoS from an L2 access layer switch:

```
(interface) mls qos vlan-based

(interface) mls qos trust cos
```

A Layer 2 access layer switch can classify and mark traffic based only on Layer 2 CoS values. As well, QoS is applied to the voice VLAN where IP Phone traffic is carried. A distribution or core layer switch can then apply QoS policies directly to the voice VLAN.

b. *(Optional)* Trust QoS from another distribution or core switch or a Layer 3 access layer switch:

```
IOS L3   (interface) no mls qos vlan-based
         (interface) mls qos trust dscp

IOS L2   (interface) no mls qos trust cos
```

The QoS information from other switches in a QoS domain can be trusted. This assumes that *every* switch in the QoS domain has been configured to enforce QoS policies consistently.

QoS is port-based on these connections because every VLAN carried over the link will have its QoS values already examined and modified. A Layer 3 switch can trust the inbound DSCP information, but a Layer 2 switch can trust only the inbound CoS values.

  c. *(Optional)* Don't trust QoS from sources outside the QoS domain:

IOS L3   (interface) **mls qos cos 0**

             (interface) **no mls qos trust**

IOS L2   (interface) **mls qos cos 0**

             (interface) **no mls qos trust**

Frames that are untagged receive CoS value 0. This also causes the ingress DSCP values to be mapped to 0 by the CoS-to-DSCP mapping. (See the next step.)

2. *(Optional; Layer 3 only)* Adjust the ingress QoS-to-DSCP mappings:

(global) **mls qos map cos-dscp 0 8 16 26 32 46 48 56**

(global) **mls qos map ip-prec-dscp 0 8 16 26 32 46 48 56**

You can make minor adjustments to the mappings so that CoS 3 maps to DSCP 26 (AF31) and CoS 5 maps to DSCP 46 (EF). The default values are slightly different and are not the standard values expected for voice traffic.

3. *(Optional; Layer 3 only)* Apply a QoS policy to the voice traffic.

  a. Define matching traffic with an ACL:

(global) **ip access-list extended** *acl-name*

(access-list) **permit tcp any any range 2000 2002 dscp 26**

(access-list) **exit**

In this case, the SCCP voice control TCP ports 2000, 2001, and 2002 are matched. These frames are given a DSCP value of 26 (AF31), even if this value was already set.

If other voice protocols are used, you can change the ACL to match against the appropriate port numbers.

  b. *(Layer 3 IOS only)* Define the QoS policy:

(global) **policy-map** *policy-name*

(pmap) **class** *class-name* **access-group** *acl-name*

The policy uses a class to match traffic from the ACL.

c. Apply the QoS policy to the voice VLAN:

```
(global) interface vlan voice-vlan

(interface) service-policy input policy-name
```

The QoS policy can be applied to all ports carrying the voice VLAN. This is an efficient way to use a QoS policy on one specific VLAN within a trunk.

4. Configure voice scheduling on the egress ports:

By default, all frames with CoS 5 are sent to the strict-priority queue. Frames with CoS 3 are sent to the lowest-priority queue. The scheduling map makes sure that the voice control frames (CoS 3) are sent to a higher-priority queue, serviced ahead of other traffic.

```
IOS L3   (interface) no mls qos vlan-based
         (interface) wrr-queue cos-map 2 1 3


IOS L2   (interface) wrr-queue cos-map 2 1 3
```

Voice QoS Example

See the QoS example in section "13-2: QoS Configuration," in Chapter 13, "Quality of Service," which presents a complete voice example, covering a variety of switch platforms in a layered network design.

Further Reading

Refer to the following recommended sources for further information about the topics covered in this chapter.

Cisco IP Telephony Design Guides

Cisco Unified Communications SRND – Network Infrastructure: http://www.tinyurl.com/dg5gxs.

Design Zone for Unified Communications at: http://www.tinyurl.com/a4yknm.

Cisco IP Telephony Books

Davidson, et al. *Voice over IP Fundamentals*. Cisco Press, 1-58705-257-1.

Deel, Nelson, and Smith. *Developing Cisco IP Phone Services*. Cisco Press, ISBN 1-58705-060-9.

Giralt, Paul and Addis Hallmark. *Troubleshooting Cisco IP Telephony*. Cisco Press, ISBN 1-58705-075-7

Lovell, David. *Cisco IP Telephony*. Cisco Press, ISBN 1-58705-050-1.

Inline Power

IEEE P802.3af DTE Power via MDI: http://www.ieee802.org/3/af/index.html

Voice Protocols

Session Initiation Protocol (SIP), RFC 2543: http://www.ietf.org/rfc/rfc2543.txt

H.323 ITU standards at http://www.itu.int/home/index.html

Multimedia Gateway Control Protocol (MGCP) v1.0, RFC 2705: ftp://ftp.isi.edu/in-notes/rfc2705.txt

Megaco: http://www.ietf.org/rfc/rfc3015.txt

Real-Time Transport Protocol (RTP), RFC 1889: http://www.cs.columbia.edu/~hgs/rtp

Voice QoS

CIM Voice Internetworking: VoIP Quality of Service, Cisco Systems, ISBN 158720050-3.

Appendix A

Cabling Quick Reference

Network cabling is always subject to distance limitations, which depend on the media used and the bandwidth supported. Table A-1 provides a quick reference by listing the maximum cabling distance of a variety of network media and cable types.

Table A-1 *Cabling Distances for Network Media and Cabling*

Media	Cable Type	Maximum Distance
10/100BASE-TX Ethernet	EIA/TIA Category 5 UTP[1]	100 m (328 ft)
100BASE-FX	MMF 62.5/125	400 m half-duplex 2000 m full-duplex
	SMF	10 km
1000BASE-CX	STP[2]	25 m (82 ft)
1000BASE-T	EIA/TIA Category 5 UTP (4 pair)	100 m (328 ft)

Table A-1   *Cabling Distances for Network Media and Cabling*

Media	Cable Type	Maximum Distance
1000BASE-SX	MMF 62.5 micron, 160 MHz/km	220 m (722 ft)
	MMF 62.5 micron, 200 MHz/km	275 m (902 ft)
	MMF 50.0 micron, 400 MHz/km	500 m (1640 ft)
	MMF 50.0 micron, 500 MHz/km	550 m (1804 ft)
1000BASE-LX/LH[3]	MMF 62.5 micron, 500 MHz/km	550 m (1804 ft)
	MMF 50.0 micron, 400 MHz/km	550 m (1804 ft)
	MMF 50.0 micron, 500 MHz/km	550 m (1804 ft)
	SMF 9/10	10 km (32,810 ft)
1000BASE-ZX	SMF	70 to 100 km
SONET	MMF (62.5 or 50.0 micron)	3 km (1.5 mi)
	SMI[4]	15 km (9 mi)
	Single-mode long reach	45 km (28 mi)
ISDN BRI	UTP, RJ-45	10 m (32.8 ft)

Table A-1   *Cabling Distances for Network Media and Cabling*

Media	Cable Type	Maximum Distance
Async EIA/TIA-232	2400 baud	60 m (200 ft)
	4800 baud	30 m (100 ft)
	9600 baud	15 m (50 ft)
	19200 baud	15 m (50 ft)
	38400 baud	15 m (50 ft)
	57600 baud	7.6 m (25 ft)
	115200 baud	3.7 m (12 ft)
Sync EIA/TIA-449 with balanced drivers, including X.21 and V.35	2400 baud	1250 m (4100 ft)
	4800 baud	625 m (2050 ft)
	9600 baud	31 m (1025 ft)
	19200 baud	156 m (513 ft)
	38400 baud	78 m (256 ft)
	56000 baud	31 m (102 ft)
	T1 (1.544 mbps)	15 m (50 ft)

[1]UTP = unshielded twisted-pair

[2]STP = single twisted-pair

[3]When using 1000BASE-LX/LH GBICs with 62.5 micron multimode fiber, you must use a mode-conditioning patch cord for distances of more than 300 m (984 ft). See www.cisco.com/univercd/cc/td/doc/product/lan/cat5000/cnfg_nts/ethernet/5421_01.htm for installation and usage information.

[4]SMI = single-mode intermediate reach.

In many cases, you might find that you need to know the pinout connections for various network cables. The RJ-45 connector is commonly used across many media, but with different pinouts for each. Table A-2 shows the pinout for an RJ-45 connector when used with specific media.

Table A-2 *RJ-45 Connector Pinouts Based on Media Type*

RJ-45 Pin	Router Console (DTE)	Ethernet UTP 10/100	Ethernet UTP 1000	Token Ring UTP	ISDN BRIS/TTE	ISDN BRIU	CT1/PRI CSU	CE1/PRI	56/64 kbps DSU/CSU*	T1/E1*
1	RTS	TX+	TP0+	GND	–	–	Rcv Ring	TX Tip	TX Ring	RX
2	DTR	TX–	TP0–	GND	–	–	Rcv Tip	TX Ring	TX Tip	RX
3	TxD	RX+	TP1+	TX+	TX+	–	–	TX Shld	–	–
4	GND	–	TP2+	RX+	RX+	Tip or Ring	Ring	RX Tip	–	TX
5	GND	–	TP2–	RX–	RX–	Tip or Ring	Tip	RX Ring	–	TX
6	RxD	RX–	TP1–	TX–	TX–	–	–	RX Shld	–	–
7	DSR	–	TP3+	GND	–	–	–	–	RX Tip	–
8	CTS	–	TP3–	–	–	–	–	–	RX Ring	–

*An RJ-48 connector is actually used in these applications.

Back-to-Back Connections

In a lab setup or in certain circumstances, you might find that you need to connect two switches or two routers to each other in a back-to-back fashion. Normally, some other active device is used to connect router interfaces. For example, an Ethernet hub or switch, a Token Ring *media attachment unit (MAU)*, and the *Public Switched Telephone Network (PSTN)* all perform an active role in interconnecting routers. If these are not available, as in a lab environment, a special cable is needed to make the back-to-back connection.

Note   It is not possible to make a back-to-back cable connect two Token Ring interfaces. Token Ring connections require an active device such as a MAU or a Token Ring switch to terminate the connection.

Ethernet Connections

Normally, a 10BASE-T or a 10/100BASE-TX host *network interface card (NIC)* connects to a switch through a *straight-through* Category 5 UTP cable. RJ-45 pins 1 and 2 form one pair, and pins 3 and 6 form another pair. To connect two Ethernet switch ports directly, however, you need a *crossover cable*.

A crossover cable connects the pair containing pins 1 and 2 on one end to the pair containing pins 3 and 6 on the other end. Likewise, pins 3 and 6 connect to pins 1 and 2. Table A-3 lists the pinout connections for both RJ-45 ends of the crossover cable.

Table A-3   *RJ-45 Connector Pinouts for Crossover Cables*

RJ-45 Pin End A	Description End A	Description End B	RJ-45 Pin End B
1	TX+	RX+	3
2	TX–	RX–	6
3	RX+	TX+	1
4	–	–	4
5	–	–	5
6	RX–	TX–	2
7	–	–	7
8	–	–	8

Asynchronous Serial Connections

An asynchronous serial connection, such as the Aux port or a line on an access server, requires an RJ-45 connection. For a back-to-back link between two async ports on two different routers, you must use a *rollover cable*. Rollover cables are usually flat eight-conductor cables with RJ-45 connectors, fashioned so that pin 1 on one end goes to pin 8 on the other end, pin 2 goes to pin 7, and so forth. Cisco normally supplies a rollover cable with a console cable kit. Table A-4 shows the pinout connections for both ends of the rollover cable.

Table A-4 *RJ-45 Connector Pinouts for Rollover Cables*

RJ-45 Pin End A	Description End A	Description End B	RJ-45 Pin End B
1	RTS	CTS	8
2	DTR	DSR	7
3	TxD	RxD	6
4	GND	GND	5
5	GND	GND	4
6	RxD	TxD	3
7	DSR	DTR	2
8	CTS	RTS	1

T1/E1 CSU/DSU Connections

You can also make back-to-back connections between two routers with integrated T1/E1 CSU/DSUs using a specially made cable. Again, the transmit and receive pairs are crossed in the cable. Table A-5 lists the pinout connections of both RJ-48 (an RJ-45 will do) ends of the cable.

Table A-5   *RJ-48 Connector Pinouts for Back-to-Back T1/E1 CSU/DSU Connections*

RJ-48 Pin End A	Description End A	Description End B	RJ-48 Pin End B
1	RX (input)	TX (input)	4
2	RX (input)	TX (input)	5
3	–	–	3
4	TX (output)	RX (output)	1
5	TX (output)	RX (output)	2
6	–	–	6
7	–	–	7
8	–	–	8

Well-known Protocol, Port, and Other Numbers

Refer to the following sections for explanations and listings of well-known numbers:

- B-1: IP Protocol Numbers

- B-2: ICMP Type and Code Numbers

- B-3: Well-known IP Port Numbers

- B-4: Well-Known IP Multicast Addresses

- B-5: Ethernet Type Codes

B-1: IP Protocol Numbers

A higher-layer protocol is identified with an 8-bit field within an IPv4 packet called *Protocol*. The IPv4 header format is shown in Figure B-1 with the Protocol field shaded. Figure B-2 shows the IPv6 header format where the protocol number is stored in the shaded Next Header field.

Well-known or assigned IP protocols are registered with the *Internet Assigned Numbers Authority* (IANA). The information presented here is reproduced with permission from the IANA. For the most current IP protocol number assignment information, refer to www.iana.org/numbers.htm under the "Protocol Numbers" link.

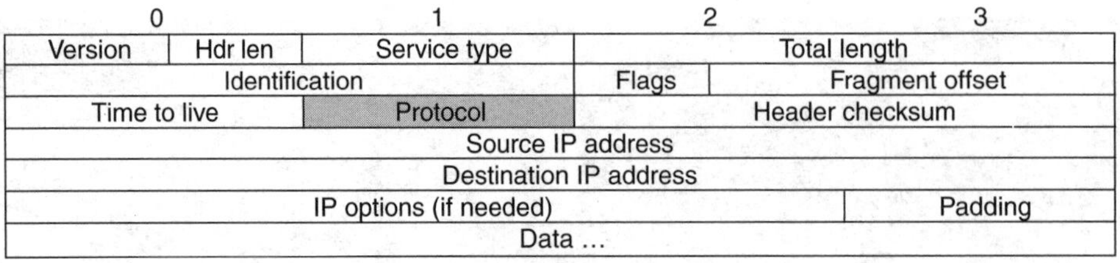

0	1	2	3
Version | Hdr len | Service type		Total length	
Identification		Flags	Fragment offset
Time to live | Protocol		Header checksum	
Source IP address			
Destination IP address			
IP options (if needed)			Padding
Data ...			

Figure B-1   *IPv4 Header Format Showing the Protocol Field*

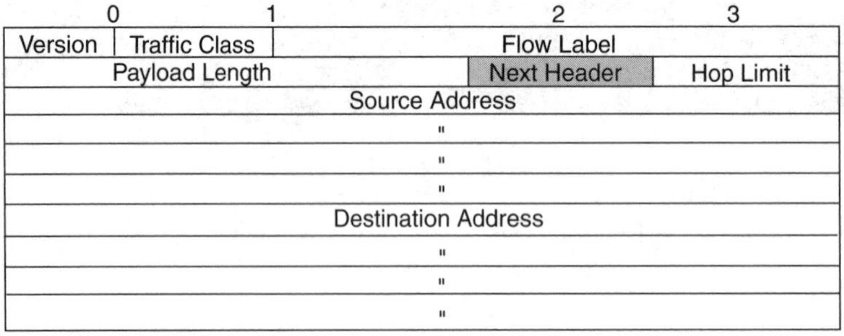

0	1	2	3
Version | Traffic Class		Flow Label	
Payload Length		Next Header	Hop Limit
Source Address			
"			
"			
"			
Destination Address			
"			
"			
"			

Figure B-2   *IPv6 Base Header Format Showing the Next Header Field*

Table B-1 shows the registered IP protocol numbers, along with the protocol keyword (or acronym), the name of the protocol, and an RFC number (if applicable).

Table B-1   *Registered IP Protocol Numbers, Keywords, Names, and Associated RFCs*

Keyword Protocol References	Number
HOPOPT IPv6 Hop-by-Hop Option RFC 1883	0
ICMP Internet Control Message RFC 792	1
IGMP Internet Group Management RFC 1112	2
GGP Gateway-to-Gateway RFC 823	3
IP IP in IP (encapsulation) RFC 2003	4

Table B-1 *Registered IP Protocol Numbers, Keywords, Names, and Associated RFCs*

Keyword Protocol References	Number
ST Stream RFC 1190, RFC 1819	5
TCP Transmission Control RFC 793	6
CBT CBT	7
EGP Exterior Gateway Protocol RFC 888	8
IGP Any private interior gateway IANA (used by Cisco for IGRP)	9
BBN-RCC-MON BBN RCC Monitoring	10
NVP-II Network Voice Protocol RFC 741	11
PUP PUP	12
ARGUS ARGUS	13
EMCON EMCON	14
XNET Cross Net Debugger	15
CHAOS Chaos	16
UDP User Datagram RFC 768	17
MUX Multiplexing	18
DCN-MEAS DCN Measurement Subsystems	19

Table B-1   *Registered IP Protocol Numbers, Keywords, Names, and Associated RFCs*

Keyword Protocol References	Number
HMP Host Monitoring RFC 869	20
PRM Packet Radio Measurement	21
XNS-IDP XEROX NS IDP	22
TRUNK-1 Trunk-1	23
TRUNK-2 Trunk-2	24
LEAF-1 Leaf-1	25
LEAF-2 Leaf-2	26
RDP Reliable Data Protocol RFC 908	27
IRTP Internet Reliable Transaction RFC 938	28
ISO-TP4 ISO Transport Protocol Class 4 RFC 905	29
NETBLT Bulk Data Transfer Protocol RFC 969	30
MFE-NSP MFE Network Services Protocol	31
MERIT-INP MERIT Internodal Protocol	32
SEP Sequential Exchange Protocol	33
3PC Third Party Connect Protocol	34

Table B-1   *Registered IP Protocol Numbers, Keywords, Names, and Associated RFCs*

Keyword Protocol References	Number
IDPR Inter-Domain Policy Routing Protocol RFC 1479	35
XTP XTP	36
DDP Datagram Delivery Protocol	37
IDPR-CMTP IDPR Control Message Transport Protocol	38
TP++ TP++ Transport Protocol	39
IL IL Transport Protocol	40
IPv6 Ipv6	41
SDRP Source Demand Routing Protocol	42
IPv6-Route Routing Header for IPv6	43
IPv6-Frag Fragment Header for IPv6	44
IDRP Inter-Domain Routing Protocol	45
RSVP Resource ReSerVation Protocol RFC 2205	46
GRE General Routing Encapsulation RFC 1701	47
MHRP Mobile Host Routing Protocol	48
BNA BNA	49

Table B-1   *Registered IP Protocol Numbers, Keywords, Names, and Associated RFCs*

Keyword Protocol References	Number
ESP Encap Security Payload RFC 2406	50
AH Authentication Header RFC 2402	51
I-NLSP Integrated Net Layer Security TUBA	52
SWIPE IP with Encryption	53
NARP NBMA Address Resolution Protocol RFC 1735	54
MOBILE IP Mobility RFC 2002	55
TLSP Transport Layer Security Protocol using Kryptonet key management	56
SKIP SKIP	57
IPv6-ICMP ICMP for IPv6 RFC 2463	58
IPv6-NoNxt No Next Header for IPv6 RFC 2460	59
IPv6-Opts Destination Options for IPv6 RFC 2460	60
Any host internal protocol IANA	61
CFTP CFTP	62
Any local network IANA	63

Table B-1   *Registered IP Protocol Numbers, Keywords, Names, and Associated RFCs*

Keyword Protocol References	Number
SAT-EXPAK SATNET and Backroom EXPAK	64
KRYPTOLAN Kryptolan	65
RVD MIT Remote Virtual Disk Protocol	66
IPPC Internet Pluribus Packet Core	67
Any distributed file system IANA	68
SAT-MON SATNET Monitoring	69
VISA VISA Protocol	70
IPCV Internet Packet Core Utility	71
CPNX Computer Protocol Network Executive	72
CPHB Computer Protocol Heart Beat	73
WSN Wang Span Network	74
PVP Packet Video Protocol	75
BR-SAT-MON Backroom SATNET Monitoring	76
SUN-ND SUN ND PROTOCOL-Temporary	77
WB-MON WIDEBAND Monitoring	78
WB-EXPAK WIDEBAND EXPAK	79
ISO-IP ISO Internet Protocol	80

Table B-1   *Registered IP Protocol Numbers, Keywords, Names, and Associated RFCs*

Keyword Protocol References	Number
VMTP VMTP RFC 1045	81
SECURE-VMTP SECURE-VMTP	82
VINES VINES	83
TTP TTP	84
NSFNET-IGP NSFNET-IGP	85
DGP Dissimilar Gateway Protocol	86
TCF TCF	87
EIGRP EIGRP CISCO	88
OSPFIGP OSPFIGP RFC 2328	89
Sprite-RPC Sprite RPC Protocol	90
LARP Locus Address Resolution Protocol	91
MTP Multicast Transport Protocol	92
AX.25 AX.25 Frames	93
IPIP IP-within-IP Encapsulation Protocol RFC 1853	94
MICP Mobile Internetworking Control Protocol	95

Table B-1   *Registered IP Protocol Numbers, Keywords, Names, and Associated RFCs*

Keyword Protocol References	Number
SCC-SP Semaphore Communications Sec. Pro.	96
ETHERIP Ethernet-within-IP Encapsulation	97
ENCAP Encapsulation Header RFC 1241	98
Any private encryption scheme IANA	99
GMTP GMTP	100
IFMP Ipsilon Flow Management Protocol	101
PNNI PNNI over IP	102
PIM Protocol Independent Multicast RFC 2362 (sparse mode)	103
ARIS ARIS	104
SCPS SCPS	105
QNX QNX	106
A/N Active Networks	107
IPComp IP Payload Compression Protocol RFC 2393	108
SNP Sitara Networks Protocol	109
Compaq-Peer Compaq Peer Protocol	110

Table B-1   *Registered IP Protocol Numbers, Keywords, Names, and Associated RFCs*

Keyword Protocol References	Number
IPX-in-IP IPX in IP RFC 1234	111
VRRP Virtual Router Redundancy Protocol RFC 2328	112
PGM PGM Reliable Transport Protocol	113
Any 0-hop protocol IANA	114
L2TP Layer Two Tunneling Protocol RFC 2661	115
DDX D-II Data Exchange (DDX)	116
IATP Interactive Agent Transfer Protocol	117
STP Schedule Transfer Protocol	118
SRP SpectraLink Radio Protocol	119
UTI UTI	120
SMP Simple Message Protocol	121
SM SM	122
PTP Performance Transparency Protocol	123
ISIS over IPv4	124
FIRE	125
CRTP Combat Radio Transport Protocol	126

Table B-1   *Registered IP Protocol Numbers, Keywords, Names, and Associated RFCs*

Keyword Protocol References	Number
CRUDP Combat Radio User Datagram	127
SSCOPMCE	128
IPLT	129
SPS Secure Packet Shield	130
PIPE Private IP Encapsulation within IP	131
SCTP Stream Control Transmission Protocol	132
FC Fibre Channel	133
Unassigned IANA	134 to 254
Reserved IANA	255

B-2: ICMP Type and Code Numbers

The Internet Control Message Protocol (ICMP) transports error or control messages between routers and other devices. An ICMP message is encapsulated as the payload in an IP packet. Figure B-3 shows the ICMP message format. Notice that in the case of an error condition, the first 8 bytes (64 bits) of the original datagram causing the error are included in the ICMP message. This provides the protocol and port numbers of the original message to be seen, making troubleshooting easier.

ICMP type codes are registered with the IANA. The information presented here is reproduced with permission from the IANA. For the most current ICMP type code number assignment information, refer to www.iana.org/numbers.htm under the "ICMP Type" link.

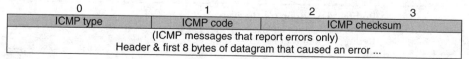

Figure B-3   *ICMP Message Format*

Table B-2 shows the assigned ICMP type numbers, ICMP codes (where applicable), a brief description, and a reference to an RFC.

Table B-2   *Assigned ICMP Type Numbers, Codes, Descriptions, and Associated RFCs*

Type	Code	Name	Reference
0		Echo Reply	RFC 792
1		Unassigned	
2		Unassigned	
3		Destination Unreachable	RFC 792
	0	Net Unreachable	
	1	Host Unreachable	
	2	Protocol Unreachable	
	3	Port Unreachable	
	4	Fragmentation Needed and Don't Fragment Was Set	
	5	Source Route Failed	
	6	Destination Network Unknown	
	7	Destination Host Unknown	
	8	Source Host Isolated	
	9	Destination Network Is Administratively Prohibited	
	10	Destination Host Is Administratively Prohibited	
	11	Destination Network Unreachable for Type of Service	
	12	Destination Host Unreachable for Type of Service	
	13	Communication Administratively Prohibited	RFC 1812
	14	Host Precedence Violation	RFC 1812
	15	Precedence Cutoff in Effect	RFC 1812
4		Source Quench	RFC 792
5		Redirect	RFC 792
	0	Redirect Datagram for the Network (or Subnet)	
	1	Redirect Datagram for the Host	
	2	Redirect Datagram for the Type of Service and Network	
	3	Redirect Datagram for the Type of Service and Host	
6		Alternate Host Address	

Table B-2 *Assigned ICMP Type Numbers, Codes, Descriptions, and Associated RFCs*

Type	Code	Name	Reference
	0	Alternate Address for Host	
7		Unassigned	
8		Echo	RFC 792
9		Router Advertisement	RFC 1256
10		Router Solicitation	RFC 1256
11		Time Exceeded	RFC 792
	0	Time to Live Exceeded in Transit	
	1	Fragment Reassembly Time Exceeded	
12		Parameter Problem	RFC 792
	0	Pointer Indicates the Error	
	1	Missing a Required Option	RFC 1108
	2	Bad Length	
13		Timestamp	RFC 792
14		Timestamp Reply	RFC 792
15		Information Request	RFC 792
16		Information Reply	RFC 792
17		Address Mask Request	RFC 950
18		Address Mask Reply	RFC 950
19		Reserved (for Security)	
20 to 29		Reserved (for Robustness Experiment)	
30		Traceroute	RFC 1393
31		Datagram Conversion Error	RFC 1475
32		Mobile Host Redirect	
33		IPv6 Where-Are-You	
34		IPv6 I-Am-Here	
35		Mobile Registration Request	
36		Mobile Registration Reply	
37		Domain Name Request	
38		Domain Name Reply	

Section B-2

Table B-2   *Assigned ICMP Type Numbers, Codes, Descriptions, and Associated RFCs*

Type	Code	Name	Reference
39		SKIP	
40		Photuris	
	0	Reserved	
	1	Unknown Security Parameters Index	
	2	Valid Security Parameters, but Authentication Failed	
	3	Valid Security Parameters, but Decryption Failed	
41 to 255		Reserved	

B-3: Well-known IP Port Numbers

Transport layer protocols identify higher-layer traffic with 16-bit fields called *port numbers*. A connection between two devices uses a source and a destination port, both contained within the protocol data unit. The *User Datagram Protocol* (UDP) header format is shown in Figure B-4 with the source and destination port fields shaded. The UDP checksum is optional for IPv4. Figure B-5 shows *Transmission Control Protocol* (TCP) header format with the source and destination port fields shaded.

0	1	2	3
UDP source port		UDP destination port	
UDP message length		UDP checksum	
Data ...			

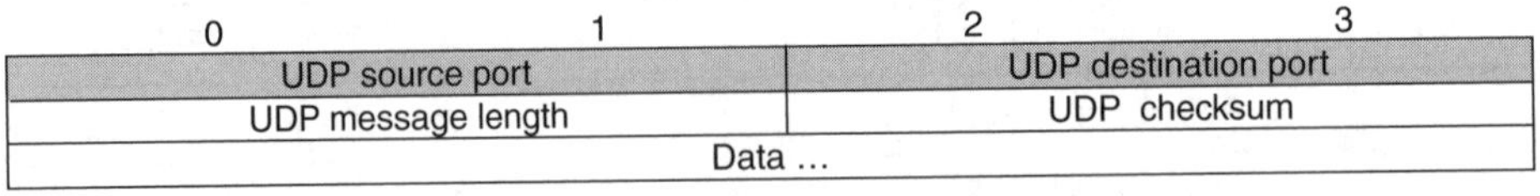

Figure B-4   *UDP Datagram Format Showing Port Fields*

0	1	2	3
TCP source port		TCP destination port	
Sequence number			
Acknowledgment number			
Hdr len	Reserved	Code bits	Window
Checksum		Urgent pointer	
Options (if necessary)			Padding
Data			
Data ...			

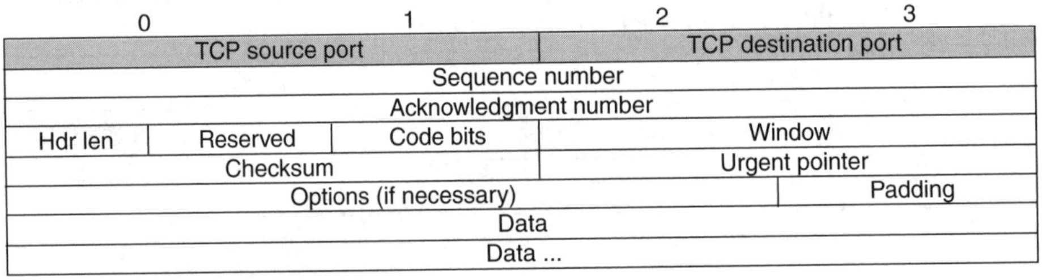

Figure B-5   *TCP Segment Format Showing Port Fields*

Both UDP and TCP port numbers are divided into the following ranges:

- Well-known port numbers (0 through 1023)

- Registered port numbers (1024 through 49151)

- Dynamic or private port numbers (49152 through 65535)

Usually, a port assignment uses a common port number for both UDP and TCP. A connection from a client to a server uses the well-known port on the server as a *service contact port*, whereas the client is free to dynamically assign its own port number. For TCP, the connection is identified by the source and destination IP addresses, as well as the source and destination TCP port numbers.

Well-known or assigned IP protocols are registered with the IANA. The information presented here is reproduced with permission from the IANA. For the most current IP protocol number assignment information, refer to www.iana.org/numbers.htm under the "Port Numbers" link.

Table B-3 shows some commonly used protocols, their port numbers, and a brief description. The IANA has recorded around 3350 unique port numbers. Because of space limitations, only a small subset of these port numbers are presented here.

Table B-3 *Commonly Used Protocols and Associated Port Numbers*

Keyword	Description	UDP/TCP Port
echo	Echo	7
discard	Discard	9
systat	Active Users	11
daytime	Daytime (RFC 867)	13
qotd	Quote of the Day	17
chargen	Character Generator	19
ftp-data	File Transfer [Default Data]	20
ftp	File Transfer [Control]	21
ssh	SSH Remote Login Protocol	22
telnet	Telnet	23
Any private mail system	Any private mail system	24
smtp	Simple Mail Transfer	25
msg-icp	MSG ICP	29
msg-auth	MSG Authentication	31
Any private printer server	Any private printer server	35

Table B-3 *Commonly Used Protocols and Associated Port Numbers*

Keyword	Description	UDP/TCP Port
time	Time	37
name	Host Name Server	42
nameserver	Host Name Server	42
nicname	Who Is	43
tacacs	Login Host Protocol (TACACS)	49
re-mail-ck	Remote Mail Checking Protocol	50
domain	Domain Name Server	53
Any private terminal address	Any private terminal address	57
Any private file service	Any private file service	59
whois++	whois++	63
tacacs-ds	TACACS-Database Service	65
sql*net	Oracle SQL*NET	66
bootps	Bootstrap Protocol Server	67
bootpc	Bootstrap Protocol Client	68
tftp	Trivial File Transfer	69
gopher	Gopher	70
Any private dial out service	Any private dial out service	75
Any private RJE service	Any private RJE service	77
finger	Finger	79
http	World Wide Web HTTP	80
www	World Wide Web HTTP	80
www-http	World Wide Web HTTP	80
hosts2-ns	HOSTS2 Name Server	81
xfer	XFER Utility	82
Any private terminal link	Any private terminal link	87
kerberos	Kerberos	88
dnsix	DNSIX Securit Attribute Token Map	90
npp	Network Printing Protocol	92
dcp	Device Control Protocol	93

Table B-3 *Commonly Used Protocols and Associated Port Numbers*

Keyword	Description	UDP/TCP Port
objcall	Tivoli Object Dispatcher	94
acr-nema	ACR-NEMA Digital Imag. & Comm. 300	104
rtelnet	Remote Telnet Service	107
snagas	SNA Gateway Access Server	108
pop2	Post Office Protocol (version 2)	109
pop3	Post Office Protocol (version 3)	110
sunrpc	SUN Remote Procedure Call	111
Mcidas	McIDAS Data Transmission Protocol	112
ident/auth	Authentication Service	113
audionews	Audio News Multicast	114
sftp	Simple File Transfer Protocol	115
uucp-path	UUCP Path Service	117
sqlserv	SQL Services	118
nntp	Network News Transfer Protocol	119
ntp	Network Time Protocol	123
pwdgen	Password Generator Protocol	129
cisco-fna	Cisco FNATIVE	130
cisco-tna	Cisco TNATIVE	131
cisco-sys	Cisco SYSMAINT	132
ingres-net	INGRES-NET Service	134
profile	PROFILE Naming System	136
netbios-ns	NetBIOS Name Service	137
netbios-dgm	NetBIOS Datagram Service	138
netbios-ssn	NetBIOS Session Service	139
imap	Internet Message Access Protocol	143
sql-net	SQL-NET	150
sgmp	SGMP	153

Section B-3

Table B-3 *Commonly Used Protocols and Associated Port Numbers*

Keyword	Description	UDP/TCP Port
sqlsrv	SQL Service	156
pcmail-srv	PCMail Server	158
sgmp-traps	SGMP-TRAPS	160
snmp	SNMP	161
snmptrap	SNMPTRAP	162
cmip-man	CMIP/TCP Manager	163
send	SEND	169
print-srv	Network PostScript	170
xyplex-mux	Xyplex	173
mailq	MAILQ	174
vmnet	VMNET	175
xdmcp	X Display Manager Control Protocol	177
bgp	Border Gateway Protocol	179
mumps	Plus Five's MUMPS	188
irc	Internet Relay Chat Protocol	194
dn6-nlm-aud	DNSIX Network Level Module Audit	195
dn6-smm-red	DNSIX Session Managementt Module Audit Redirect	196
dls	Directory Location Service	197
dls-mon	Directory Location Service Monitor	198
src	IBM System Resource Controller	200
at-rtmp	AppleTalk Routing Maintenance	201
at-nbp	AppleTalk Name Binding	202
at-3	AppleTalk Unused	203
at-echo	AppleTalk Echo	204
at-5	AppleTalk Unused	205
at-zis	AppleTalk Zone Information	206
at-7	AppleTalk Unused	207

Table B-3 *Commonly Used Protocols and Associated Port Numbers*

Keyword	Description	UDP/TCP Port
at-8	AppleTalk Unused	208
qmtp	The Quick Mail Transfer Protocol	209
ipx	IPX	213
vmpwscs	VM PWSCS	214
softpc	Insignia Solutions	215
dbase	dBASE UNIX	217
imap3	Interactive Mail Access Protocol (version 3)	220
http-mgmt	http-mgmt	280
asip-webadmin	AppleShare IP WebAdmin	311
ptp-event	PTP Event	319
ptp-general	PTP General	320
pdap	Prospero Data Access Protocol	344
rsvp_tunnel	RSVP Tunnel	363
rpc2portmap	rpc2portmap	369
aurp	AppleTalk Update-Based Routing Protocol	387
ldap	Lightweight Directory Access Protocol	389
netcp	NETscout Control Protocol	395
netware-ip	Novell NetWare over IP	396
ups	Uninterruptible power supply	401
smsp	Storage Management Services Protocol	413
mobileip-agent	MobileIP-Agent	434
mobilip-mn	MobilIP-MN	435
https	HTTP protocol over TLS/SSL	443
snpp	Simple Network Paging Protocol	444
microsoft-ds	Microsoft-DS	445
appleqtc	Apple QuickTime	458
ss7ns	ss7ns	477

Section B-3

Table B-3   *Commonly Used Protocols and Associated Port Numbers*

Keyword	Description	UDP/TCP Port
ph	Ph service	481
isakmp	isakmp	500
exec	Remote process execution	512
login	remote login by Telnet	513
shell	cmd	514
printer	spooler	515
ntalk	ntalk	518
utime	unixtime	519
ncp	NCP	524
timed	timedserver	525
irc-serv	IRC-SERV	529
courier	rpc	530
conference	chat	531
netnews	readnews	532
netwall	For emergency broadcasts	533
iiop	iiop	535
nmsp	Networked Media Streaming Protocol	537
uucp	uucpd	540
uucp-rlogin	uucp-rlogin	541
klogin	klogin	543
kshell	krcmd	544
appleqtcsrvr	appleqtcsrvr	545
dhcpv6-client	DHCPv6 Client	546
dhcpv6-server	DHCPv6 Server	547
afpovertcp	AFC over TCP	548
rtsp	Real Time Stream Control Protocol	554
remotefs	rfs server	556
rmonitor	rmonitord	560

Table B-3 *Commonly Used Protocols and Associated Port Numbers*

Keyword	Description	UDP/TCP Port
monitor	monitor	561
nntps	nntp protocol over TLS/SSL (was snntp)	563
whoami	whoami	565
sntp-heartbeat	SNTP HEARTBEAT	580
imap4-ssl	IMAP4 + SSl (use 993 instead)	585
password-chg	Password Change	586
eudora-set	Eudora Set	592
http-rpc-epmap	HTTP RPC Ep Map	593
sco-websrvrmg3	SCO Web Server Manager 3	598
ipcserver	SUN IPC server	600
sshell	SSLshell	614
sco-inetmgr	Internet Configuration Manager	615
sco-sysmgr	SCO System Administration Server	616
sco-dtmgr	SCO Desktop Administration Server	617
sco-websrvmgr	SCO WebServer Manager	620
ldaps	LDAP protocol over T LS/SSL (was sldap)	636
dhcp-failover	DHCP Failover	647
mac-srvr-admin	MacOS Server Admin	660
doom	doom Id Software	666
corba-iiop	CORBA IIOP	683
corba-iiop-ssl	CORBA IIOP SSL	684
nmap	NMAP	689
msexch-routing	MS Exchange Routing	691
ieee-mms-ssl	IEEE-MMS-SSL	695
cisco-tdp	Cisco TDP	711
flexlm	Flexible License Manager	744
kerberos-adm	Kerberos administration	749

Section B-3

Table B-3   *Commonly Used Protocols and Associated Port Numbers*

Keyword	Description	UDP/TCP Port
phonebook	Phone	767
dhcp-failover2	dhcp-failover2	847
ftps-data	FTP protocol, data, over TLS/SSL	989
ftps	FTP protocol, control, over TLS/SSL	990
nas	Netnews Administration System	991
telnets	Telnet protocol over TLS/SSL	992
imaps	imap4 protocol over TLS/SSL	993
ircs	irc protocol over TLS/SSL	994
pop3s	POP3 protocol over TLS/SSL (was spop3)	995
sunclustermgr	SUN Cluster Manager	1097
tripwire	TRIPWIRE	1169
shockwave2	Shockwave 2	1257
h323hostcallsc	H323 Host Call Secure	1300
lotusnote	Lotus Notes	1352
novell-lu6.2	Novell LU6.2	1416
ms-sql-s	Microsoft SQL Server	1433
ms-sql-m	Microsoft SQL Monitor	1434
ibm-cics	IBM CICS	1435
sybase-sqlany	Sybase SQL Any	1498
shivadiscovery	Shiva	1502
wins	Microsoft Windows Internet Name Service	1512
ingreslock	ingres	1524
orasrv	Oracle	1525
tlisrv	Oracle	1527
coauthor	Oracle	1529
rdb-dbs-disp	Oracle Remote Data Base	1571
oraclenames	oraclenames	1575

Table B-3 *Commonly Used Protocols and Associated Port Numbers*

Keyword	Description	UDP/TCP Port
ontime	ontime	1622
shockwave	Shockwave	1626
oraclenet8cman	Oracle Net8 Cman	1630
cert-initiator	cert-initiator	1639
cert-responder	cert-responder	1640
kermit	kermit	1649
groupwise	groupwise	1677
rsvp-encap-1	RSVP-ENCAPSULATION-1	1698
rsvp-encap-2	RSVP-ENCAPSULATION-2	1699
h323gatedisc	h323gatedisc	1718
h323gatestat	h323gatestat	1719
h323hostcall	h323hostcall	1720
cisco-net-mgmt	cisco-net-mgmt	1741
oracle-em1	oracle-em1	1748
oracle-em2	oracle-em2	1754
tftp-mcast	tftp-mcast	1758
www-ldap-gw	www-ldap-gw	1760
bmc-net-admin	bmc-net-admin	1769
bmc-net-svc	bmc-net-svc	1770
oracle-vp2	Oracle-VP2	1808
oracle-vp1	Oracle-VP1	1809
radius	RADIUS	1812
radius-acct	RADIUS Accounting	1813
hsrp	Hot Standby Router Protocol	1985
licensedaemon	Cisco license management	1986
tr-rsrb-p1	Cisco RSRP Priority 1 port	1987
tr-rsrb-p2	Cisco RSRP Priority 2 port	1988
tr-rsrb-p3	Cisco RSRP Priority 3 port	1989

Section B-3

Table B-3   *Commonly Used Protocols and Associated Port Numbers*

Keyword	Description	UDP/TCP Port
stun-p1	Cisco STUN Priority 1 port	1990
stun-p2	Cisco STUN Priority 2 port	1991
stun-p3	Cisco STUN Priority 3 port	1992
snmp-tcp-port	Cisco SNMP TCP port	1993
stun-port	Cisco serial tunnel port	1994
perf-port	Cisco perf port	1995
tr-rsrb-port	Cisco Remote SRB port	1996
gdp-port	Cicso Gateway Discovery Protocol	1997
x25-svc-port	Cisco X.25 service (XOT)	1998
tcp-id-port	Cisco identification port	1999
dlsrpn	Data Link Switch Read Port Number	2065
dlswpn	Data Link Switch Write Port Number	2067
ah-esp-encap	AH and ESP Encapsulated in UDP packet	2070
h2250-annex-g	H.225.0 Annex G	2099
ms-olap3	Microsoft OLAP	2382
ovsessionmgr	OpenView Session Manager	2389
ms-olap1	MS OLAP 1	2393
ms-olap2	MS OLAP 2	2394
mgcp-gateway	Media Gateway Control Protocol Gateway	2427
ovwdb	OpenView NNM daemon	2447
giop	Oracle GIOP	2481
giop-ssl	Oracle GIOP SSL	2482
ttc	Oracle TTC	2483
ttc-ssl	Oracle TTC SSL	2484
citrixima	Citrix IMA	2512
citrixadmin	Citrix ADMIN	2513
call-sig-trans	H.323 Annex E call signaling transport	2517

Table B-3 *Commonly Used Protocols and Associated Port Numbers*

Keyword	Description	UDP/TCP Port
windb	WinDb	2522
novell-zen	Novell ZEN	2544
clp	Cisco Line Protocol	2567
hl7	HL7	2575
citrixmaclient	Citrix MA Client	2598
sybaseanywhere	Sybase Anywhere	2638
novell-ipx-cmd	Novell IPX CMD	2645
sms-rcinfo	SMS RCINFO	2701
sms-xfer	SMS XFER	2702
sms-chat	SMS CHAT	2703
sms-remctrl	SMS REMCTRL	2704
mgcp-callagent	Media Gateway Control Protocol Call Agent	2727
dicom-iscl	DICOM ISCL	2761
dicom-tls	DICOM TLS	2762
citrix-rtmp	Citrix RTMP	2897
wap-push	WAP Push	2948
wap-pushsecure	WAP Push Secure	2949
h263-video	H.263 Video Streaming	2979
lotusmtap	Lotus Mail Tracking Agent Protocol	3007
njfss	NetWare sync services	3092
bmcpatrolagent	BMC Patrol Agent	3181
bmcpatrolrnvu	BMC Patrol Rendezvous	3182
ccmail	cc:mail/lotus	3264
msft-gc	Microsoft Global Catalog	3268
msft-gc-ssl	Microsoft Global Catalog with LDAP/SSL	3269
Unauthorized Use by SAP R/3	Unauthorized Use by SAP R/3	3300 to 3301
mysql	MySQL	3306

Table B-3   *Commonly Used Protocols and Associated Port Numbers*

Keyword	Description	UDP/TCP Port
ms-cluster-net	MS Cluster Net	3343
ssql	SSQL	3352
ms-wbt-server	MS WBT Server	3389
mira	Apple Remote Access Protocol	3454
prsvp	RSVP Port	3455
patrolview	Patrol View	4097
vrml-multi-use	VRML Multiuser Systems	4200 to 4299
rwhois	Remote Who Is	4321
bmc-reporting	BMC Reporting	4568
sip	SIP	5060
sip-tls	SIP-TLS	5061
pcanywheredata	PcANYWHEREdata	5631
pcaywherestat	pcANYWHEREstat	5632
x11	X Window System	6000 to 6063
bmc-grx	BMC GRX	6300
bmc-perf-agent	BMC PERFORM AGENT	6767
bmc-perf-mgrd	BMC PERFORM MGRD	6768
sun-lm	SUN License Manager	7588
http-alt	HTTP Alternate (see port 80)	8080
cp-cluster	Check Point Clustering	8116
patrol	Patrol	8160
patrol-snmp	Patrol SNMP	8161
wap-wsp	WAP connectionless session service	9200
wap-wsp-wtp	WAP session service	9201
wap-wsp-s	WAP secure connectionless session service	9202
wap-wsp-wtp-s	WAP secure session service	9203
wap-vcard	WAP vCard	9204

Table B-3   *Commonly Used Protocols and Associated Port Numbers*

Keyword	Description	UDP/TCP Port
wap-vcal	WAP vCal	9205
wap-vcard-s	WAP vCard Secure	9206
wap-vcal-s	WAP vCal Secure	9207
bmc-perf-sd	BMC-PERFORM-SERVICE DAEMON	10128
h323callsigalt	h323 Call Signal Alternate	11720
vofr-gateway	VoFR Gateway	21590
quake	quake	26000
flex-lm	FLEX LM (1–10)	27000 to 27009
traceroute	traceroute use	33434
reachout	REACHOUT	43188

B-4: Well-Known IP Multicast Addresses

Some client server applications use a multicast packet to send large streams of data to many hosts with a single transmission. The multicast packet uses special addressing at Layer 3 and Layer 2 to communicate with clients that have been configured to receive these packets. The multicast packet contains a Class D IP address to specify the group of devices that are to receive the packet. This group is known as the *multicast group*, and the IP address translates directly to a multicast Ethernet address. The Ethernet multicast address has the first 24 bits set to 01-00-5E, the next bit is set to 0, and the last 23 bits are set to match the low 23 bits of the IP multicast address. Figure B-6 shows how Layer 3 multicast addresses translate to Layer 2 Ethernet addresses.

Section B-4

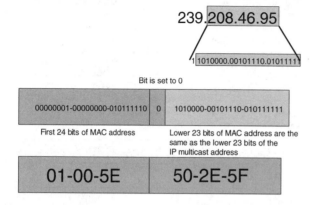

Figure B-6   *Layer 3-to-Layer 2 Multicast Translation*

Well-known or assigned IP protocols are registered with the IANA. The information presented here is reproduced with permission from the IANA. For the most current IP protocol number assignment information, refer to www.iana.org/numbers.htm under the "Multicast Addresses" link.

Host extensions for IP multicasting (RFC 1112) specifies the extensions required of a host implementation of the Internet Protocol to support multicasting. The multicast addresses are in the range 224.0.0.0 through 239.255.255.255. Current addresses are listed in the table that follows.

The range of addresses between 224.0.0.0 and 224.0.0.255, inclusive, is reserved for the use of routing protocols and other low-level topology discovery or maintenance protocols, such as gateway discovery and group membership reporting. Multicast routers should not forward any multicast datagram with destination addresses within this range, regardless of its TTL.

Table B-4 shows the registered multicast addresses, along with the application, and the RFC number (if applicable) or other reference.

Table B-4   *Registered Multicast Addresses and Associated Applications, RFCs, and References*

Group, Application, and References	Address
Base address (reserved) RFC 1112	224.0.0.0

Table B-4 *Registered Multicast Addresses and Associated Applications, RFCs, and References*

Group, Application, and References	Address
All systems on this subnet RFC 1112	224.0.0.1
All routers on this subnet	224.0.0.2
Unassigned	224.0.0.3
DVMRP Routers RFC 1075	224.0.0.4
OSPFIGP OSPFIGP all routers RFC 2328	224.0.0.5
OSPFIGP OSPFIGP designated routers RFC 2328	224.0.0.6
ST Routers RFC 1190	224.0.0.7
ST Hosts RFC 1190	224.0.0.8
RIP2 Routers RFC 1723	224.0.0.9
EIGRP Routers	224.0.0.10
Mobile agents	224.0.0.11
DHCP Server/Relay agent RFC 1884	224.0.0.12
All PIM routers	224.0.0.13
RSVP-ENCAPSULATION	224.0.0.14
all-cbt-routers	224.0.0.15
designated-sbm	224.0.0.16
all-sbms	224.0.0.17

Table B-4   *Registered Multicast Addresses and Associated Applications, RFCs, and References*

Group, Application, and References	Address
VRRP	224.0.0.18
IPAllL1Iss	224.0.0.19
IPAllL2Iss	224.0.0.20
IPAllIntermediate Systems	224.0.0.21
IGMP	224.0.0.22
GLOBECAST-ID	224.0.0.23
Unassigned	224.0.0.24
router-to-switch	224.0.0.25
Unassigned	224.0.0.26
Al MPP Hello	224.0.0.27
ETC Control	224.0.0.28
GE-FANUC	224.0.0.29
indigo-vhdp	224.0.0.30
shinbroadband	224.0.0.31
digistar	224.0.0.32
ff-system-management	224.0.0.33
pt2-discover	224.0.0.34
DXCLUSTER	224.0.0.35
DTCP Announcement	224.0.0.36
Zeroconfaddr	224.0.0.37 to 224.0.0.68
Reserved	224.0.0.69 to 224.0.0.100
cisco-nhap	224.0.0.101
HSRP	224.0.0.102
MDAP	224.0.0.103
Unassigned	224.0.0.104 to 224.0.0.250
mDNS	224.0.0.251
Unassigned	224.0.0.25 to 224.0.0.255

Table B-4   *Registered Multicast Addresses and Associated Applications, RFCs, and References*

Group, Application, and References	Address
VMTP Managers Group RFC 1045	224.0.1.0
NTP (Network Time Protocol) RFC 1119	224.0.1.1
SGI-Dogfight	224.0.1.2
Rwhod	224.0.1.3
VNP	224.0.1.4
Artificial Horizons – Aviator	224.0.1.5
NSS (Name Service Server)	224.0.1.6
AUDIONEWS (Audio News Multicast)	224.0.1.7
SUN NIS+ Information Service	224.0.1.8
MTP (Multicast Transport Protocol)	224.0.1.9
IETF-1-LOW-AUDIO	224.0.1.10
IETF-1-AUDIO	224.0.1.11
IETF-1-VIDEO	224.0.1.12
IETF-2-LOW-AUDIO	224.0.1.13
IETF-2-AUDIO	224.0.1.14
IETF-2-VIDEO	224.0.1.15
MUSIC-SERVICE	224.0.1.16
SEANET-TELEMETRY	224.0.1.17
SEANET-IMAGE	224.0.1.18
MLOADD	224.0.1.19
Any private experiment	224.0.1.20
DVMRP on MOSPF	224.0.1.21
SVRLOC	224.0.1.22
XINGTV	224.0.1.23
microsoft-ds	224.0.1.24
nbc-pro	224.0.1.25
nbc-pfn	224.0.1.26

Table B-4   *Registered Multicast Addresses and Associated Applications, RFCs, and*
References

Group, Application, and References	Address
lmsc-calren-1	224.0.1.27
lmsc-calren-2	224.0.1.28
lmsc-calren-3	224.0.1.29
lmsc-calren-4	224.0.1.30
ampr-info	224.0.1.31
Mtrace	224.0.1.32
RSVP-encap-1	224.0.1.33
RSVP-encap-2	224.0.1.34
SVRLOC-DA	224.0.1.35
rln-server	224.0.1.36
proshare-mc	224.0.1.37
Dantz	224.0.1.38
cisco-rp-announce	224.0.1.39
cisco-rp-discovery	224.0.1.40
gatekeeper	224.0.1.41
iberiagames	224.0.1.42
nwn-discovery	224.0.1.43
nwn-adaptor	224.0.1.44
isma-1	224.0.1.45
isma-2	224.0.1.46
telerate	224.0.1.47
Ciena	224.0.1.48
dcap-servers RFC 2114	224.0.1.49
dcap-clients RFC 2114	224.0.1.50
mcntp-directory	224.0.1.51
mbone-vcr-directory	224.0.1.52
Heartbeat	224.0.1.53

Table B-4 *Registered Multicast Addresses and Associated Applications, RFCs, and References*

Group, Application, and References	Address
sun-mc-grp	224.0.1.54
extended-sys	224.0.1.55
pdrncs	224.0.1.56
tns-adv-multi	224.0.1.57
vcals-dmu	224.0.1.58
Zuba	224.0.1.59
hp-device-disc	224.0.1.60
tms-production	224.0.1.61
Sunscalar	224.0.1.62
mmtp-poll	224.0.1.63
compaq-peer	224.0.1.64
iapp	224.0.1.65
multihasc-com	224.0.1.66
serv-discovery	224.0.1.67
Mdhcpdisover RFC 2730	224.0.1.68
MMP-bundle-discovery1	224.0.1.69
MMP-bundle-discovery2	224.0.1.70
XYPOINT DGPS Data Feed	224.0.1.71
GilatSkySurfer	224.0.1.72
SharesLive	224.0.1.73
NorthernData	224.0.1.74
SIP	224.0.1.75
IAPP	224.0.1.76
AGENTVIEW	224.0.1.77
Tibco Multicast1	224.0.1.78
Tibco Multicast2	224.0.1.79
MSP	224.0.1.80

Table B-4 *Registered Multicast Addresses and Associated Applications, RFCs, and References*

Group, Application, and References	Address
OTT (One-way Trip Time)	224.0.1.81
TRACKTICKER	224.0.1.82
dtn-mc	224.0.1.83
jini-announcement	224.0.1.84
jini-request	224.0.1.85
sde-discovery	224.0.1.86
DirecPC-SI	224.0.1.87
B1Rmonitor	224.0.1.88
3Com-AMP3 dRMON	224.0.1.89
ImFtmSvc	224.0.1.90
NQDS4	224.0.1.91
NQDS5	224.0.1.92
NQDS6	224.0.1.93
NLVL12	224.0.1.94
NTDS1	224.0.1.95
NTDS2	224.0.1.96
NODSA	224.0.1.97
NODSB	224.0.1.98
NODSC	224.0.1.99
NODSD	224.0.1.100
NQDS4R	224.0.1.101
NQDS5R	224.0.1.102
NQDS6R	224.0.1.103
NLVL12R	224.0.1.104
NODS1R	224.0.1.105
NODS2R	224.0.1.106
NODSAR	224.0.1.107
NODSBR	224.0.1.108

Table B-4 *Registered Multicast Addresses and Associated Applications, RFCs, and References*

Group, Application, and References	Address
NODSCR	224.0.1.109
NODSDR	224.0.1.110
MRM	224.0.1.111
TVE-FILE	224.0.1.112
TVE-ANNOUNCE	224.0.1.113
Mac Srv Loc	224.0.1.114
Simple Multicast	224.0.1.115
SpectraLinkGW	224.0.1.116
Dieboldmcast	224.0.1.117
Tivoli Systems	224.0.1.118
pq-lic-mcast	224.0.1.119
HYPERFEED	224.0.1.120
Pipesplatform	224.0.1.121
LiebDevMgmg-DM	224.0.1.122
TRIBALVOICE	224.0.1.123
Unassigned (Retracted 1/29/01)	224.0.1.124
PolyCom Relay1	224.0.1.125
Infront Multi1	224.0.1.126
XRX DEVICE DISC	224.0.1.127
CNN	224.0.1.128
PTP-primary	224.0.1.129
PTP-alternate1	224.0.1.130
PTP-alternate2	224.0.1.131
PTP-alternate3	224.0.1.132
ProCast	224.0.1.133
3Com Discp	224.0.1.134
CS-Multicasting	224.0.1.135
TS-MC-1	224.0.1.136

Section B-4

Table B-4   *Registered Multicast Addresses and Associated Applications, RFCs, and References*

Group, Application, and References	Address
Make Source	224.0.1.137
Teleborsa	224.0.1.138
SUMAConfig	224.0.1.139
Unassigned	224.0.1.140
DHCP-SERVERS	224.0.1.141
CN Router-LL	224.0.1.142
EMWIN	224.0.1.143
Alchemy Cluster	224.0.1.144
Satcast One	224.0.1.145
Satcast Two	224.0.1.146
Satcast Three	224.0.1.147
Intline	224.0.1.148
8x8 Multicast	224.0.1.149
Unassigned	224.0.1.150
Intline-1	224.0.1.151
Intline-2	224.0.1.152
Intline-3	224.0.1.153
Intline-4	224.0.1.154
Intline-5	224.0.1.155
Intline-6	224.0.1.156
Intline-7	224.0.1.157
Intline-8	224.0.1.158
Intline-9	224.0.1.159
Intline-10	224.0.1.160
Intline-11	224.0.1.161
Intline-12	224.0.1.162
Intline-13	224.0.1.163
Intline-14	224.0.1.164

Table B-4 *Registered Multicast Addresses and Associated Applications, RFCs, and References*

Group, Application, and References	Address
Intline-15	224.0.1.165
marratech-cc	224.0.1.166
EMS-InterDev	224.0.1.167
itb301	224.0.1.168
rtv-audio	224.0.1.169
rtv-video	224.0.1.170
HAVI-Sim	224.0.1.171
Nokia Cluster	224.0.1.172
host-request	224.0.1.173
host-announce	224.0.1.174
ptk-cluster	224.0.1.175
Proxim Protocol	224.0.1.176
Unassigned	224.0.1.177 to 224.0.0.255
"rwho" Group (BSD) (unofficial)	224.0.2.1
SUN RPC PMAPPROC_CALLIT	224.0.2.2
SIAC MDD Service	224.0.2.64 to 224.0.2.95
CoolCast	224.0.2.96 to 224.0.2.127
WOZ-Garage	224.0.2.128 to 224.0.2.191
SIAC MDD Market Service	224.0.2.192 to 224.0.2.255
RFE Generic Service	224.0.3.0 to 224.0.3.255
RFE Individual Conferences	224.0.4.0 to 224.0.4.255
CDPD Groups	224.0.5.0 to 224.0.5.127
SIAC Market Service	224.0.5.128 to 224.0.5.191
Unassigned	
IANA	224.0.5.192 to 224.0.5.255
Cornell ISIS Project	224.0.6.0 to 224.0.6.127
Unassigned IANA	224.0.6.128 to 224.0.6.255

Table B-4   *Registered Multicast Addresses and Associated Applications, RFCs, and References*

Group, Application, and References	Address
Where-Are-You	224.0.7.0 to 224.0.7.255
INTV	224.0.8.0 to 224.0.8.255
Invisible Worlds	224.0.9.0 to 224.0.9.255
DLSw Groups	224.0.10.0 to 224.0.10.255
NCC.NET Audio	224.0.11.0 to 224.0.11.255
Microsoft and MSNBC	224.0.12.0 to 224.0.12.63
UUNET PIPEX Net News	224.0.13.0 to 223.0.13.255
NLANR	224.0.14.0 to 224.0.14.255
Hewlett Packard	224.0.15.0 to 224.0.15.255
XingNet	224.0.16.0 to 224.0.16.255
Mercantile & Commodity Exchange	224.0.17.0 to 224.0.17.31
NDQMD1	224.0.17.32 to 224.0.17.63
ODN-DTV	224.0.17.64 to 224.0.17.127
Dow Jones	224.0.18.0 to 224.0.18.255
Walt Disney Company	224.0.19.0 to 224.0.19.63
Cal Multicast	224.0.19.64 to 224.0.19.95
SIAC Market Service	224.0.19.96 to 224.0.19.127
IIG Multicast	224.0.19.128 to 224.0.19.191
Metropol	224.0.18.192 to 224.0.19.207
Xenoscience, Inc.	224.0.19.208 to 224.0.19.239
HYPERFEED	224.0.19.240 to 224.0.19.255
MS-IP/TV	224.0.20.0 to 224.0.20.63
Reliable Network Solutions	224.0.20.64 to 224.0.20.127
TRACKTICKER Group	224.0.20.128 to 224.0.20.143
CNR Rebroadcast MCA	224.0.20.144 to 224.0.20.207
Talarian MCAST	224.0.21.0 to 224.0.21.127
WORLD MCAST	224.0.22.0 to 224.0.22.255
Domain Scoped Group	224.0.252.0 to 224.0.252.255

Table B-4 *Registered Multicast Addresses and Associated Applications, RFCs, and References*

Group, Application, and References	Address
Report Group	224.0.253.0 to 224.0.253.255
Query Group	224.0.254.0 to 224.0.254.255
Border Routers	224.0.255.0 to 224.0.255.255
ST Multicast Groups RFC 1190	224.1.0.0 to 224.1.255.255
Multimedia Conference Calls	224.2.0.0 to 224.2.127.253
SAPv1 Announcements	224.2.127.254
SAPv0 Announcements (deprecated)	224.2.127.255
SAP Dynamic Assignments	224.2.128.0 to 224.2.255.255
DIS transient groups	224.252.0.0 to 224.255.255.255
MALLOC (temp - renew 1/01)	225.0.0.0 to 225.255.255.255
VMTP transient groups	232.0.0.0 to 232.255.255.255
Static Allocations (temp - renew 03/02)	233.0.0.0 to 233.255.255.255
Administratively Scoped IANA RFC 2365	239.0.0.0 to 239.255.255.255
Reserved IANA	239.0.0.0 to 239.63.255.255
Reserved IANA	239.64.0.0 to 239.127.255.255
Reserved IANA	239.128.0.0 to 239.191.255.255
Organization-Local Scope RFC 2365	239.192.0.0 to 239.251.255.255
Site-Local Scope (reserved) RFC 2365	239.252.0.0 to 239.252.255.255
Site-Local Scope (reserved) RFC 2365	239.253.0.0 to 239.253.255.255
Site-Local Scope (reserved) RFC 2365	239.254.0.0 to 239.254.255.255
Site-Local Scope RFC 2365	239.255.0.0 to 239.255.255.255
rasadv	239.255.2.2

B-5: Ethernet Type Codes

A listing of commonly used Ethernet type codes is maintained by the IANA. The information presented here is reproduced with permission from the IANA. For the most current Ethernet type code number assignment information, refer to www.iana.org/numbers.htm under the "Ethernet Numbers" link. Table B-5 shows the Ethernet type code numbers in hexadecimal format, along with a description.

Table B-5   *Ethernet Type Codes*

Hex Value	Description
0000 to 05DC	IEEE 802.3 Length Field
0101 to 01FF	Experimental
200	XEROX PUP (see 0A00)
201	PUP Addr Trans (see 0A01)
400	Nixdorf
600	XEROX NS IDP
660	DLOG
661	DLOG
800	Internet IP (IPv4)
801	X.75 Internet
802	NBS Internet
803	ECMA Internet
804	Chaosnet
805	X.25 Level 3
806	ARP
807	XNS Compatibility
808	Frame Relay ARP (RFC 1701)
081C	Symbolics Private
0888 to 088A	Xyplex
900	Ungermann-Bass net debug
0A00	Xerox IEEE802.3 PUP
0A01	PUP Address Translation
0BAD	Banyan VINES
0BAE	VINES Loopback (RFC 1701)

Table B-5   *Ethernet Type Codes*

Hex Value	Description
0BAF	VINES Echo (RFC 1701)
1000	Berkeley Trailer negotiation
1001 to 100F	Berkeley Trailer encapsulation/IP
1600	Valid Systems
4242	PCS Basic Block Protocol
5208	BBN Simnet
6000	DEC Unassigned (experimental)
6001	DEC MOP Dump/Load
6002	DEC MOP Remote Console
6003	DEC DECNET Phase IV Route
6004	DEC LAT
6005	DEC Diagnostic Protocol
6006	DEC Customer Protocol
6007	DEC LAVC, SCA
6008 to 6009	DEC Unassigned
6010 to 6014	3Com Corporation
6558	Trans Ether Bridging (RFC 1701)
6559	Raw Frame Relay (RFC 1701)
7000	Ungermann-Bass download
7002	Ungermann-Bass dia/loop
7020 to 7029	LRT
7030	Proteon
7034	Cabletron
8003	Cronus VLN
8004	Cronus Direct
8005	HP Probe
8006	Nestar
8008	AT&T
8010	Excelan

Table B-5   *Ethernet Type Codes*

Hex Value	Description
8013	SGI diagnostics
8014	SGI network games
8015	SGI reserved
8016	SGI bounce server
8019	Apollo Domain
802E	Tymshare
802F	Tigan, Inc.
8035	Reverse ARP
8036	Aeonic Systems
8038	DEC LANBridge
8039 to 803C	DEC Unassigned
803D	DEC Ethernet Encryption
803E	DEC Unassigned
803F	DEC LAN Traffic Monitor
8040 to 8042	DEC Unassigned
8044	Planning Research Corp.
8046	AT&T
8047	AT&T
8049	ExperData
805B	Stanford V Kernel exp.
805C	Stanford V Kernel prod.
805D	Evans & Sutherland
8060	Little Machines
8062	Counterpoint Computers
8065	Univ. of Mass. @ Amherst
8066	Univ. of Mass. @ Amherst
8067	Veeco Integrated Auto.
8068	General Dynamics
8069	AT&T

Table B-5 *Ethernet Type Codes*

Hex Value	Description
806A	Autophon
806C	ComDesign
806D	Computgraphic Corp.
806E to 8077	Landmark Graphics Corp.
807A	Matra
807B	Dansk Data Elektronik
807C	Merit Internodal
807D to 807F	Vitalink Communications
8080	Vitalink TransLAN III
8081 to 8083	Counterpoint Computers
809B	Appletalk
809C to 809E	Datability
809F	Spider Systems Ltd.
80A3	Nixdorf Computers
80A4 to 80B3	Siemens Gammasonics Inc.
80C0 to 80C3	DCA Data Exchange Cluster
80C4	Banyan Systems
80C5	Banyan Systems
80C6	Pacer Software
80C7	Applitek Corporation
80C8 to 80CC	Intergraph Corporation
80CD to 80CE	Harris Corporation
80CF to 80D2	Taylor Instrument
80D3 to 80D4	Rosemount Corporation
80D5	IBM SNA Service on Ether
80DD	Varian Associates
80DE to 80DF	Integrated Solutions TRFS
80E0 to 80E3	Allen-Bradley
80E4 to 80F0	Datability

Table B-5   *Ethernet Type Codes*

Hex Value	Description
80F2	Retix
80F3	AppleTalk AARP (Kinetics)
80F4 to 80F5	Kinetics
80F7	Apollo Computer
80FF to 8103	Wellfleet Communications
8107 to 8109	Symbolics Private
8130	Hayes Microcomputers
8131	VG Laboratory Systems
8132 to 8136	Bridge Communications
8137 to 8138	Novell, Inc.
8139 to 813D	KTI
8148	Logicraft
8149	Network Computing Devices
814A	Alpha Micro
814C	SNMP
814D	BIIN
814E	BIIN
814F	Technically Elite Concept
8150	Rational Corp
8151 to 8153	Qualcomm
815C to 815E	Computer Protocol Pty Ltd
8164 to 8166	Charles River Data System
817D	XTP
817E	SGI/Time Warner prop.
8180	HIPPI-FP encapsulation
8181	STP, HIPPI-ST
8182	Reserved for HIPPI-6400
8183	Reserved for HIPPI-6400
8184 to 818C	Silicon Graphics prop.

Table B-5 *Ethernet Type Codes*

Hex Value	Description
818D	Motorola Computer
819A to 81A3	Qualcomm
81A4	ARAI Bunkichi
81A5 to 81AE	RAD Network Devices
81B7 to 81B9	Xyplex
81CC to 81D5	Apricot Computers
81D6 to 81DD	Artisoft
81E6 to 81EF	Polygon
81F0 to 81F2	Comsat Labs
81F3 to 81F5	SAIC
81F6 to 81F8	VG Analytical
8203 to 8205	Quantum Software
8221 to 8222	Ascom Banking Systems
823E to 8240	Advanced Encryption System
827F to 8282	Athena Programming
8263 to 826A	Charles River Data System
829A to 829B	Inst Ind Info Tech
829C to 82AB	Taurus Controls
82AC to 8693	Walker Richer & Quinn
8694 to 869D	Idea Courier
869E to 86A1	Computer Network Tech
86A3 to 86AC	Gateway Communications
86DB	SECTRA
86DE	Delta Controls
86DD	IPv6
86DF	ATOMIC
86E0 to 86EF	Landis & Gyr Powers
8700 to 8710	Motorola
876B	TCP/IP Compression (RFC 1144)

Table B-5   *Ethernet Type Codes*

Hex Value	Description
876C	IP Autonomous Systems (RFC 1701)
876D	Secure Data (RFC 1701)
880B	PPP
8847	MPLS Unicast
8848	MPLS Multicast
8A96 to 8A97	Invisible Software
9000	Loopback
9001	3Com(Bridge) XNS Sys Mgmt
9002	3Com(Bridge) TCP-IP Sys
9003	3Com(Bridge) loop detect
FF00	BBN VITAL-LanBridge cache
FF00 to FF0F	ISC Bunker Ramo
FFFF	Reserved (RFC 1701)

Index

Symbols

(*, G) common shared tree structure, 141

(S, G) shortest path tree structure, 141

6000 series Catalyst switches, password recovery process, 33-34

802.1Q trunking, native VLAN switching, 96

802.1X port authentication, configuring, 186

A

access layer, 17-18
  configuring for voice QoS, 256-259
access ports, 91
accessing
  modules, 34
  switch devices, SSH, 184-185
ACEs (access control entries), 227
ACLs (access control lists)
  configuring, 183-184
  VACLs, 176-178

active commands, disabling, 3

adding entries to switching table, 53-54

AF (Assured Forwarding) service levels, 223

aggressive mode (UDLD), 115

aging time, configuring on switching table, 54

assigning IP management address, 28

assigning VLAN ports
  dynamic assignment, 91-93
  static, 91

asynchronous back-to-back connections, 268

authentication
  configuring, 180
  example, 182
  port authentication, configuring, 185-186
  RADIUS, configuring, 181-182
  TACACS, configuring, 181

automatic IP management address assignment, 28

B

C

J-K-L

326 manual system time configuration

manual system time configuration, 48-49

mapping internal DSCP values to egress CoS values, 244

marking

Layer 2 frames, 222-223

Layer 3 frames, 223-226

MaxAge timer, adjusting, 125

MaxAge timer (STP), 124

maximum cabling distances, 263-265

messages, logging, 193

syslog, configuring, 194-198

syslog, displaying information, 198

microflow policers, configuring, 234-235

microflows, 227

modes of VTP operation, 100-101

modules

accessing, 34

powering on/off, 35

resetting, 35

viewing, 34

monitoring environmental conditions, 214

more command, 4

moving system files, 39-40

MST (Multiple Spanning Tree), 112

MTU (maximum transmission unit), 59

mtu parameter, configuring Ethernet VLANs, 89

multicast addressing

IGMP snooping, 142-145

tree structures, 141

multicast broadcast floods, controlling, 169

N

name parameter, configuring Ethernet VLANs, 89

native VLAN (802.1Q), switching, 96

navigating

IFS, 36-38

STP topology, 127-130

nested Telnet sessions, 6

network management, SNMP, 199

configuring, 199-202

displaying information, 206

example, 205-206

notifications, 203

RMON support, 204-205

saving configuration file to TFTP server, 203

traps, 203-204

network media

connector pinouts, 266

maximum cabling distances, 263-265

normal mode (UDLD), 115

normal range, VLAN numbers, 88

notifications, SNMP, 203-204

NSF (Non-Stop Forwarding), 132

configuring, 133-134

displaying information about, 135

NSF/SSO mode, 43

NTP (Network Time Protocol)

stratum, 47

system time, configuring, 49-50

O-P

operating systems, alias command backward compatibility, 41

out-of-profile traffic, 227

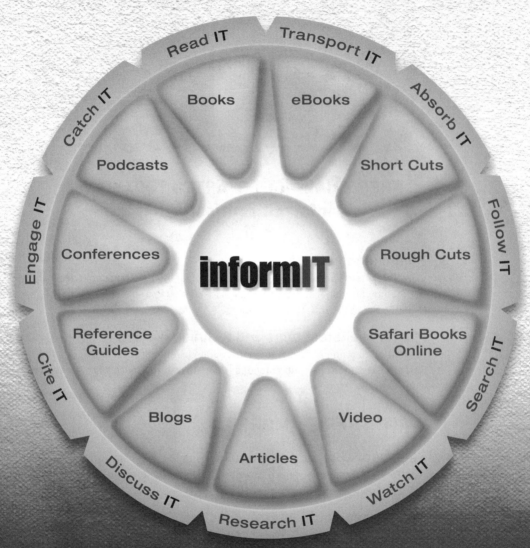

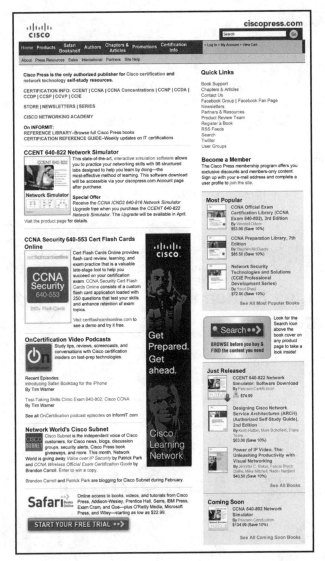

Cisco LAN Switching Configuration Handbook
Second Edition

A concise reference for implementing the most frequently used features of the Cisco Catalyst family of switches

Steve McQuerry, CCIE® No. 6108
David Jansen, CCIE No. 5952
David Hucaby, CCIE No. 4594

ciscopress.com

FREE Online Edition

Your purchase of **Cisco LAN Switching Configuration Handbook** includes access to a free online edition for 45 days through the Safari Books Online subscription service. Nearly every Cisco Press book is available online through Safari Books Online, along with more than 5,000 other technical books and videos from publishers such as Addison-Wesley Professional, Exam Cram, IBM Press, O'Reilly, Prentice Hall, Que, and Sams.

SAFARI BOOKS ONLINE allows you to search for a specific answer, cut and paste code, download chapters, and stay current with emerging technologies.

Activate your FREE Online Edition at www.informit.com/safarifree

> **STEP 1:** Enter the coupon code: FHETREH.

> **STEP 2:** New Safari users, complete the brief registration form.
> Safari subscribers, just log in.

If you have difficulty registering on Safari or accessing the online edition, please e-mail customer-service@safaribooksonline.com